Still the New World

Still the New World

AMERICAN LITERATURE IN A CULTURE OF CREATIVE DESTRUCTION

PHILIP FISHER

HARVARD UNIVERSITY PRESS

CAMBRIDGE, MASSACHUSETTS

LONDON, ENGLAND

1999

Designed by Gwen Nefsky Frankfeldt

Library of Congress Cataloging-in-Publication Data

Fisher, Philip.
Still the new world : American literature in a culture
of creative destruction / Philip Fisher.
p.   cm.
Includes bibliographical references (p.   ) and index.
ISBN 0-674-83859-9 (hardcover : alk. paper)
1. American literature—History and criticism—Theory, etc.
2. Literature and society—United States—History.
3. Conflict of generations in literature.
4. Social change in literature.
5. Future in literature.   I. Title.
PS25.F55   1999   98-37746
306'.0973—dc21

Contents

Still the New World

Introduction

Painting a Fence in America: Tom Sawyer Starts a
New but Temporary Business

Of all American literature the scene that stays longest in many readers' minds is the one in which Tom Sawyer paints Aunt Sally's fence. Tom himself does only a few brush strokes before he enterprisingly enlists the neighborhood boys passing by. They compete to take turns at a task that only a short time earlier would have seemed as bad a way to spend time as breaking rocks in a juvenile prison. They fall under the spell of Tom's way of seeing the adventure and pay him for the privilege of participating. Tom has started a small business where none had existed a day before. One day later the enterprise has shut down. Improvised and temporary, it has done its job by letting Tom redesign his own, once onerous chore.

Mark Twain's scene could be called a young person's guide to the American orchestra. If we had the national wit to do so, it would have been passed out in translation to every newly arrived settler at Ellis Island, the Mexican border, and the major coastal airports. Since *Tom Sawyer* is one of the first books read out loud to a child in the United States, the scene does reach the ears of many of the nation's newly arrived internal settlers, the children of the next generation who are, in America, wise to take their clues from their fellow immigrants rather than from their parents, who might be called, in settler language, the old-timers. The wisdom of old-timers is usually out of date as soon as its lessons have been learned.

Like his contemporary Leo Tolstoy, who wrote a set of simple parables, among them "How Much Land Does a Man Need?" in an attempt to reach into every corner of European society with his message, Twain in his sly and quick-witted style created, in Tom Sawyer's fence-painting, an almost biblical parable for the economic mind in an as-yet half-finished culture. Twain knew, as did Ralph Waldo Emerson, that there are different truths when we know ourselves to be late in time, near the completion of the world (or of our own country), ready to fit a few last details somehow onto a crowded page, and when, being near the beginning of time, we find ourselves still studying a sketch of what might someday be realized, but only if we have the freedom and the power to grasp the consequences of being truly in a still new world. Both Emerson and Twain thought that it was still the new world, still early in time and history, still fresh, and that America needed to be taken as a model because with a still lightly marked out and occupied vast land, it could remind even the old world that it too was lightly sketched on a young planet.

At first it might seem that Emerson and Twain should be seen as the philosophers of a newness based uniquely on the thin population of an enormous land, the philosophers of cheap land and careless uses, the philosophers of moving on and using up. If so, the thickening of population, the end of free or nearly free land, the marking out of major cities, the fixing of rules and paths within the professions and occupations would quickly have changed the nation into yet one more old world with the cement of regulations and the depression of the young face to face with a completely owned and crowded social space. They might have been, like Frederick Jackson Turner with his frontier hypothesis, pessimists, but in disguise, because the very conditions of newness they celebrated would have to be acknowledged to be rapidly evaporating as the sketch was progressively filled in. The heady philosophy of Emerson and Twain would turn out to be true only for the initial settler phase, a false fire that served its uses and then vanished under settled conditions that would be permanent and solid, if unexciting.

Introduction

Intellectuals in our own century, drawing on the nineteenth-century lines traced in the sand by Turner, Twain, and Emerson, were always more comfortable with the nostalgic pessimism of Turner than they were with the fresh buoyancy of Emerson or the zest of the young Mark Twain. To consider the frontier decisive at just that moment when the 1890 census had declared that the frontier was closed and the unique frontier experience ended, along with the frontier's ability to instill democratic habits of self-reliance and self-organized society, turned out to appeal to many twentieth-century intellectuals, who seem always to prefer the description of unavailable conditions, those of a past already vanished or a future remote in a utopian distance.

We might ask if Emerson and Twain had been saved from the same depressing encounter with an already filled world only by the temporary near-emptiness of the American map. The answer, I think, is a resounding No. I want to argue that a merely temporarily unfinished newness made it possible to sketch the philosophy for a new, permanently unsettled rhythm of creation and destruction. With the onset of a richly inventive modern technology that presumed destructive restlessness, along with an economy that was committed to giving free rein to that destructive restlessness, the possibility opened up that in American culture the initial, unfinished newness would define the terms of a more permanent newness guaranteed by the one genuine permanent revolution, that of competitive technological capitalism.

America became a culture willing to pay the deep costs of obsolescence and ghost towns as part of what might be called the bargain of invention. The airplanes that crisscross the skies in America today fly over tens of thousands of miles of rusting and little-used railroad tracks. Some of the tracks themselves have been covered with asphalt to make recreational trails for bicyclists and weekend hikers.

The engines of the trains that used to ride those tracks have been turned into scrap iron. One century earlier those very locomotives had ended the useful life of the mighty Mississippi steamboats that seemed like a fantasy of power and modernity in Mark Twain's youth, but had already become obsolete by his adult years. The canals in America have refilled with dirt. The wharves, along with the towns that grew up because of those wharves and the dirt roads that led to the towns, are all grassed over as surely as graves. The farms of New England existed briefly on the site of what had been forests, but new forests have now, two hundred years later, once again replaced those farms. When the telegraph came, it buried the pony express along with the horses and riders who had once made up the pony express. A century later, geosynchronous satellites, cellular phones, computers, and the Internet have begun to eat away at the wired telephone system that had, in its time, buried the Morse code, the key operators, and the wired system of the great Western Union Telegraph monopoly.

All cultures met this ever renewed technological revolution of the past century and a half with a mixture of embrace and resistance. The structural instability that accompanied rapid technological change led in many societies to ever stronger resistance and nostalgia. Uniquely, in the culture of the United States there has been for the whole of the past hundred and fifty years a clear stake in newness itself that overwhelmed the party of nostalgia, delay, opposition, and elegiac celebration of a vanishing or vanished past in favor of a rush to the future.

The nineteenth century witnessed many land rushes in which settlers massed at the borders of newly opened territories. The gold rush to California and Nevada around 1850 no less than the rush to the Internet in the 1990s can be taken as sample instances of the energy that speeds up the possibility of change, if not the actual change itself. Workers rushed into Pittsburgh between 1880 and 1910 to work in the mills before there were houses for them to live in. A mere sixty years later, the forty miles of steel mills stretched out along the banks of the rivers were turned to scrap and leveled between 1970 and 1990, the ground being left cleared and empty. No legal or government policies encouraged or sped up the rush to build. No organized social policy resisted the rush to destroy the hundred-year tradition of steel-making in Pittsburgh. Once under way, the rush to build or to level accelerated as though with a hunger for the goal no matter what the goal.

The acceleration of frame-making and frame-breaking because of technology, occurring within a country still thinly settled, offered a unique line of sight for philosophical reflection, and created ideas and parables for the explanation or imagination of this new condition. By a remarkable gift of timing, the philosophy suited to this condition, and therefore seemingly doomed slightly later by the short-lived process of sketch and settlement that had been linked to the physical newness of the United States with its as-yet unpopulated and profoundly unsettled early conditions, turned out to make a bold, even better, fit with that restlessly accelerated technological transformation which, with its permanently unsettled conditions, would guarantee that, in effect, it would always be a new world.

The young would always find themselves in a cultural landscape unknown to their grandfathers, piloting themselves by rules and skills that baffled those who were supposed to pass on wisdom and skill to them, but who had found late in life that the hand tools to which their muscles were tuned, and on which their skills were honed, were all gone, and the skills that went with them were obsolete in a land of power drills, electric nail guns, and composite materials used in new ways. Each generation of carpenters can teach its own sons and daughters less and less. Often it is the old who must go to school to the young, the grandfather asking the fourteen-year-old how to use the portable telephone, the satellite television, the new microwave oven. The word "pilot" itself would shift in the shifting frame and come to refer to aviators rather than Mississippi steamboat pilots.

Philosophical Parables: Frederick Jackson Turner or Tom Sawyer

Just slightly offstage in many debates about American culture is the choice between two parables. On the one side stands Turner's frontier hypothesis with its announcement that we have come too late. Only the freely available land out west, Turner claimed, provided a safety valve for the rising pressures within the settled lands to the east. Only that same frontier could offer a rigorous school for democratic habits, while eliciting the energies to challenge the unbroken fields, or ground not even yet civilized to the status of fields.

One part of the immediate success and enduring popularity of Turner's frontier hypothesis must be found in its subtle allegory of what we might call limited-resource capitalism. A global version of Turner's hypothesis haunts recent apocalyptic pictures of exhausted resources such as the Club of Rome Report.

Land exists before it is owned, and many people prefer to blur the distinction between raw land, uncleared and isolated, and a thriving farm, well stocked, shrewdly managed, and linked to a market for its crops. Only a minute fraction of the raw land in America has, even today, become fully improved and fully productive. Nor is there any need for most land to be fully valued and exploited.

Oil in the ground is finite; once owned, it might seem unchanged by mere ownership. John D. Rockefeller did not create the oil he learned how to market. Nor did he create the automobile that provided the frame within which the oil had a value impossible to imagine earlier.

Gold and silver are the simplest examples of scarce, buried treasure. The one who finds them stakes his claim, and defends that eternal claim against all others. A significant part of wealth in the early American economy was based on these already existing resources such as land, oil, or gold that fell into the hands of those who could build a fence around them by means of legal claims. The earliest wealth in the new world came from the fur trade, in which the animal is seized, killed, and skinned, but never possessed and nurtured as farm animals are. Wealth from limited resources, from the whales in the ocean, the bison on the prairie, the oil in the ground, or the land itself, can always seem unjustly distributed and easily wasted or exhausted. Force and violence often seize it; guns and fences defend it against those who arrive slightly later.

Turner's elegiac warning about the closing of the frontier resonated as a parable for all the limited resources that, unclaimed, might seem to guarantee the promise of American life, but once claimed might build a ring of fences around the freedom of all who came after this short time of seizing, claiming, and fencing. The image of monopoly capitalism had its strongest evidence in the possibility of a monopoly of oil, like that of Rockefeller's Standard

Oil, or a monopoly of silver, or, worst of all, a monopoly of land, as had occurred in England with its aristocracy of large landowners.

If Turner's image of the closing of the frontier stood for the potential exhaustion of ownership rights over all limited resources—water rights in the West, oil, gold, furs, land, silver, iron ore, copper, and waterfalls for the generation of electricity or for the running of factory machines through water wheels and belts—then Turner's "closing" meant the closing of all possible access to future enterprise and opportunity. If the frontier, in this wider sense, had closed around 1890 or 1910, then society itself would soon have been as locked in as England was through the operation of its class system. The promise of democratic mobility would have turned out to be only a short prelude to one more depressingly rigid economic world in which there were open positions only at the bottom. This is the larger allegory of limited-resource capitalism that gave weight to the seemingly more limited pessimism of Turner's hypothesis. It is this wider account of limited-resource capitalism, often taken to be the whole of capitalism by its critics, that accounts for the attention that made Turner's hypothesis the single most important historical idea ever proposed by an American intellectual.

Looking only at the creation of wealth in eighteenth- and nineteenth-century America, we might miss the flaw in using land and oil, furs and slaves, gold and water rights as representative examples of wealth. But this is where an alternative parable, Twain's famous scene of Tom Sawyer whitewashing Aunt Sally's fence, offers a decisive counter-image to Turner's closed frontier with its hidden claim that all opportunity bears the spiritual burden of limited and only temporarily unclaimed resources.

Tom, ordered to paint the fence by Aunt Sally, manages to perform the task so that his young friends passing by, instead of pitying him chained to the task, beg for a turn and ultimately pay Tom for the right to do what had earlier seemed to them the worst possible way to spend a fine day. We might, initially, be tempted to say that Tom Sawyer tricks the boys into painting the fence. Should we think of him as the very model of a huckster, an advertising man arriving in a small town, packaging his shoddy product to sell to the gullible rubes? Isn't this a parable of the capitalist exploiting the labor of others, getting them to pay for the privilege of working for him by duping them into believing that fence-painting is fun? The morals of Tom Sawyer are often seen as shoddy compared to those of the sentimentalized but upright Huck Finn.

In fact, the reality of Tom Sawyer, standing by his well-painted fence, is more interesting than this naive account would suggest. Tom's question to the first boy who stops to watch him paint is this: "What do you call work?"[1] The boy who hears this Socratic question, Ben Rogers, has just paused in his game of pretending to be a steamship, the *Big Mississippi*, drawing nine feet of water. The impersonation takes skill, practice, and imagination to bring off. It also takes the participating imaginations of any spectators who come to feel that Ben is not doing a bad job of convincing them that a small boy can sound like, act like, and navigate like a Mississippi River steamboat gliding down the road in a village.

It might seem that, unlike Ben Rogers, Tom Sawyer uses his imagination to prey on the imaginations of others so that they become his customers (in their eyes), buying the right to paint, while becoming his employees (in his eyes), relieving him of the need to paint the fence himself. In fact, Tom does not get out of work. He cannot, for example, leave the scene for a day of fishing. Instead, he becomes a manager, a salesman, a negotiator, and a supervisor, and this requires him to work hard all day and to bring a wide range of talents and knowledge into play. He participates in the larger job of painting the fence, but in a new way that keeps him engaged in the task and on the spot until the last inch of fence has received its third coat of paint. Tom's boss, Aunt Sally, ends up satisfied beyond her wildest dreams.

Not only is the specific job done better than Aunt Sally expected, but its very nature has been changed crucially. No longer a routine, solitary labor, it is now an event, almost a festival, not different in kind from an Amish barn raising that turns merely building a barn into a community and communal feast, or a spelling bee in school that turns practicing spelling into a social event. Tom changes the frame, sinking the dull work into a larger game or social event that converts drudgery into excitement mixed with participatory pleasure.

Tom ends the day with a pile of treasure, and this "profit" might seem to be the exploitative aspect of his day at the fence. He now has "a dead rat and a string to swing it with," a piece of bottle glass to look through, a dog collar, four pieces of orange peel, and a dilapidated old window sash.

If there is a trick here, hasn't Tom been the one tricked? Are the pieces of orange peel or the dead rat really forms of wealth? Isn't an act of imagination, or what we now call in philosophy an act of seeing-as, required to see the orange peel as treasure just as much as it is required to see painting a fence as fun? When Tom first negotiates with Aunt Sally's slave, Jim, before Ben Rogers appears, he offers to swap jobs with Jim, to trade work for work. Tom will take Jim's place and fetch water from the town pump if Jim will paint the fence while Tom goes to get the water.

Jim refuses the swap until Tom ups his offer, throwing in a marble and finally offering to show Jim his sore toe. This sore toe, now reimagined as a form of wealth—as a desirable possession rather than as a painful defect—turns the tide, and Jim agrees to trade jobs.

The world that Mark Twain pictures here is a world saturated with the imagination and with the pleasures of the imagination. It is also a world imagined as a market where each thing might be seen as a "good" for sale or for barter. A sore toe might be a hindrance if, for example, you were to enter a race, and it might be treasure, if you charge others to see it or swap it for something that someone else has imagined into wealth, such as a dead rat that a boy saw without the ordinary adult disgust. In the light of his imagination the boy saw the rat as a potential toy. He tied a string around it so as to swing it and began to carry it around with him as wealth, to own or to swap, if he can convince someone else's imagination to see it as a valuable asset just as he does. Is a sore toe only a negative fact about my foot? Is a dead rat only to be seen as an adult might see it upon finding it in the kitchen sink?

Tom Sawyer's sly opening question to Ben Rogers—What do you call work?—is part of a series of questions: What do you consider wealth? property? pleasure? Is the common positive or negative value of a sore toe, a dead rat, or an unpainted fence merely one of many possible values that might, if the right visionary imagination enters the world, change fundamentally the toe, the rat, the un-painted fence in a way that creates not just a new personal account, but a new social fact once other imaginations also see the toe, the rat, or the unpainted fence just as the first inventor of this new way of seeing it did? Only the existence of a market can make clear the question of whether other imaginations can be made to see it the same way. We might define the world of Tom Sawyer and Huck Finn as a world without parents but with a fully functioning market system for the imagination.

Tom's question is answered at the end of the chapter by Twain's explicit account. "Work consists of whatever a body is *obliged* to do and . . . Play consists of whatever a body is not obliged to do. And this would help him to understand why constructing artificial flow-ers or performing on a treadmill is work, while rolling ten pins or climbing Mont Blanc is only amusement."[2]

At this point we might see Twain's point as the freedom to rename or to recategorize and reframe the already fixed things and actions of life. Is a dead rat wealth or a disgusting object that we might have to pay someone else to dispose of so as to avoid touching it ourselves? This, too, would bring the dead rat into the market, but not as a toy on a string. Can work really be revisualized as play? And can a small boy impersonate a Mississippi steamboat and use his hands, his voice, his way of gliding along the street to mimic the steamboat-ef-fect so that his friends, who have already seen steamboats, will be reminded of what they already know are details of the steamboat experience? At some point he might even ask for payment—a bottle cap or a cricket in a bag—for seeing him "do" the steamboat.

Ben Rogers, in his steamboat phase, might best be described by a contemporary of Twain's, the French poet Arthur Rimbaud, who wrote the famous line "Je est une autre" ("I is an other"). Rimbaud's poem continued a statement that might as easily be about manufac-turing as about magic: "si le cuivre s'eveille clarion, il n'y a rien de sa faute."[3] The brass and leather that "wake up" to find themselves "trumpet" or the wood that "wakes up" to find itself "violin" or "matchstick" or "gunstock" must first have been imagined to be possible as and transformable into trumpet, gunstock, violin, or matchstick. This habit of imagining is common to both poetry and industry. The thing as it now stands is not regarded as fixed or final. Henry David Thoreau in *Walden* speaks of the ground being made to "say" beans.

Rimbaud and Tom Sawyer might seem an unlikely pair. But Twain should not be seen as a light-hearted aesthete engaged in what we call repicturing the already existing world out of boredom and cunning in order to make it new within his own subjectivity. Rimbaud trained himself to this end. And Rimbaud's early life as a poet led more naturally than most people think to his later life as a hard-nosed colonial businessman. "I accustomed myself to pure hallucination; I saw clearly a mosque instead of a factory, a drummers' school consisting of angels, coaches on the road of the sky, a drawing room at the bottom of a lake."[4]

Twain does not force the familiar into new shapes. His is the necessary way of seeing and looking, at the most literal level, for a fast-changing world. In Twain's lifetime the city of Cincinnati was imagined as the Queen of the American West (now the Midwest) because of its key location within the river, canal, and lake system of transportation. Its access to the Ohio and Mississippi routes that would link the entire country through water, flat-boats, canals, rivers, locks, and steam power would, some day, make Cincinnati a great metropolis, perhaps the greatest in the country. The highways of America seemed for the moment to be made of water. Cincinnati was, in the key phrase, "just about to become" the great city of the American heartland. Land values reflected what this or that block of property would be worth "as soon as" the full value of the city became actual rather than potential.

Long before Cincinnati's triumph could occur, the highways of America turned to steel, and Chicago, the junction point of the rail system and the great lakes, became the city of promise, the place "about to become" or "sure to become" the key city of the Midwest. Later, the highways of the country turned to concrete and asphalt and the interstate highways and tractor trailer trucks that moved goods along them from coast to coast undid Chicago just as the rails had undone Cincinnati.

Technological change that rewrites the framing conditions of action also reassembles wealth and value along the path of change.

Boom towns become backwaters or, even worse, ghost towns. Such technological change in a society embracing it rather than impeding its dynamic makes an entirely different parable out of Tom Sawyer's whitewashing of the fence or the young boy's manufacturing of a valuable toy out of a dead rat and a string. Technological change creates far more than the rise and fall of value. It creates ever new things undreamed of ten years or ten minutes earlier. It creates as well frames within which facts that were not facts until then settle themselves and assemble. Where frames change several times within one lifetime, those who thrive on such variability come to the front and those who fear instability move to the side. Mark Twain changed from his own Tom Sawyer–like boyhood to a businessman-author who followed or created every shift of the literary market between 1865 and 1900. The energy that comes not just from mobility but also from the love of mobility rose to the surface in Twain and in his countrymen and country women. For such people what "might be" becomes as strong a category as what is, or even a stronger one. What used to be becomes nothing. All that now exists is studied with a knowledge that it might not be much longer.

Discounting Future Gains and Losses: Premature Enterprise

One important detail of such a world is the fact that a zone of time comes into existence that becomes decisive for all attempts to set value. This is the phase between the start-up of an idea that, so it is claimed, might just change everything, and the full acceptance or final rejection of the idea, the moment when its promise is, at last, either realized or exposed as empty. This intermediate zone of time between the possible and the realized (or discarded) takes on enormous importance. During this time of possibility, the value of all things becomes a wager, both those things that will, if they are actualized, rise in value, and those that will fall in value, even to zero, like the carriage trade after the widespread distribution of the automobile. Economists use the concept of discounted future return to talk about the present moment's relation to an uncertain future. Land values anticipate what might be their worth in advance of the actual change of circumstance. This swampland that you see on your left might be the best site for a new feedlot once the railroad station is built over there—if the railroad is built at all and if its projection that it will take business away from the nearby canal turns out to be correct. The price at which the seller offers the swampland to you already includes a mark-up for the someday-to-be-built railroad station. He wants part of that future profit now.

That piece of land far out from town and of little value now because of that very distance might be the best land for a new airport, and if so the value of all the land nearby would increase by a factor of ten, except the houses that would become almost worthless because the airport noise would destroy the semirural tranquillity that gives them their current value. But are those houses worthless *now*, already, just because there is the idea of using the land for a future airport in someone's mind, or because the scheme has been mentioned in the newspaper or passed by the city council? Do the towns along the canals have to be seen as future ghost towns now, in the present, even before the first railroad track has been laid? This point where knowledge, the future, and value intersect is a key topic within the epistemology of rapidly changing worlds, the epistemology of capitalism.

In a technological world that accepts what the economist Joseph Schumpeter called the "creative destruction" of what already exists and currently satisfies needs in its own way, the future and the possible, the promising idea and the articulated plan, have a complex reality long before they are real. Fictions that in stable systems are the marks of fraud and the work of charlatans are in unstable systems the sketch, or one possible sketch, of what will turn out to be the real just slightly later in one lifetime. Equally important is the fact that everything that is now fully real becomes potentially unreal because it is or might be threatened by some new scheme of things in which it would disappear or become merely decorative, as horses are today now that they are no longer primarily used for farm work. What does not exist, but might someday, takes on a half-real, half-unreal quality long before it exists. But all that now exists is equally half-real, half-unreal because it exists under the threat that it might soon become obsolete or be discarded.

Each person has to discount, as economists put it, both the possible future and the not quite secure present wealth that has no guarantee of longevity once or if the frame alters. And it certainly will alter. This discounting and this insecurity of what in a stable system would seem guaranteed impose upon us one ever-changing calculation within this zone of time. The license to operate a radio station seemed a license to print money in the golden days of radio when the television set that would destroy radio was just in its early stage of development. The skills of a jazz musician in a world where jazz was the popular music would be devalued with the coming of rock-and-roll and the conversion of jazz into an esoteric art with a coterie audience.

An even more complex problem of this zone of time has been described by the economic historian Robert Fogel in his book on the railroads in nineteenth-century America.[5] The land grants to the railroads have commonly been described as a massive, corrupt give-away. But as Fogel demonstrates, the fact that an economic idea is certain to be correct *at some point in the future* lures speculators into building what he refers to as a "premature enterprise." Built too early or even in existence before the freight loads and the nearby towns and farms that can only be created at a later moment by the very existence of the railroad itself, the enterprise must be an economic catastrophe for the interval right after completion. The channel tunnel—or Chunnel—between England and France, the Panama Canal, and most other large scale-enterprises are "premature" in Fogel's sense. With the tendency of all important future-shaping projects to occur too soon because the idea is widely seen as correct and the future profits as enormous, the intervening time in which it is impossible to value all affected objects for the near-term future, and while investors wait for the full play of forces to work themselves out and align the system correctly, guarantees a disastrous early phase of existence and a significantly extended crisis of values.

One consequence of premature but relatively certain future enterprises is that, in the aftermath of success, it can seem that an absurd "free gift" like the wide swath of land along the railroad right-of-way was given away to tempt speculators into what was, in any case, a sure thing. A sure thing: except for the timing. The later "actual" values of land and rights are then, by critics, reimagined as the obvious values right from the start, whereas they are, in fact, the very information that only the unfolding process could have produced.

A culture rich in premature enterprises, in mirages created by discounted future values and future losses, rich in frames insecure even in the moment of their first triumph, in monopolies ambushed from behind (as Western Union was by the telephone), exists with the imagination decisively present in all acts of valuing. In a culture of this kind the strength of the imagination, as Mark Twain describes it among the boys of *Tom Sawyer*, becomes a primary *social* asset. In the lability and "what if" of the bargaining process, one's imagination does not primarily convince oneself, but, rather, convinces someone else; Jim is convinced of the value of seeing Tom's sore toe (after Tom has realized brilliantly that just this might be his best asset at the moment), and Tom is convinced by the imagination of the boy who could picture the dead rat as a treasure in the same moment that the owner of the rat is convinced by Tom that fence-painting could be a good time, worth paying for. Bargaining reveals that a market exists. In the act of bargaining each person's preferences are revealed, often even to himself.

Of course, what makes the day spent painting seem like a good time is, in part, the transformation of solitary work into a social event with its line-up of would-be painters waiting their turn. Once a crowd assembles, all benefit from the excitement of the talk, bargaining, and trading that makes up the second-order pleasure of any activity. It was the social life of the town pump, the place to talk and laugh and exchange gossip, that made Jim prefer the task of getting water over that of painting a fence. What Tom Sawyer has done is to embed the mere task in a far larger social enterprise in which the brush strokes are only one detail. He has, in the vocabulary of Emerson's famous essay of the late 1830s, drawn a larger circle around the fixed circle that everyone else took as the final limit.

Emerson's Circles: "The Coming Only Is Sacred"

Tom Sawyer's solution to Aunt Sally's order to whitewash the fence matches almost perfectly the dynamic described by Emerson in the

1839 essay "Circles." Emerson could be said, here in this early work, to have articulated the fundamental philosophy of enterprise capitalism and therefore the philosophy for the wider American culture long before his more explicitly economic account in the late essay "Wealth." Tom Sawyer drew a larger circle around the small cliché of a "hated task" just as he did around the small circle called a "sore toe." The circle that we find reality arranged in with its parts all fitted close together as though they had always been this way, or were, in any case, at last just right, seems fully occupied end to end. This circle that defines the world just-as-it-is when we find it, is itself the result of the play of earlier imaginations. The resulting world has been projected, a state of matter under some spell or another of the imagination. In fact it is the outcome of the sedimentation of thousands of years of different imaginations. But to the eye it seems fixed and satisfactory. There seems at first no place for us within this circle or for the activity of our minds. The circle is Emerson's term for this apparent completeness and perfection of the world just as it is now. We might choose to regard any change as a destruction of this perfect circle. Perhaps even our own birth is such a disturbance.

But then, in Emerson's image, we create a new and larger circle. A new idea or invention surrounds and dissolves the earlier fixed places for these limited facts. This new circle makes a new world. For Emerson steam is such a new idea. The railroad, coal, the telephone, the airplane, the personal computer, the Internet also count as new ideas in Emerson's sense. As does Tom Sawyer's realization that his sore toe might be used as a desirable bargaining chip.

Even in moral life, for Emerson, every new virtue "extinguishes [the other] in the light of a better . . . There is no virtue which is final; all are initial." The life that results is a "series of surprises." In America, economic life has been the best and most fully achieved model for the rapid play of this series of surprises. "In nature," as Emerson wrote, "every moment is new; the past is always swallowed and forgotten; the coming only is sacred. Nothing is secure but life, transition, the energizing spirit."[6]

This thrilling philosophy of what Emerson calls "the coming"—the next-on, the promising, unfolding world—is the natural constitution for an unfinished land. Emerson's genius is to take the material incompleteness of the United States in the mid-nineteenth century as a philosophical truth suggested by, but not limited to, American newness. Intellectuals in the nineteenth century too easily believed the tired claim of Emerson's contemporary Arthur Schopenhauer that we live near the end of time. For European pessimists like Schopenhauer, we find ourselves born tired in the last days of the world. The pyramids were built long ago; the Greeks and the Romans have passed away. We moderns are lesser beings living on a nearly exhausted earth. This is the familiar intellectual melancholy of the poetry of Matthew Arnold. Schopenhauer was the most popular philosopher in Europe during the second half of the nineteenth century.

The Emersonian imagination sees that the next-on world will shatter and rewrite this circle that now seems already finished and fixed in its array. Emerson sees, also, that it is ideas and inventions that, in large part, define the circle. "The things which are dear to men at this hour are so on account of the ideas which have emerged on their mental horizon, and which cause the present order of things, as a tree bears its apples. A new degree of culture would instantly revolutionize the entire system of human pursuits."[7]

Without the lively fact of technology and a system of creative destruction that can—and will—undo the blockade that the present always sets up in the face of the future, Emerson would have no actual instance of this claim other than the waves of religious ideas that had transformed culture and the meanings of culture in the past. Now, in the middle of the Industrial Revolution, he can use the word "train" to call up in every mind what such a transformation might look like.

> There are no fixtures in nature. The universe is fluid and volatile. Permanence is but a word of degrees. Our globe seen by God is a transparent law, not a mass of facts. The law dissolves the fact and holds it fluid. Our culture is the predominance of an idea which draws after it this *train* of cities and institutions. Let us rise into another idea; they will disappear. The Greek sculpture is all melted away, as if it had been statues of ice; here and there a solitary figure or fragment remaining, as we see flecks and scraps of snow left in

cold dells and mountain clefts, in June and July. For the genius that created it creates now somewhat else. The Greek letters last a little longer, but are already passing under the same sentence, and tumbling into the inevitable pit which the creation of new thought opens for all that is old. The new continents are built out of the ruins of an old planet; the new races fed out of the decomposition of the foregoing. New arts destroy the old. See the investment of capital in aqueducts made useless by hydraulics; fortifications, by gunpowder; roads and canals, by railways; sails, by steam; steam by electricity.[8]

Just as the whole political history of the United States ought to be seen as a struggle to be worthy of the Declaration of Independence, so too the whole of American culture and economic life is a, so far, successful attempt to live up to this Emersonian manifesto for a genuine culture of newness and nextness, a manifesto for the always "coming" or "oncoming" world on the horizon of the imagination.

The thrill of creative destruction, of overcoming the old arts, of superseding the revered fact, of watching the old world crumble, the old roads fall into disuse and finally into invisibility: these lyrical ideas of Emerson's are, it is clear from the word "train" and the word "electricity," centered on the new technology. He never sees technological change as merely additive. There is never a new toaster on the kitchen shelf without a disused oven nearby that no longer is used to brown the bread. And for Emerson the world of invention would be less thrilling if each new invention somehow could fit in without destroying the order of the old world—the old kitchen in this case. The destruction of the oven and the realignment of the whole circle of tasks within the kitchen once one new fact exists is an essential part of the value of this small instance of newness. Nothing around it will ever be the same again.

For Emerson, the arts and ideas of culture are part of the restlessness of the frame in which life reshapes itself. Hydraulics is an art, just as the brilliant masonry of the Roman aqueduct had been. One art creates the beauty of the fast-moving Yankee clipper ship with its thin wood and perfectly designed sails. Another art sank those ships forever (or made them merely a decorative feature of harbors and leisure time) once the ingenuity of the steam engine with its indifference to winds and calms and its ability to move large cargoes in heavy ships had taken over the shipping lanes of the earth.

The marble statues of Greece are changed now into a few fragments that we hold in museums. Only Emerson could liken the white marble of ancient statues to the bits of snow left in high mountain cliffs in June and July. The freezing of the water in this way is seen as an interruption, brief and fragile, of the fluid life of water before and after its brief moment as snow. The last remaining snow, these last remaining bits of marble, have been passed over by the seasons of life. And in Emerson's mind we are now living in the heat of June and July, not in the last days of the Schopenhauerian November or December of humankind. "It is a mischievous notion that we are come late into nature; that the world was finished a long time ago."9

The young in Emerson's reckoning "owe us a new world," and owe us, at the same time, the destruction of the world that we have comfortably come to see as fixed and finished around us, our comfortable circle. Emerson glides from the material and technological forms of creative destruction, which few would deny, although many would spend their lives and energies opposing and delaying, to the destruction of arts and ideas by new arts and ideas, which still fewer would welcome and most would deny, to the encircling and surpassing of moral values, which almost all would regret and oppose. It is at this point that he approaches Tom Sawyer and that Tom Sawyer becomes the true son of Emerson.

Emerson writes: "One man's justice is another's injustice . . . One man thinks justice consists in paying debts, and has no measure in his abhorrence of another who is very remiss in this duty and makes the creditor wait tediously." To this point Emerson's reader can see and probably buy into the familiar meanings that are held in the words "justice," "debts" and "duty." Emerson then draws a new circle around the words and, at the same time, around us. "But that second man has his own way of looking at things; asks himself which debt must I pay first, the debt to the rich, or the debt to the poor? the debt of money, or the debt of thought to mankind, of genius to nature? . . . If a man should dedicate himself to the payment of notes, would not this be injustice? Does he owe no debt but money?

And are all claims on him to be postponed to a landlord's or a banker's?"[10]

Unfortunately, Emerson suddenly tips over into the language of the scoundrel and the charlatan. So exploitive and self-serving a new definition of the word "debt," however faithful it might be to the idea of drawing a more imaginative circle around the fixed arrangements of the world, has to arouse suspicion. Our skepticism here would be confirmed by the failure of other imaginations to respond and create a social fact out of so one-sided a proposal. Tom Sawyer's friend is able to convince at least Tom to see the rat on a string as a prize possession. Such a convergence of imaginations is the essential meaning of a market. Emerson's debtor is likely to find himself in jail long before he convinces twelve of his neighbors, who make up the jury trying him for fraud, that his "debt" to nature and to thought took reasonable preference over his debt to his landlord.

The essential limits to the idea of ever new circles can be defined as the creation of social facts, those believed in by many people; and the essential ground for the creation of facts is manufacturing, especially the creation of entirely new technological frames within which a range of human activities take place, advance in importance, or, in the end, retire into the background or disappear.

Making a Law for Newness: The Charles River Bridge Case

The parable of an ever new America that we find in Mark Twain's account of the whitewashing of the fence along with the philosophical celebration of nextness and the "coming" world that we find everywhere in Emerson, but above all in "Circles," might seem to be resonant but isolated examples within nineteenth-century American culture. Counter-instances and alternative parables could easily be produced. What, in any case, can the works of Emerson mean within a culture that cared so little for philosophy or for intellectual defense of its mundane, eager inclinations?

In the late 1830s a long-fought judicial case was settled by the Supreme Court in a ruling that, we might say, wrote into law the premises of Emerson's "Circles," an essay written in lecture form in the same years. In the Charles River bridge decision the court affirmed the right of later improvements to exist even where their creation necessarily led to the destruction of the value of whatever means had served until then to fulfill the need. In his book *Privilege and Creative Destruction* Stanley Kutler offered a profound analysis of this watershed decision, which deserves to be known as one of the classic turning points in the creation of a legal framework for a society of permanent newness. I will draw on Kutler's book for both the details and the analysis presented in the following pages.[11]

In the early years of the Massachusetts Bay Colony the only connection between Boston and the emerging cities to the north and west was by means of a ferry operated by Harvard College under a grant from the legislature. When a toll bridge was built between Charlestown and Boston, connecting Cambridge, Concord, Medford, and other cities to Boston, the bridge's creation destroyed the future profits anticipated by the owners of the ferry monopoly. This is the simplest instance of creative destruction, because the bridge represents a genuine improvement over the ferry and if the ferry owners' rights to a permanent monopoly right were to be recognized, progress would cease. Turnpike owners could stop free highways. Canals could block railroads. The railroads themselves could later block airports, as they in fact tried to do. The coal and rail industries could block natural gas pipelines no matter how beneficial the cleaner fuel might be for home heating.

The legislature in Massachusetts provided that an annual payment should be made to Harvard College out of the tolls collected at the new bridge as compensation for the destruction of the ferry monopoly. Over time the toll bridge from Charlestown to Boston, built in 1786 for roughly $50,000, had so much traffic that stock in the bridge was worth $300,000. The value of the stock was based on the expectation of the flow of future tolls.

Forty years into the toll bridge's prosperous life, a new bridge was proposed. It would be located right beside the old one and would charge tolls only until its costs were paid, becoming then a free bridge. This new bridge would destroy the value of the stockholders' shares in the old toll bridge. It would have undergone creative destruction by a mere duplicate bridge, not by a technological advance.

For ten years the courts argued the case of the Charles River bridges. Justice Roger Taney in 1837 presided over a Supreme Court that ruled in favor of the new bridge and the legislature that had permitted it. In so doing it liquidated the annual payments to Harvard College for the even earlier destruction of the ferry. No compensation would now be paid to the already enriched stockholders of the first toll bridge.

The ruling affirmed progress over existing property that requires a future that does not change for it to hold its own present value. Each act of building also destroys. The interstate highway system built after 1950 destroyed the value of thousands of restaurants, gas stations, and hotels lining the old roads along which traffic had earlier passed. No compensation for the loss of expected future business would ever be paid.

The Charles River bridge case, as Stanley Kutler has shown in his important book, sets a philosophic and legal tone for the American relation to property. One important fact about Lincoln's Emancipation Proclamation was that with a stroke of a pen it destroyed the largest amount of property—ownership rights in slaves—existing in the South without any compensation. The value of the slave embodied the expected future work and the owner's profit from that work over the slave's lifetime. Lincoln drew a new circle, in Emerson's vocabulary, and the property vanished.

The Charles River bridge case set out the legal arguments and created the precedent for a culture in which privilege granted in the past would be secondary to the good of society understood as its right to the best possible future. That a bridge became the occasion for this precedent is symbolic. It is the pressure of technology and the opportunity that it creates under situations of a rapidly changing horizon of invention that make sense of the preference for the future over the past. A society satisfied with its traditional crafts and way of life would never affirm the instability that the local destruction of patterns of behavior and long-nourished skills would entail. Only a society that intends to train and pension off one and only one generation of riverboat pilots, jazz musicians, train firemen, and typist-clerks could contemplate with excitement the Emersonian ruling that Chief Justice Taney's Court handed down. They made creative destruction part of the law of the land.

New Men and Women for a Society of Creative Destruction

The turbulence and promise of a world of legal change matched to the inventive practices of technology and enterprise capitalism had profound consequences for the democratic personality that might not only endure but thrive within such conditions. America has always signaled the right to a new start. Mobility is made easier if community bonds are light. Sameness of features creates a society where it is always easy on the first or second day to know your way around. Bankruptcy laws encourage what in a card game always exists as the right to discard a bad hand and ask for a new deal. The most important social revolution of the twentieth century was appropriately named the New Deal.

The changing frame of ferries, toll bridges, free bridges, carts, wagons, canals, trains, roads, and highways encourages the travelers on those ever-shifting paths to imagine themselves changed, putting older selves "out of business" for the chance of a fresh start. If ideas can be circled, in Emerson's metaphor, then not only does natural gas encircle Pennsylvania coal and oil, which had themselves earlier encircled whale oil of the kind the saner partners in *Moby Dick* sought before they were encircled by Captain Ahab's mad quest for vengeance on a single whale, but the family that burns the whale oil to light their farmhouse in Massachusetts might draw a circle around their years in New England and flee to the new territory of the West.

Democratic personality under the spell of a new kind of freedom composed first and foremost of two nonpolitical facts—immigration and enterprise—wrote itself out in an entirely new alphabet, shorn of the old-world notion of status or character with its fixed sense of place, its steep costs for change, and its intergenerational responsibilities and culture.

In the same decade that the Charles River bridge case was finally settled in the Supreme Court, Emerson wrote his essay "Circles" and Mark Twain passed the early years of his life that are the basis of

Tom Sawyer. As he wrote in the opening sentences of his *Autobiography*: "I was born the 30th of November, 1835, in the almost invisible village of Florida, Monroe County, Missouri. My parents removed to Missouri in the early 'thirties; I do not remember just when."[12] The town was so faint on the map that he speaks of it as "almost invisible." Such a move was so little burnt into the family memory that he thinks of it only as some time in the early thirties.

Twain's parents had not spent their early lives in Florida, Missouri, and their parents had never seen the place. Twain himself would move on to the West, to Hartford, and finally spend almost a third of his later years in Europe. The word Twain uses for his parents' mobility is a richly nuanced one: they "removed" to the town. This might mean only a second move: to move and then to "remove," or move again. But it also suggests wiping the slate clean, removing the past, or at least the traces of the past. The family's life has been written on a blackboard and not on parchment. A swipe of a wet cloth each night and the slate is clean, the details removed.

The village of Florida in 1835 had roughly one hundred residents. "Most of the houses were of logs . . . There was a log church, with a puncheon floor and slab benches. A puncheon floor is made of logs whose upper surfaces have been chipped flat with the adz. The cracks between the logs were not filled; there was no carpet; consequently, if you dropped anything smaller than a peach it was likely to go through."[13]

It was villages of this kind, slightly to the north of Missouri, that Alexis de Tocqueville had passed through on his journey of 1830 prior to the writing of his great book *Democracy in America*. In his notebooks for this journey Tocqueville gave us the first keen-sighted portrait of the citizens of a world of immigration, enterprise, and creative destruction—citizens who have taken to "removing."

When his journey took him to the outer limits of settlement in the West of his day, an area now known to us as Ohio, he met a new kind of man and woman. Although these were poor, hard-working farmers, the word "peasant," he remarked, was never used. This old-world term implied a settled culture's way of life with its fixed positions, its limited horizon of thought, and an accompanying heritage matched to a predictable future to be inculcated into the children of the next generation. Instead of peasants he found settlers who had "escaped" (as he put it) from earlier poverty and an earlier way of life. Each family lived in a log house made from the first few downed trees. These "miserable" and "isolated" dwellings revealed to the approaching traveler at night glimpses of the hearth fire within through the unplugged chinks in the walls.

An ignorant and simple folk might be imagined inside such crude dwellings. Nothing could be further from the truth. The pioneer within this "primitive and wild" setting is the product of "the labor and experience of eighteen centuries. He wears the dress and speaks the language of cities; he is acquainted with the past, curious about the future, and ready for argument about the present; he is, in short, a highly civilized being, who consents for a time to inhabit the backwoods, and who penetrates into the wilds of the New World with the Bible, an axe, and some newspapers."[14]

In the notebooks from his journey, Tocqueville explained that these settlers were the products of a "second immigration." Most of them came from New England. They were immigrants at one remove. It was in Ohio, where even the new world of the eastern states was just another kind of old world, that the full taste of a democracy of reiterated immigration could be experienced. "The inhabitants of Ohio arrived only yesterday in the place where they live. They have come without knowing one another, and with different morals and conceptions. The greater part of them have not come to stay. No common tie binds them together. There is not one among them who could talk about his life to people who would understand him. No one has had the time to establish a way of life, to win a reputation, or to establish an influence of any permanence on the strength of his services or his virtues."[15] Tocqueville's description would apply today to the many casually entered and exited temporary societies that make up American life. We find ourselves still commonly involved in one or another "second immigration." Eighteen-year-old students newly arrived in a college dormitory where they will spend four years together with other newly arrived strangers, newly retired New Yorkers moving into a condominium complex in Florida for their years as senior citizens, job hunters leaving the declining industrial area around Pittsburgh for a Denver suburb where most other residents have arrived within the past five years and the suburb itself did not exist twenty years earlier: these and many other categories of second immigration would fit the terms of Tocqueville's Ohio of the 1830s. If anything, there is even more Ohio in the United States than there used to be.

Astonished by this world with its blunt logic, Tocqueville notes that "in Ohio everyone has come to make money . . . The whole of society is an industry."[16] Free of memory and shared experience, the settlers lack leaders who might have some claim to respect and veneration based on a history of their earlier deeds. To our, and to his surprise, Tocqueville concludes emphatically: *and yet the society prospers*. He means, by this, far more than mere financial prosperity. This Ohio world of the "transitory and the temporary" thrives in richly human terms. Here the self-organized initiative, the local improvisation, the newly formed and temporary association of citizens thrives on an as-needed basis.

The Ohio of the French observer's profound description, a place of which it can be said that "no one was born there," has truly earned the title of the "new world." As former New Englanders flooded into the territory, they reaffirmed both immigration and enterprise. What in Tocqueville's day was a "second immigration" might be, in ours, the fifth or tenth in the family history of earlier settlers. Under modern conditions we find even the second or third immigration within a single lifetime.

Florida and California in the decades after the Second World War became the new Ohios of the 1950s and 1960s. The cities of the North or the strong states within the New South drew the same crowds of new settlers as the land rush of Oklahoma had a century earlier. New patterns of going away to college and retiring to warmer climates meant that even the separable phases of a single life invited second and third and fourth immigrations, with the last adventure of resettlement often started at the age of retirement. How, in America, could we have grown used to the word "settler" for describing such unsettled lives lived out amid so many unsettled conditions? What Tocqueville viewed as the conditions of immigration reaffirmed in the lives of his Ohio pioneers have as strong an appeal today.

Introduction

The thickly rooted, tacit culture that has often been nostalgically invoked in talk of community and communitarian principles was nowhere to be seen in Tocqueville's West. As he observed in a shocking sentence, in Ohio no one *"could talk about his life to people who would understand him."* "Rules of behavior seem uncertain." He saw that there was no list of old families, no long-admired leading citizens whose grandfathers and fathers had also served well. There was not even the "moral power exercised over a people's spirit by the memory of a whole life spent *before its eyes* in doing good."[17] Instead of the memory of whole lives, the settlers in Ohio had to rely on the stories and claims that each person chose to tell or to make up about an unseen earlier life. In fact, the stories strangers told each other of their earlier deeds were just as likely to be tall tales, crude lies, or carefully cleaned up versions of lives decidedly not lived under each other's inspection. This self-invention, including a change of name, is one of the advantages of a second immigration, or what Twain had called a "remove."

Social life bound to these strange premises continues to flourish even today in the United States: immigration; segmented lives whose phases are passed among entirely new, made-up communities like those of a college campus, an army barracks, a retirement community, or a freshly landscaped new suburban development; economic enterprise along with a toleration of the clean slate offered by bankruptcy laws; the world of strangers; a core notion of freedom that implies mobility, flight, and economic ambition; and finally, a somehow portable, minimal culture summed up, in Tocqueville's day, by the triad of "the Bible, an axe, and some newspapers." Today that minimal portable culture might require a high school diploma instead of the Bible, a personal computer instead of an axe, and a cable-connected television set instead of the newspapers that kept the Ohio pioneers hooked up to the news of the world and to the civic life of their political society.

In the pages that follow I will examine the culture and the aesthetics of a society of first and second immigration, enterprise, creative destruction, and an ever shifting census of persons, things, and ways of life. The mental world defined in the 1830s by Emerson's circles,

27

the prototype of Tom Sawyer's fence as it existed in Twain's first years in Florida, Missouri, the bridges over the Charles River, and the settlers Tocqueville found in Ohio created a profound literary culture, but one that took its leading signals in an entirely new way from economic life rather than from religious or traditional, past-centered cultural foundations. Among the questions that will concern me here the following are central. They amount to an attempt to define representation and in particular the representation of persons in American culture between the century from Emerson's "Circles" or Walt Whitman's *Leaves of Grass* to William Faulkner's *The Sound and the Fury*.

1. What are the features of a democratic social space in cultural life, and how might a society come to prefer such a minimal social space to the thick detail of a culture that is passed on from generation to generation?

2. What is the link between immigration, a culture of invention, and such a democratic social space? As I will try to show, invention can be thought of as an immigration of objects or techniques. The young of each new generation should also be regarded as immigrants once the frame of economic or social life changes too rapidly for the parental generation to predict and pass on needed life skills. Immigration in its most profound sense means that any person born or entering a culture will spend adult years amid a changed census of persons, things, and ways of life. Learning what already exists, including the past, is of less use than cultivating a "loose inkling of types," in Whitman's phrase.

3. Because our history, especially the early paradox of slavery in a democratic culture, falls short of the requirements of a democratic social space, we are forced to ask about the effects of the breaks within or alternatives to a democratic social space. This will be the subject of Chapters 3 and 4, where I separately analyze slavery, professionalism, the hierarchy of performer and audience, and the key alternative of a traditional, and to outside spectators, opaque culture in its ritualized form.

4. In much of the book I will be asking what account literature can give of a person under these new conditions. I will begin

addressing this question in the chapter on Whitman and will continue in the final chapters on detail, voice, and state in realism.

5. The aesthetic equivalent of a culture of "removing" can be found in abstraction. What features of abstraction make it uniquely suited to a democratic social space?

6. What alternatives are there to abstraction? What alternative aesthetic modes of representation challenge the dominant abstraction? In chapters on regionalism and realism in Parts III and IV I will answer this question by examining the claims of thick, or natal, culture, on the side of regionalism, and of strongly isolated individual persons, experiences, places, and moments of time within what we call realism.

7. Can we say that abstraction is a sign that a society like that of the United States has, in anthropological terms, managed to do without culture altogether—without "ways" in the sense of fixed means of explaining, acting, and encompassing the central issues of life: economic survival, relational life, the connection of the past to the future? What is the relation of a democratic social space and its aesthetic of abstraction to traditional ideas of culture in which continuity over time, the weight of the past, and the strong linkage between generations amount to a set of requirements no longer met and, in fact, inimical to a society of invention, enterprise, and immigration with its bias towards the next-on world? Can a society of creative destruction, a society of "removing," be said to be a "culture" at all?

Finally, it might be expected that in a book where I make so strong a claim for an aesthetics of abstraction as the cultural side of an ever new world I would lead up to an analysis of American painting in the twentieth century. In an earlier book, *Making and Effacing Art*, I made just these claims for the great generation of American painters following World War II.[18] In that book I took up the effect that museums have had on art that is now created with the intent of securing a place in these visible histories of the past. The museum creates abstraction by resettling past objects away from their religious, civic, and familial cultural locations. We could think of the objects in museums as immigrants or, to use Twain's term, "removed" objects. The museum has effaced features of the objects of the past, giving them a newer, abstract minimal identity as objects in a museum with new features that suit the world in which they have now been socialized.

To speak metaphorically, the United States is itself a museum, gathering but abstracting persons from what had earlier been stable cultures of a familiar kind. The pressure and the freedom of the resocialization (the "removing") of persons and things into an ever-changing frame where years from now many even newer persons and things will define the texture and meaning of the whole is the deep and optimistic subject of both *Making and Effacing Art* and this complementary study of American literary culture in the period of invention, enterprise, and immigration. Both claim that ours is still the new world.

PART ONE

American Abstraction

chapter one

Democratic Social Space

Democratic Social Space versus the Classic State

When we think of the United States in the 1880s, a hundred years after the Constitution, one nation from the Atlantic to the Pacific, the simplest thing to say in terms of every theory of nationalism that had dominated European thinking in that hundred years is that there could not possibly be any such single country. The theories of the state from Montesquieu's *L'esprit des lois* of 1748 to the Romantic theory of nationhood in the early nineteenth century had spelled out the conditions for the creation of a people or a nation. None of those conditions existed in the 1880s in what was fast becoming the most powerful nation in the world.

First of all, Americans were not a *Volk.* They had no common racial origin and no common history. Open to immigration and flooded by immigrants in the century between 1820 and 1920, America was a patchwork of peoples. In addition, with no shared religion, no deep relation to a common language, no shared customary way of life with its ceremonies and manners, no single style of humor or common inherited maxims and unspoken rules, the continental nation lacked just those features that any Romantic theory of the nation-state required. The radical choice to people the continent rapidly through immigration so as to "hold the land" by force of numbers blocked the patient creation over time of a historically or racially unified people. If patience and selection were historically essential, Americans were not, and would never be, a *Volk*.

Second, if Americans were not a people, America itself was not a land, because as political thought since Montesquieu's *L'esprit des lois* had recognized, climate was, in a sense, destiny. The vast American continent was many climates rather than one. As a location it was made up of many environments, and could properly be the home to a collection of nations, as Europe was, but not to one. If mountains produced liberty, as Montesquieu thought, and coastal geographies, societies of trade; if differences between hot, temperate, and cold climates produced distinct temperaments and laws, then the variation within the fertility of the land, the strongly marked tropical and northern climates, the flat midlands and the coastal mountains should have provided room for Swiss-style democracy and Tartar despotisms, for frugal and independent Dutch-style nations of traders around Philadelphia, New York, and Boston, and for voluptuous and hot-blooded societies of honor in the Deep South.

If climate and terrain, along with relative fertility, produce the entire system that we call "a way of life," with its system of laws, form of government, religion, and structure of ideas, then once again, just as in the case of immigration, American geography rules out a single nation in any traditional sense. Montesquieu had written that "l'empire du climat est le premier de tous les empires."[1] Within Montesquieu's powerful determinism, certainly the most important before Marx's, there could not logically be one system of laws, or one people within a geography so vast and diverse, with climates and ways of life as profoundly different as the frugal village life of New England, driven by its nearly half year of winter, and the almost tropical plantation society of southern America, with communities varying from the farming populations of the fertile Midwest to the coastal trading societies of the East and West Coasts. Montesquieu's was the single most important book of political thought to have appeared in the generation before the creation of American independence. In the first two years after its appearance in Geneva, twenty-two printings were needed. In its profoundly rational and detailed empirical elaboration of the material basis of society, Montesquieu's book became itself the climate for the invention of America as an independent political entity of a new kind.

In the same hundred years between 1780 and 1880 a single German nation was created out of a confusing mass of small and middle-sized principalities. In some ways this state was formed as a culture before it existed as a political nation. Luther, Goethe, and Schiller; Kant, Hegel, and Fichte; German poetry, German Romanticism, German philosophy, and German music built a common identity before political structures existed to translate that identity into economic or nation-state terms. For such a culture state there is also no equivalent in America, and even now there is no poetry, music, or philosophy that plays a significant part in what we think of as American identity. Even if culture was permitted as an alternative to geography or to *Volk* as the base for a nation, America would come up empty.

The same Romantic theory of the state in which, from above, the "Genius" of a people might be concentrated and expressed in its few Beethovens, Kants, and Goethes, and then become a common point of reference for society as a whole, had also claimed that in language could be found an unconscious philosophy and shared spirit which even in the absence of externalization in the works of a few geniuses would stabilize and shape a common consciousness. The particular American English that has been learned and reshaped by all immigrants is not, however, like French, Italian, German, or Russian, a "language" at all, but rather a new type of colonial language—a world language more and more purged of those qualities of a people and a history that we think of as rooted, shared experience. It is a shared language of what we now call "communication," rather than a thickly sedimented historical product of a way of life. American English is always a second language, a language by adoption. Insofar as the English language in use in America implied the historical experience of England or even the experience of English landscape and climate, it was an impediment rather than a starting point.

In America since at least the mid-nineteenth century there has always been a higher percentage of language learners than language speakers. Immigrants master a kind of minimal competence, a language of necessity. Where a culture has a high percentage of immigrants, as many cities and states have had throughout the last century and a half, language itself comes to exist in a shortcut version that is the best available shared medium. Even more important, so many people live in a kind of language anxiety because they are newcomers embarrassed about accent or lack of competence that a widespread desire to relax in silence, a desire to spend more and more time outside language, becomes a social fact.

Some observers of the American city in the early twentieth century (when the percentage of foreign-born was at a peak not reached again until our own time) claimed that a kind of barbarism of language existed. Children deprived of the nuance and wealth of tone and expression of the parental language used a sketchy, minimal version of the new language that they had not yet learned. Novels of the early twentieth century through the thirties often feature a loud street world of shouted taunts and dares, bragging, bluster, and curses, clipped and slaughtered in pronunciation. In many cities a half-language became the residue language of a generation that fell between the stools of an abandoned parental language that they no longer wished to speak and a very partially acquired new language that they knew they spoke clumsily and inarticulately.

The role of the immigrants' basic survival English in forming an awkward relationship to the act of speaking itself in later generations that live in the shadow of language embarrassment is one of the great unstudied cultural facts in America. The silent hero or heroine in American novels and films is only one fact among many within a culture that needed alternative paths outside language to communicate meaning and tone in a polyglot and minimally shared language world. Other expressive paths were used whenever becoming articulate was a great burden. We do not have to share the idea that the minimal language is a form of barbarism or that immigrant children necessarily sound like those in the Studs Lonigan trilogy or Stephen Crane's *Maggie* to see how impossible it was for a shared rich language world to develop in America and create a common social space.

One reason that the American entertainment industry has been so agile and successful worldwide is that American immigration and the hunt for shared ground domestically has meant that Hollywood profits from the internal distillation of traits within the United States. Italian, Irish, Mexican, African, Chinese, Korean, Russian, and German descendants who intermarried in all possible combinations make the domestic market a model for the world market. The common cultural ground that makes a film work in Kansas, Los Angeles, Florida, Seattle, Boston, and Alabama also makes it relatively easy for that film to succeed in Paris, Hong Kong, Berlin, Buenos Aires, and Tokyo. The same is true for American television story-telling series and American music. They also profit from our internal distillation of taste and temper. What Whitman called the loose inkling of types, the thin demand on personality in America, produced a rich visual world of film and television because the visual was inevitably a common ground for a nation where so many citizens had only a minimal skill in language. American music, from jazz to rock, has been a world of sound rather than words, or of words so entrapped in manner and style that the words themselves are nothing, as in the buried language of rock music. The culture that has taken over the world entertainment market is not a language culture because languages are one of the most stubborn residual homes of mutual incomprehensibility and traditional rooted habits of thought and feeling. Instead it is a visual and a sound culture in which words play only a small part and often project, as in a Disney cartoon, a minimal shared core of meaning less rich than the absorbing visual world in which it is nested. Fortunately for the language-embarrassed cities of the early twentieth century, the first form of the modern entertainment industry was both visual and silent: the silent films of Charlie Chaplin and Mack Sennett.

To review quickly as I have done the eighteenth- and nineteenth century vocabularies of nationalism is to see that without a single *Volk*, without a single environment or climate, without a culture, and without, in the deep Romantic sense, a language, the national fact of America meant that somehow the problem of identity had been solved by other means, by unprecedented means. My premise in what follows is that it was in the creation of a democratic social space, a homogeneous, cellular medium of life, that this was done. I also want to propose that it was within economic life—within free enterprise capitalism—that there arose a remarkable solution to what we might call the problem of the production or manufacture of a democratic social space. In other words, in the pages that follow I will be proposing and then testing the idea that the vast geography of America and the radical mixture of immigrants within that geography steered themselves towards a common identity by means that were—instead of religious, ideological, cultural, historical, or linguistic—fiercely economic and, in the end, profoundly dependent upon the mass production and broad distribution that capitalism created.

Once a capitalism of shared goods is interwoven with the rush to the future, the next-on state of things that accelerated technological change makes possible, the stake in culture or stable culture as a world inherited from the past declines in value. The future that newcomers and old-timers alike face as another new world into which they must immigrate redistributes advantages away from those settled toward the young and the new, those with a minimal stake in the preservation of the present frame, whether that frame be the horse and buggy, the silent movie, the telegraph, the clipper ship, the current style of painting, or the popular music of this or that decade for the brief moment that it was the present.

Abstraction and the Minimal Culture of Immigration

In a country lacking a single *Volk*, a coherent geography and climate, or a strong common culture of reference, the unity that resolved the two great diversities—that of geography and that of population—was a unity that had about it a quality of abstraction. It was a uniformity rather than a unity. What would have been called, a few years ago, American conformity, or even American blandness or thinness of character, was a resolution of a diversity so unmanageable that only by the creation of an almost mechanically applied pattern could it be composed or settled. Like the basic English of communication, this thinness of character solved the problem of a common ground different from, but drawing on the, thick, historically burdened identities that each and every family had begun its American career by leaving behind.

This easy, light-fitting American personality Whitman celebrated as "the loose drift of character, the inkling through random types."[2] In the novels of Charles Dickens we are aware of the paradoxical, close connection between a brittle, memorable uniqueness of character and the city crowd. Unforgettably sharp simplification of personality has to do with a close-packed competition for attention and for space within memory under circumstances where most people are strangers and all are quickly forgotten. That American conditions have produced the opposite of Dickensian high-definition personality has to do both with the uncrowded social space into which each new person has to insert himself or herself and with the subtraction of differences from diverse immigrant groups that is the first stage of personal self-characterization in American life. Cultivation, even manufacture, of difference plays the part in the nineteenth-century European city culture of Baudelaire, Dickens, and Dostoevsky that subtraction of difference played in the United States. This Whitman catches in his wonderful phrase "the loose drift of character." The "making of americans," as Gertrude Stein called it, was achieved first of all by those thousands of negations by which the children of Italian Americans, German Americans and Chinese Americans erased letter by letter the accent, style of laughter, customs and costumes of family life, dress, and idiom of the old country so as to be, at last, simply American. In every American personality there exists a past history of abandoned differences. The deep topic of American culture is not difference, but abandoned difference.

What the young of newly arrived families assimilated to was not an alien past of some other, dominant group. Instead, the young joined themselves to a generation of their peers, those locals who were also in flight from their own parental culture and bent on the creation of a future that would be their own. Any such future, once realized, would feel not alien at all, but like "our own world." That world, in its turn, would be lost to the next-on generation of their children, who would, once again in combination with the children of the newly arrived, set out on the generational project that Emerson turned into a command: "The Young owe us a new world." Above all else they owe themselves, not us, a new world.

Wherever the process of subtraction of "old-world" details takes place, it imposes submission not to some other "old world" and its details, but to the loose flow of character that Whitman named as his subject. The new generation will make up their own common fund of stories and songs that they will share and use to define their sense of life. The child of Croatian parents in Chicago in 1920 did not give up the old Croatian stories to submit himself to the old Serbian stories or the old stories of the Ottoman Empire, as had happened in the chain of conquests back home. Instead, the immigrants who arrived between 1890 and 1920 found their children huddled around the radio listening to the new stories of their generation: *The Shadow, The Lone Ranger, Fibber McGee and Molly.*

In turn, the children of the radio generation would find their children out at the movies or watching television to get the common stories of their generation, a generation that included the children of all those who had arrived in the meantime. The radio was the first guarantee in America that new stories, new personalities, and new music could be beamed out across the nation and received on any cheap, small, listening device. The original crystal-set radios could be made at home by winding copper wire around an oatmeal box and attaching the coil to a small galena crystal and listening through an earphone. Once these cheap devices, including the tube and transistor sets that followed, had come into existence, the new music of jazz and swing could take a generation by storm. The stories, sports events, national heroes, and notorious criminals of each generation would be unique to the people of that generation and their time. A common, new world grew up that saved an immigrant culture from the need to assimilate to, rather than assimilate with. Every young person, whether first or tenth generation, joined the culture that was equally new and exciting to them all.

The immigrant generation of what Woody Allen's movie had called "Radio Days" was saved by radio and movies from any mere submission to yet another old culture, whether Anglophone culture or the culture of nineteenth-century American "classics." Longfellow, Emerson, Whittier, Hawthorne, and Cooper represented a past that had always had a faux antique feeling. It always did seem really past: Hiawatha and the Village Blacksmith, *The Scarlet Letter* and Chingachgook are each set into a picture-frame past. American classics were always a safe past away from the reader. The whaling industry was gone. The Mississippi steamboats of Mark Twain's youth were extinct. New England Culture was quaint and thin. The accumulated stories of this literature had no more hold on the native young, listening in their rooms at night to *The Shadow* or watching *LA Law*, than they had on the new immigrants of Chicago and Los Angeles in the great periods of immigration and their aftermath: 1890 to 1940 and 1975 to the present.

Even jazz, movies, Broadway musicals, and radio did not, in their turn, become a museum of classic, shared experiences to be passed on to the next generation, or discussed between the generations. New music, new visual styles, television, records, and CDs quickly made the swing music of the 1940s, the films of John Ford, and the screwball comedies of the 1930s seem as antique as *The Scarlet Letter*.

By choosing to have *no tradition*, no deep and permanent stories, no old songs, no traditional dances and ceremonies, a democratic culture, aided by the dynamic of technology and what we now call entertainment, proceeded to level in every generation the playing field between the natives and the newly arrived. The deep meaning of having a Constitution is the privilege not to have a tradition or a traditional culture. A Constitution spells out the minimal limits for whatever new world, new practices we may in the future choose to create. It does not guard, as tradition does, a warehouse of old recipes for living and thinking. To have a Constitution is to be able to say good riddance to culture in the anthropologists' sense of the word.

The invention of entertainment and the consolidation of the entertainment industry, which is now charged with providing new stories, new visual forms, new means of linking the next-on generation together, meant that for the first time an alternative existed to the idea of tradition and culture. At the same time, an alternative also existed to the old sacrificial act of giving up one's own "old ways" of dress, songs, and traditions only to submit to those of someone else's old culture.

In America the rise of the entertainment industry necessarily and fortunately went hand in hand with the lifetime of the most massive immigrant generation in our history, the generation of 1890 to 1920, a generation whose children's lives set the tone for the national culture down to the war years of the early nineteen-forties.

The new entertainment industry of those years made possible their assimilation into a culture that was as new to residents who had arrived earlier as it was to those fresh from Ellis Island. The marriage in America of an immigrant culture and an entertainment industry was one of the luckiest strokes imaginable for a democracy at the cultural level. It was a fated combination.

It was the generation of the 1920s that was the first "generation" in the United States. Americans had, for the first time, the means to become aware of themselves as a generation. With their new dances, films, music, jazz-age, lost-generation stories, they were also the first generation to profit from the energies of the wave of immigration that was now settling down in a new culture in the American cities and towns.

What we call the erasure of differences within personality and within distinct traditions was only half of the larger story of a world in which all the young would, in effect, immigrate into their own generation's cultural world and define that world by how little it would share with that of their parents, whether those parents were "old-world" or simply "old-fashioned." After the 1920s every generation has its own short-lived cultural identity within which it thrives and comes to feel at home, but which it fails to stabilize and pass on because the very idea of transmission became obsolete, considered an impediment to the rapid assimilation of newcomers. Technology-driven change and immigration are a second marriage made in heaven.

Jefferson's Map

When we look at the passage from American nature to American settlement or from land to property we see a similar erasure of traits rather than cultivation of features.

But the diversity of geography did not undergo abstraction by the step-by-step, three-generation-long process of surrender of difference that characterized immigration. With one stroke Thomas Jefferson in 1785 created the land ordinance that would govern the western territories. He based the future American map on a one-mile square (640-acre) section that could be subdivided to yield

A SECTION OF LAND — 640 ACRES.

A rod is 16½ feet.
A chain is 66 feet or 4 rods.
A mile is 320 rods, 80 chains or 5,280 ft.
A square rod is 272¼ square feet.
An acre contains 43,560 square feet.
"   "   "   160 square rods.
"   "   is about 208¾ feet square.
"   "   is 8 rods wide by 20 rods long,
or any two numbers (of rods) whose
product is 160.
25x125 feet equals .0717 of an acre.

Thomas Jefferson's map of a 640-acre section of land. (Courtesy of the Chicago Title and Trust Company.)

farms of 20, 40, 80, 160, or 320 acres, or, in the other direction, could be multiplied to define state borders that look as though drawn with a ruler. Jefferson set down a mechanical grid over the surface of America that made the United States the first nation with property lines that could be read easily from an airplane at 30,000 feet. The resulting American surveyor's grid divided the geography and oriented the lines of western states as well as those of city streets with no regard whatsoever for terrain.[3]

Far more important than the literal map that Jefferson created was the progressive definition and realization of a democratic social space. Democratic society grounds itself in what we might call a Cartesian social space, one that is identical from point to point and potentially unlimited in extent. In this it differs from the Greek *polis*, which both Plato and Aristotle limited in size to a few thousand people; to a number that could gather and speak together, see one another in one place and act in common. Democratic social space has no clear logic of limitation because it begins with the modern notion of political representation: the mechanical idea of sampling. American politicians, including American Presidents, who often seem ordinary, even banal, should be thought of in this sense as "samples" of the society rather than as its few best men and women. They are representative in the way that John Q. Public is, and not as Achilles was.

Representation, of course, also implies an identity from point to point so that one part can stand for or represent the whole. Democratic social space would, ideally, be a universal and everywhere similar medium in which rights and opportunities were identical, a space in which the right and even the ability to move from place to place would be assured. In this important sense, a democratic social space requires an ever more sophisticated and effortless system of transportation alongside a less and less developed sense of place, region, or home. The history of American society is to a larger extent than most histories a history of transportation. Canals, covered wagons, the romance of the horse, the continental railroad system, the Mississippi steamboats, the interstate highway system, the Mack truck, the private passenger car, the airport system: the history of the development of a truly national life is embedded in the rapid building and rapid wearing out of a grid along which movement could occur. Place in America, by contrast, has often been casual, the crossroads of one or another system of movement. The system has always been more fundamental than the cross-points on the grid. The erasure of place in the aftermath of systems that turned out to be only temporary is one of the fundamental American stories, the story of "ghost towns."

Along with mobility, the right to enter or to exit is equally fundamental to a Cartesian social space. Similarity, representation, the absence of limits, openness to immigration and expatriation, internal mobility: these are essential features, and conspicuously Cartesian features, of a continuous and democratic social space.

Thomas Jefferson's picture of America as a nation of independent family farms—self-sufficient, not so large that they could not be worked by family members alone; stable; neither increasing nor decreasing in size or wealth; contented and independent—was one of the first and most enduring images of democratic social space. All farms would be very similar because each would provide completely for the needs of the family. The larger society might be made up of an unlimited number of such households. Such farms are also isomorphic. A family could move from one such farm in Virginia to another in Nebraska and reduplicate their way of life, carry it on without resistance other than that from changes in landscape and climate.

Thoreau's *Walden* was a Jeffersonian experiment to define the unit of self-sufficient life without the complication of sexual or familial life. It is the repeatable pattern for a nation of self-sufficient poet-farmers. An entire earth could be carpeted from end to end with reduplications of Thoreau's experiment, but, given the abstemious nature of asexuality, Thoreau's pattern could work for one generation only. Jefferson's democratic social space, unlike Thoreau's, provides for both self-sufficiency and reproduction. It is, therefore, the most compact imaginable truly Cartesian unit.

The modern American suburb is another such Cartesian democratic social space. Everywhere across the varied geography and climate the suburbs are comfortably the same, equipped with the same schools and parks for children; the same shopping centers with the same stores selling Levis, Tide, and power lawn mowers; the same array of churches and car dealers; the same fraternal organizations and specialized doctors. The reduplication of housing types with identical appliances, the familiar street names with the same automobiles on those streets, anchors a modern social space that has identity from point to point. Because of this identity it invites mobility, which becomes nearly cost-free. Ultimately, wherever you move, the new place will be enough like the old to feel very quickly "like home." It is an interesting American invention, both semantic and literal, to live not "at home" but in a place that feels "like home."

To describe the suburb, that great American invention of the last hundred years, and an invention whose essence from the start is tied into the consequences of transportation systems that let you live "near," but not in or at, various places, is to point out that modern capitalism, however much Jefferson feared it, turned out to be the very means for achieving a Jeffersonian America. An army of traveling salesmen began, in the nineteenth century, to visit, one by one, the tens of thousands of Jeffersonian farms, selling each of them its own McCormick reaper, Singer sewing machine, or copy of Mark Twain's latest book. Soon the Sears and Roebuck catalogue sat on every kitchen table. But the climactic national object was Henry Ford's Model T, which Ford smartly observed you could have in any color you wanted as long as it was black. What sounds at first tyrannical in Ford's remark is in the end a profound conclusion drawn from the ethos of democratic uniformity. The black Model T and the Jeffersonian map of 640 acre sections are solutions by alternative means to the same underlying problem.

The everyday world of standardized products that could be duplicated in unlimited numbers made possible a way of life that was cellular and unlimited. Daniel Boorstin, in his book *The Americans: The Democratic Experience*, has told the history of the Singer sewing machines and the Ford Model T; of Levis, bottles of Coca-Cola, telephones and television sets. But he has also written of such larger social units capable of replication everywhere as the Woolworth's five-and-dime, the A & P, the McDonalds, the movie theaters in every town showing the same film from coast to coast, and, later, television programs sent into every living room at 9:00 on Tuesday night. Boorstin has pointed out that "no American transformation was more remarkable than these new American ways of changing things from objects of possession and envy into vehicles of community."[4] The phrase is a startling one, but it captures a historical novelty. Within a democratic social space possessions would be used not for stratification and differentiation, but as tokens of communality, or in Boorstin's words, "vehicles of community." In combination they would make up a fixed collection of cheap, everyday objects and experiences that, once replicated across an almost unmanageable geography and an almost unprecedented immigrant culture, would produce a democratic social space of everyday familiarity. Mass production, exact replication, and mass culture made up a twentieth-century Jeffersonian ideal for a society no longer devoted to agriculture as a way of life, a society without farmers.

The landscape of forty-acre Jeffersonian farms stretching like the cells of the social body from border to border, or the modern American suburban way of life, which is an updated model of the Jeffersonian ideal, or, more accurately, an adaptation of it to an economy where all work is done outside the home: both of these social formulas assume that any democratic politics or any democratic poetics requires an underlying, everyday context of an undifferentiated and democratic social space. They both assume, at the same time, what Thoreau's atomistic model assumes, that such a social space and social practice must be open to the newcomer, to the immigrant, to anybody who chooses to be included. In effect, it is a society without a border, just as Descartes's is a space without any edge or boundary. The Jeffersonian square has no natural boundary. At the same time, the cultural sameness from point to point is secured, not by ideology, religion, language, or culture, but by the box of Kellogg's Corn Flakes on the kitchen table, *Sesame Street* on the television screen at 4:30, the package of Marlboro cigarettes in the shirt pocket, and the same ten songs on every car radio on a certain summer day everywhere in America.

Undamaged Social Space: Atomistic, Unbounded, Transparent, Unopposed

Four characteristics of an undamaged democratic social space are particularly important for the analysis that follows.

1. It is atomistic or cellular and therefore identical from place to place. This makes possible representation in both the political and the aesthetic sense because it permits sampling. Realism, especially in its reliance on the "slice of life" or, as it could better be called, the "sample," or in its interest in the "type," the typical, and the everyday is dependent on the cellular nature of social reality, which guarantees both that units are complete and that they replicate other units of experience while remaining internally "self-reliant." In the chapter on Whitman as well as the final chapters on realism I will explore the consequences of this replication.

2. The social space is unbounded. Open to immigration and equally to expatriation or internal mobility—that continuation of immigration into later generations—it has no natural or final size. In the chapter on regionalism I will deepen my account of this condition, but the primary fact of immigration, along with what we might call the "immigration of objects and systems" that modern technology confronts us with, should be seen as the single most important social fact that argues for abstraction as the defining aesthetic fact within a democratic social space. It may seem whimsical to refer to invention and newness within technology as an "immigration of objects," as though the automobile, the computer, the Boeing 747, and penicillin were, like the millions of persons lined up at Ellis Island or the Mexican border, immigrants. In fact, the consequence of an ever new culture of objects and systems is identical to that of an ever new body of citizens with their strangeness. Both cases require that one element of citizenship is constant adaptation to a new world on the part of both immigrants themselves and the former immigrants now called natives. Technological change and the capitalism that forces it quickly into actuality level the playing field between old-timers and newcomers because both face the deep life problem of adaptation to an unexpected world. In a culture of rapidly changing frame and technology, all are immigrants.

One important conclusion is that it is precisely the simultaneous commitment to immigration and to technological and economic restructuring that makes either of the two considered separately, tolerable, even welcome. The prior and necessary commitment to immigration, because of the empty land that needed to be held, made the second commitment to dizzy technological creative destruction thinkable, even comfortable, in America in a way that was true of no other country. From the other direction, it was precisely the social will to have an ever new world of objects and the systems around objects that made the accommodation of massive immigration relatively easy and even comfortable. In that sense it is a deep and important insight that in American culture, we need to speak of an immigration of persons and of things, that is, of all things invented and set in place in one lifetime.

3. The social space is transparent and intelligible. First of all, this is true because of the uniformity. This is one meaning of what many European travelers regarded as democratic manners, one detail of which was the setting aside of all sumptuary laws and the reduction of social relations to the informality of a first-name basis. Within uniformity, all places and individuals replicate the features of one's own life. The lives of others become spontaneously intelligible to me. From any one Jeffersonian farm or from a house in any one twentieth-century suburb, we look out to others engaged in the same actions, whether those involve repairing a fence, bringing in the hay before a storm, or, in the modern suburb, washing the car in the driveway or cutting the grass on a summer evening. The neighborhood is a sphere of intelligibility or transparency.

Another way to say this is to note that social life must be unencoded, or rather, it must appear unencoded. All social acts are, of course, part of a code. They are not given in nature. However, it is only where there are two or more codes that we are forced to become aware that everything is a system of signs and therefore artifactual, subject to choice and change. Where there are both civil and ecclesiastical codes (Stendhal's "red" and "black") or where there are class codes (aristocratic and bourgeois and proletariat), each becomes aware of his or her own way of life as a learned and differentiating way of acting. But where there is only one code there is the feeling not of codes, but of life itself. Where there are two systems of belief there are "religions," but where there is only one there is only how things are and must be. Social life, when uniform, creates a transparency that we call familiarity, and it is this feeling of familiarity that lets us move from point to point without much effort. Familiarity is the experience in which so much of the content of what is new repeats what we already know that its novelty has no strangeness. It is comfortable. This is the special intelligibility and transparency of ways of life that conquered the geographical variety of the American continent, making the American suburb basically similar from Boston to Los Angeles. It feels "like" home everywhere. The subject of transparency and encoding will dominate the third and fourth chapters of this book. Walt Whitman's and Herman Melville's works will be used as examples of the ways in which literature in America has been conscious of the social meaning of transparency and of the paths to transparency. In the case of Melville's *Benito Cereno* the alternative to transparency, the mystification of a culture of rituals, will be linked to slavery and the peculiar consequences of the most significant defect in the democratic social space of the United States in its first centuries, from the founding of the colonies to the Civil War.

4. The final characteristic of a democratic social space is particularly important for literature and intellectual life. Such a Cartesian space provides for no observers, for no oppositional positions. There are no outsiders. Everyone present is already a member, a participant, a citizen. Each one, whether he or she likes it or not, is already represented, both in the House of Representatives and in Walt Whitman's poetry. No one is able to reflect from an external point of view on society itself. There are, therefore, no intellectuals, no critics, no utopian imaginations (to use Karl Mannheim's term).[5] There cannot, then, in the modern period, be a strong and effective Marxist reflection of the society, challenging it in the name of an as-yet unrealized alternative to itself. One of the important puzzles of American experience has always been taken to be precisely this question of why, unlike Europe, Asia, and South America, the United States did not develop a strong Marxist challenge over the hundred years between 1860 and 1960. But Marxism is only an instance of the fact that within a democratic social space there cannot be organized self-consciousness and self-criticism, that is, a recognized intellectual class, and, in America, there never has been one.

The observer is a symptom of a divided social space, one that provides for a here and a there, an analyst who knows and a patient who acts (to use the example of the divided social space of a psychoanalytic interview). In a divided social space there is both society and a standing point beyond it from which it can be passed into consciousness. It is not a feature of every society that it provides such a point, although European societies, in the modern period, commonly did. In Chapter 4 I will explore the alternative of a culture of experts and performance, the culture that came to represent the primary alternative to a democratic social space after the Civil War, as slavery had before the war.

These four features—(1) uniformity; (2) openness to entry and mobility; (3) transparency and intelligibility; and (4) the absence of an observer position that makes self-awareness and criticism possible—are oversimplified in this sketch and require careful refinement. But since I will be using them only as a set of characteristics that in America were absolutely required by the democratic ethos and at times contested or absent in the actual society, they will be heuristic claims, not to be taken as social facts.

Damaged Social Space: Slavery, Regionalism, Hierarchy

We must notice not only the features of this Cartesian, open, democratic social space but also the actual damaged space within which representation both in the political and in the aesthetic sense—literature, painting, and philosophy—took place. A constant struggle or civil war between the democratic requirements placed on social life, along with the underlying social forces (immigration and technological transformation) that supported those demands on the economic plane and guaranteed the political drive for self-reliance and equality on the political plane, on the one hand, and the actual, damaged social space within which much of life takes place, on the other hand, is one of the profound themes of American culture. This civil war of self-representation was only literally a war in the 1860s, but it was and is a continuous "cold war" between democratic self-demands and equally urgent democratic self-disappointments.

The first example of a damaged social space that I will use here will be the spatial structure of slavery, since this is clearly the most radical contradiction possible for a society constructing a democratic social space. For Harriet Beecher Stowe in *Uncle Tom's Cabin*, a social space guaranteed to be universal by the permanent passions and unalterable emotional facts of mortality and family life had been torn like a piece of paper into scraps that had flown in different directions, never to be reassembled. The family of Uncle Tom, and with it the wider society, was that seamless paper, torn by slave sales into forever separated scraps. But for Stowe the social space, even in one location, was split, just as the landscape of manor house and slave quarters, upstairs and downstairs, was in her careful spatial map of Simon Legree's plantation, where Tom meets his death and the American journey its end. Stowe's segregation of spaces leads to a nation of patches and island-like worlds of differential laws, social codes, and ways of life. What we call her "regionalism" is in fact a literary form based on the damaged social space that opens up once the fact of slavery exists. The South was the first "region" in America. It was the difference of slavery that made it so; and it is because of the South that "regions" existed at all in the American imagination.

Stowe's novel depicts islands and patches of social fact scattered across a great expanse traversed only by flight and forced resettlement. But I will use her method and her social map here only as a background to make visible an alternative representation: that of Melville in *Benito Cereno*. Melville invented in his story as profound an account of the consequences of a damaged social space within democratic assumptions as has ever been given. Unlike Stowe's novel, in which the social space dissolves in favor of ever more distinct patches, Melville's is a story of a superimposed space, a layered space of what in military terms we call occupation. Because of slavery, in Melville's story, the doubled and damaged social space creates within America the requirement of consciousness. For Melville, as for Hegel, slavery is the route to thought. It is because of slavery that we cannot nationally aspire to the extraordinary united state that Whitman defined: a nation asleep. By sleep he meant existence without consciousness.

Although slavery is the decisive and permanent model for the failure of democratic space, and equally the decisive place where the strategies that we find in Stowe and Melville for the repair of democratic space within representation were produced, it is not the only example of a damaged social space. Here I will mention only one other because it will be the subject of a later chapter. Democratic social space was equally challenged by the hierarchical social space of professionalism and performance in the period after the Civil War. In fact, within American experience, we could say that once the fundamental damage of slavery was at least formally repaired by Lincoln's Emancipation Proclamation, the problem of the first hundred years of American politics gave way to the dominant democratic problem of the second hundred years: an economy that required a division into the single expert and the mass of citizens, and a culture of performance divided along similar lines between a star and an audience. Economy and culture reflected each other; both featured the structure of the one and the many.

The public world of leader and crowd, of master and mass (as opposed to the master and man of slavery) was a public world that, because of the tradition of political and religious oratory in America, had its key image in the speaker and his audience. Performer and audience define the world of both entertainment and professionalism, along with the larger worlds of mass politics and religious revival, and even the world of radical politics, from the time of the abolitionists, through the temperance movement, to the civil rights and anti-Vietnam movements of the 1960s. This antidemocratic space of speaker and audience has been, as the example of Martin Luther King, Jr., would show, decisive even where the goal has been a more democratic social life. Even American philosophy was invented in public by Emerson and William James as lectures given to crowds. James sometimes addressed almost a thousand people.

The crowd, the star, the fans—the one and the many—these spatial translations of the new professionalism were the second most important instance of a damaged social space within American culture. As I will argue, it was the economy, by means of mass production, enterprise, and a capitalism obsessed with production rather than accumulation, that became the domain in which the democratic social space was maintained and extended in just that period when the cultural life put increasing strain on its integrity and wholeness.

The later problem of cultural hierarchy I have only mentioned here to sketch the larger implications of the more permanent problem of a civil war within representation. It will be, along with regionalism, the subject of a later pair of chapters.

The artistic, literary, or conceptual responses to a damaged space can be seen as what we might call—taking over the single most important aesthetic category of the last hundred years—composition. This term from painting means literally to compose, or to quiet down, to calm, to tranquilize. That we require composition or calming of spatial reality tells us that reality is agitated, divergent, swarming, and various. Composition, in the sense that I will use it here, means a repair of space. Within the term "composition" is included the political term for what was attempted in the southern states after the Civil War: Reconstruction. Composition is the reconstruction of social space, the repair of social and perceptual experience.

One final feature of a democratic social space must be made clear at the outset. A peculiar consequence of any exception is that it makes the condition of the whole exceptional, as even the most localized illness makes the whole body sick. Health is only a state of the whole. Where any one part of the society is torn by the structure of slavery into two distinct notions of human and political standing, then the whole of the society is torn. As long as slavery exists in the southern states, every northern man becomes a White Man. His own identity takes on the torn form of southern reality. If any part of the society is a slave society, it must be so as a whole because the northern, democratic identity could not exist (even for itself) unless that identity was universal. The society cannot be undivided unless it is undivided everywhere; but it is divided, if it is divided anywhere. Slavery in the South made it true that every northerner was, in effect, a member of a slave-owning society, but one who individually did not happen to own slaves, just as many people in the South had individually decided not to own slaves.

A remarkable example of this contamination of the total space by the local exception can be seen in Whitman's "I Sing the Body Electric." Celebrating the sexual body, listing its parts, refusing to deny any of its moments or acts, Whitman needs at the center of his poem a social moment in which the body in its nakedness stands before us to be seen. The painter Thomas Eakins would, in the next generation, use the artist and his model for this affirmation or, more famously, the bodies of young men at a swimming hole. Whitman chooses, however, a slave auction where male and then female bodies are prized, studied in their every detail, and given value in the cash appraisal of a higher or lower price. To place this scene at the center of his poem as the moment to begin his inventory of the parts of the body is, as Whitman notes, to "help the auctioneer" because "the sloven does not half know his business" ("I Sing the Body Electric," sec. 7). Speaking to men, whom we know to be the potential purchasers of the slaves, Whitman then begins his mission to help the auctioneer: "Gentlemen look on this wonder . . ."

The poet at this moment becomes a white man, a gentleman among other white gentlemen. He hires himself out as an assistant auctioneer. Whatever value his poetic description will confer will raise the price of the slave who stands exposed before him. Having finished with the wonder of the male slave, he turns to help sell the female. That these two astonishing scenes take place within a New York poet's celebration of the beauty and spirituality of the sexual body—the body *electric*—illustrates the consequences of the exception within what is required as a uniform medium of social space.

chapter two

Whitman and the Poetics of a Democratic Social Space

What I Assume You Shall Assume

About Whitman's *Leaves of Grass* Emerson was right. Here at last was the first work of art to spring from the rich soil of democracy. A hundred and fifty years later "Song of Myself" is still the greatest single work of art ever written in America and one of the two greatest works of poetic modernity, the other being Baudelaire's *Les fleurs du mal*. Whitman was the only artist that America has ever had who understood the profound thrill of democratic uniformity. He saw and celebrated the paradoxical, braided relation between individuality and uniformity that in his new kind of poetry might match at last the robust populism of the American economy.

Whitman is a grounding fact for all later American culture, as Homer was for Greek culture, or as Shakespeare became for England. But because of the self-formulation involved in modern political society, Whitman's poem is more than these earlier models. It is similar to the Constitution in being an outline, a projection forward in time of the conditions of democratic personality and experience, just as the Constitution is a permanent frame for whatever political conditions might occur in later generations of whatever people call themselves Americans.

Walt Whitman's poetic or Lincoln's political idea of the *United States* stressed, as Allen Grossman has shown, the first word—indicating unity—over the second, in which the sovereignty and differences of the plural states are secured.[1] The deepest account of that unity was atomistic and uniform. This is clear in the second and third lines of Whitman's "Song of Myself": "What I assume you shall assume, / For every atom belonging to me as good belongs to you."[2] These radical words, which at first seem merely intellectual because of the philosophical term "assume," are expanded in the seventeenth section of Whitman's poem, where they stand as his aesthetics.

> These are really the thoughts of all men in all ages and lands, they
>   are not original with me,
> If they are not yours as much as mine they are nothing, or next to
>   nothing,
> If they are not the riddle and the untying of the riddle they are
>   nothing,
> If they are not just as close as they are distant they are nothing.
>
> This is the grass that grows wherever the land is and the water is,
> This the common air that bathes the globe.
>
>   "Song of Myself," sec. 17

In this aesthetics of identity each person becomes transparent to every other within society. How can it be difficult to know another if all "assume" the same? If thoughts are valid they must be "yours as much as mine" or they "are nothing." What is the relation of such thoughts and feelings, then, to other "common" or everyday elements of culture? Is the same Whitman who saw "the western turkey shooting [which] draws old and young, some leaning on their rifles, some sitting on logs." ("Song of Myself," sec. 15), present also in spirit today to see the Monday night football game that everyone can watch at the same moment on television? Is he present at the restaurants at which every thirst can at the same moment be quenched with the same refreshing drink? In not being "original," Whitman moves at once to the indefinitely repeatable unit: the grass. His aesthetics, by coming to rest on the grass from which his life's work takes its title, is a profound account of the common, and it imposes the requirement that the common be expanded until it fills out the real.

The extremity of Whitman's claim and the unexpected forms in which he restates its most radical side imply that he never held back from the requirements of democracy understood as an aesthetics of its social space. The merely intellectual side of that aesthetics he faces up to at once, as in the lines from the thirtieth section of the "Song of Myself": "(Only what proves itself to every man and woman is so, / Only what nobody denies is so.)" But the intellectual is only the most easily democratized realm of the personality. Descartes or, earlier, the proofs of Euclidean geometry aimed at and made possible a similar undeniability that implied that any mind would assent. In this, Whitman's intellectual "commonness" resembles our increasing stress, over the two centuries of democratic experience, on universal rights possessed by the individual to which any society must defer.

This intellectual accord Whitman calls "the pass-word primeval" when he writes, "I give the sign of democracy, / By God! I will accept nothing which all cannot have their counterpart of on the same terms" ("Song of Myself," sec. 24). In these words there is an immediate opening out onto a world of *having* that lies beyond thinking, and, in that world of what we each have, Whitman's new "word of the modern, the word En-Masse" (sec. 23) is underwritten by its partner term, mass production. There is an economic as well as a metaphysical ground to his aesthetics. If from Ruskin and Carlyle we have learned to sneer at the "cheap and nasty" that to their mid-nineteenth-century eyes seemed the only outcome of an industrial system, Whitman will take over the very term of scorn with all its economic weight to write, "What is commonest, *cheapest*, nearest, easiest, is Me, / Me going in for my chances, spending for vast returns, / Adorning myself to bestow myself on the first that will take me . . ." ("Song of Myself," sec. 14; emphasis added).

Myself

What could the primal word of individualism, "myself," mean to Whitman if he accepts the deep proclamation of the common? His

"Song of Myself" has no autobiography, no history of himself, no self-characterization, no list of personal and formative experiences. As he makes clear at the beginning of "Song of Myself," such things are not the "Me myself." In section four he talks of what others seem to want to know about him: "the effect upon me of my early life," or "my dinner, dress, associates," or "the real or fancied indifference of some man or woman I love." What the "askers" demand of him is the story of "ill-doing or loss or lack of money, or depressions or exaltations." All of these things come and go, "But they are not the Me myself" (sec. 4).

These are exactly the very things that make up Rousseau's *Confessions* or Wordsworth's autobiographical poem *The Prelude*, which appeared for the first time in 1850, the very moment of Whitman's "now." *The Prelude* depicts the autobiography of the poet's mind by means of childhood events, phases of life, personal crises and their resolution, accounts of friends, unique places of deep personal meaning, thoughts, philosophy of art, and a handful of the deepest experiences that made him the artist that he finally became. By discarding such things as no more than what other people—"Trippers and Askers"—want to know about us, Whitman has broken out of the heroic prison of individuality that autobiography implies. Rousseau, Goethe, Augustine, and Wordsworth were famous men whose autobiographies were meant to adjust and fill in an already rich public knowledge of, and interest in, their lives and ideas. The norm of autobiography rests on this prior fame and centrality to a generation. No one before Whitman became famous by means of a "song of myself" that preceded and caused the very world-famous individuality that in all other cases had been the premise and not the outcome of the autobiographical moment.

Whitman, in this fourth section, discards more than the personal details that others might want to know. People also want to know the effect on him of the "latest dates, discoveries, inventions, societies, authors old and new," his views on the realm of opinion and influence, his take on the public everyday world such as a newspaper would represent it. "My Life and Opinions" is, then, a second discarded model. This too is not the "Me myself." But Whitman includes, climactically, a startling set of phrases: "Battles, the horrors of fratricidal war, the fever of doubtful news, the fitful events" (sec. 4), and in these words presages the Civil War. For later readers the words wrap up and throw away as unimportant to the "Me myself" the war itself and all the national chaos of "fratricidal war." This also, is not the "Me myself." It merely "come[s] to me days and nights and go[es] from me again." Even the deepest catastrophic facts are not the "Me myself." It is clear that Whitman has discarded both classic models of a literature about *Myself.*

Even more surprisingly, when Whitman writes a classic sentence in the tradition of Montaigne and Rousseau—"I am the man, I suffer'd, I was there" (sec. 33)—we seem to have reached the high poetry of Rousseau's claim: "I am acquainted with others, myself I know." For Rousseau this difference argues for confession and for a style of autobiography based on a new intimacy of reader and writer, an intimacy made secure by the writer taking as his one subject what he alone knows completely and intimately, his own inner life. When Montaigne says, "Who touches this book, touches a man," he means by this claim the details of eating, sleeping, aches and interests, doubts and play, marriage bed and friendships. The inner and the outer man, his dailyness, his ways of thought, his memories, in all their ordinariness, their comedy and their poetry, are in plain view in his book.

Behind Whitman's words "I am the man, I suffer'd, I was there," lies the staggering fact that these resonant words are spoken not about a proud moment of his own experience, but out of his claim to be able to be someone else, in this case the brave captain of a crippled ship, crowded with passengers, enduring a storm and three days adrift until finally, after rescue, they come ashore safely, having eluded the death they had expected. The man that Whitman says "I am" in this case is the skipper who "knuckled tight and gave not back an inch, and was faithful of days and faithful of nights, / and chalk'd in large letters on a board, *Be of good cheer, we will not desert you*" (sec. 33).

These words, in which the true voice of this man appears, speaking for himself, call up one of the few other sets of italicized words in the poem, the child's question, *"What is the grass?"* ("Song of Myself," sec. 6). The skipper is one of the few persons in the poem given a scene rather than a one-or two-line portrait. We know him through a three-day ordeal, and through an act of writing in chalk on a board these words in his own plain, deeply human idiom without a touch of hierarchy or command. The skipper is a perfect democrat in the face of death. The words "We will not desert you" mean that we the crew will not use our skills as sailors to set off in the small boats, leaving you passengers behind. Even more, these words speak man to man—"Be of good cheer"—and they presume no speech from on high as would, for example, "Attention all passengers!" or "The Captain wants to assure you that . . ."

This skipper, who is, in his words and acts, in crisis and outcome given full human reality quite different from the ordinary picture of a captain proud at his wheel—the timeless, general professional picture of the poem's early sections—is exactly the catalyst for Whitman's fantastic claim: "I am the man, I suffer'd, I was there." The story that Whitman takes over here is a classic newspaper thriller, as are each of the seven stories that surround it: for example, the fireman crushed when the building collapses on him, but rescued lovingly by his fellows; the slave in flight captured by dogs and riders who beat him with the ends of their whips; the artillery-man at the bombardment of his fort with the dying general saying (again in italics in the poem) *"Mind not me mind—the entrenchments"* (sec. 33). These stories of noble courage remind us of boys' magazine accounts of famous last words. Patriotic, Victorian anecdotes, they fall in line with "I regret that I have but one life to give for my country" or "I have just begun to fight." Whitman calls this "the courage of heroes," but it sounds now more like the courage of the heroic genre, the *poncif* of heroes. We can almost see the newspaper illustration, the words printed beneath the single image of the nobility of powerful men, captains and generals one and all.

To put it bluntly, it is not only that Whitman says these words, at a moment of appropriating the experience of others, but that he uses the journalistic formula of a big, heart-wrenching story, a front-page story in the classic sense of the new mass journalism. In popular journalism, public servants like firemen, the captains of ships, and generals defending forts are seen as noble, selfless, self-sacrificing mannequins carrying out an ideal of duty and service.

These same ideals Mark Twain would show up as the wide-eyed idealizing of the small boy looking at the heroic riverboat captains in *Life on the Mississippi* and then initiate us into at least part of the reality of that world, where the adult knows that these same captains, in their vanity, race to set records, overheating the steam engines until they explode and kill the passengers.

This is one paradox of Whitman's relation to the tradition of intimacy and autobiography. It is a paradox or limit of a very different kind from what we now are so much aware of in Rousseau: that in claiming to be completely candid even about the most shameful acts of his life, both sexual and moral, he was often guaranteeing that we would not look closely at his many lies, omissions, and wild distortions. Rousseau is part of the normal paradox of what Starobinski called transparency and obstacle, or what we might more simply call the bargain of truth-telling.

Whitman's paradox is also quite different from the paradox of Montaigne: that a book about himself is so filled with quotations from other writers, so engaged with his reading of the ideas, anecdotes, and jests of others. In some ways this represents an unusually candid picture of individuality within the net of a culture and a language that was always there before we were born and by means of which, and in spite of which, we somehow have our own experiences.

In 1855 Whitman's book begins with the words "I celebrate myself; and sing myself." Ten years later, in a revised edition, the volume begins with a short poem that sets a far more startling idea in front of us: "Oneself I sing. A single separate person." Naturally, the poem "Song of Myself" still began with the original line, but from then on *Leaves of Grass* began with the paradoxically empty word "oneself," and claimed to be about a separate person even in using the word "oneself" which like "one" is the pronoun of anonymity, the pronoun that we use to avoid passive constructions or the absence of any real pronoun whatsoever.

"One walks by putting the left foot in front of the right."
"Walking is done by putting the left foot in front of the right."
"One wonders how he could have done so vicious a crime."
"One starts and leaves the rest to chance."

"Start and leave the rest to chance." The use of the "one" con-
struction is, oddly enough, not a democratic choice, but a fussy,
aristocratic refusal to be personal. Like the royal "We," the use of
"one" tags a social world false in its avoidance of, or superiority to,
the use of "I." The fastidious word "one" guards the place of a
pronoun without proposing any particular self—I or you or she or
he. Whitman is clear about the act of singing: "*I sing*"; but reserved
about its object "*Oneself* I sing."

The play of this substitution of "oneself" for "myself" sets free the
extraordinary speculative and nuanced range of independence and
interpenetration within democratic culture of what we should never
too crudely see as individuals. "Oneself" embraces the mass, the
crowd, the fusion of the self into patterns of work and profession in
which the self is both visible and yet surrendered to the impersonal
system of work: the baker, the firefighter, the surgeon. It touches on
the overlaying of selves in acts of sympathy and the fusion of selves
in sexual love. It embraces eagerly the experiences that fall under
the words "everyone" or "anyone," which are still experiences of the
distinct individual even though everyone is standing in the same
rain, or is chilled by the same air when the temperature reaches zero
or trembles inside on the day that the war against secession was
declared by Lincoln.

The paradox of Whitman's "I am the man, I suffer'd, I was there,"
with its three uses of the word "I" and its—at some level—three lies
standing in a vigorous row, touches both the heart of his strength
in opening up a remarkably nuanced, transpersonal self and the
heart of his evasiveness, weakness, egotistical appropriation, his
occupation and evacuation of others. As an idler within a crowded
city and a great reader of newspapers, he is a spectatorial owner of
second hand experiences turned into a universal man. But it is the
universal of the newsstand and street corner. That is its weakness.
At the same time it is the profound notion of how the barriers
between myself and yourself and herself had been thinned out,
made porous under democratic conditions and under the conditions
of American life between 1840 and 1890.

One detail of that thinning out was the fact that the central event
of Whitman's and every other citizen's life in the period was the

Civil War. The war provided not only the most important *uniform* and profession of those years because it fused hundreds of thousands of soldiers—uniformed in blue or gray, each with his rifle—and developed in the standardization of war matériel the fundamentals of the system of mass production of identical objects that would be the key to the capitalism of the hundred years that followed the Civil War. The war also fused every nonsoldier into a "civilian"—that wartime term very different from citizen or settler, man or woman, democrat or republican. The civilian and the soldier are the only remaining common terms of wartime.

The nation became a nation of newspaper readers during the war, lifted or depressed by the day-to-day battles of Gettysburg and Antietam, the sieges, the low points and the victories. The newspapers created a new form of inner life in this first war of telegraphed news. Accounts of battles in previous wars had taken weeks or months to reach those who waited at home. Now the telegraph and newspapers put every civilian on the battlefield, every day and every night. A new collective mood and identity constituted a new meaning for the word "everybody" in the sense of "everybody is talking about . . ." or "everybody is worried that," or "everybody is hoping that . . ."

When Mathew Brady exhibited his photographs of Antietam in his New York Gallery, Oliver Wendell Holmes wrote in the *New York Times* of October 20, 1862: "If he has not brought bodies and laid them on our door yards and along our streets, he has done something very like it . . . It seems somewhat singular that the same sun that looked down on the faces of the slain blistering them, blotting out from the bodies all semblance to humanity, and hastening corruption, should have thus caught their features upon canvas, and given them perpetuity forever, but it is so." By means of this same sun, the telegraph wires, and the press runs of the city dailies, these images returned to create the wartime "everybody."

The mass entertainment, the stars of baseball and film, that followed later, along with the new mass products like Coca-Cola and the Kodak camera or the bicycle that "everybody" wanted to own, filled in the territory opened up by the focused public attention of the war, with its two new technologies of inner life: the telegraph to transmit everywhere, instantaneously, and the newspaper to distribute to each person his own individual copy of what everyone would be thinking about that day. Neither would have worked alone. It required the speed of the telegraph and the individual copy that each person could take in for himself to establish the common life of the mind and spirit.

The porosity between individuals that such a common life of things and moods makes possible was one of Whitman's deep subjects within the surprising emphasis on what he called "myself." This porosity has nothing to do with the modern theme of the loss of self or Durkheim's lugubrious word *anomie*. Instead, Whitman's is a strong and pleasurable abstraction in the way that geometry, instead of being an "anomie" of matter, is a brilliant, distinct, pleasurable, new geography of matter. Whitman's celebration of many of the conditions that would make up the melancholy and elegiac side of sociology, from Emile Durkheim's book on suicide to David Riesman's *The Lonely Crowd*, and that even today make up one of the standard formulas of intellectual melancholy, remains immune from this cliché. He gives instead his remarkable celebration of just those conditions of a fluid boundary of the self that only later were called the "loss" of some imagined traditional, stable self.

Myself, Yourself, Now and Forever

Whitman works out the most remarkable implication of his aesthetics in his poem "Crossing Brooklyn Ferry," where the transparency and cellular identity that he assumes between himself and all of his countrymen is extended into the future to become the form of continuity for national identity through time. The poem depends on Whitman's dazzling arrogance in looking forward generations and even centuries to those who will see the same things, have the same feelings, and look back to him, knowing that he also saw and felt just those things.

The great litany is designed around a syntax that repeats the formula "just as you . . . so I." Nothing that Whitman claims stands so remote from our own thinking as his extension of transparency over time. He writes some fifty years after Hegel's *Phenomenology of Spirit*, and Whitman himself includes a short poem in *Leaves of Grass* that has the subtitle "After Reading Hegel." Yet, even having read, did Whitman take seriously the book that historicized the inner life, even perception, in a radical way that later authors down to Michel Foucault would only spell out in detail?

For a late-twentieth-century reader who has been encouraged to think that sexuality, or even the humanist idea of "Man," is a historical formula of relatively local meaning, the swagger of Whitman in his confidence that "just as you feel when you look on the river and sky, so I felt . . ." ("Crossing Brooklyn Ferry," sec. 3) seems either naive or simply incredible. For us the very act of looking, or stopping to notice this or that, the composition of a scene into foreground and background, is historically determined and filtered through categories such as the picturesque, the sublime, the beautiful, the Impressionist moment, and so on. But for Whitman the politics of any aesthetics within a democratic social space requires that there exist experiences across time that not only will happen in identical ways, but will be noticed, will arouse attention, and will even produce the same feelings within people living centuries apart. In our usual view of history nothing is more of a cliché than the idea that the very act of noticing a landscape at all and pausing before it is a historical invention of European thought. With an amusing pedantry, following Jacob Burckhardt's *Civilization of the Renaissance*, we date this "invention" to April 26, 1335, when the poet Petrarch climbed Mount Ventoux just to enjoy the beauty of the landscape that would, from the mountain, be spread out before him.

Unlike Petrarch, Whitman on his Brooklyn Ferry crossing imagines himself to be doing only what anyone would do or see. He imagines himself to be having an inevitable, natural, and therefore timeless experience. In Whitman's aesthetics it is impossible to imagine that the sublimity of experience in the Alps was a novel experience at a certain moment or that a trip to the seashore was, as a desirable experience, a recent invention, or that before Baudelaire the moments of morning and evening twilight were moments when one forgot to look. Our modern historicizing of aesthetic experience tells us that before J. M. W. Turner on a foggy day a painter would have said only: I can't paint today; nothing to see. But after Turner, that "nothing" became itself an object of attention for the first time. What Whitman implies in "Crossing Brooklyn Ferry" is that a democratic aesthetics requires that America will have no history of the senses because not only will the small sensory facts of experience repeat themselves, but they will remain, over time, the subject of our acts of noticing. One step further: we will "feel" them in the same way once that act of attention takes place. "Just as you are *refresh'd* by the *gladness* of the river and the *bright* flow, I was *refresh'd* . . ." ("Crossing Brooklyn Ferry", sec. 3; emphasis added). These words of highly complex pleasure—"refresh'd," "gladness, bright"—are imagined to be stable elements of subjectivity over time, as permanent as hydrogen, iron, and gold. To make believable his claims Whitman has to answer one question: Where can he point to such unhistoricized moments of experience?

One of the things that Whitman, unlike Emerson, needs to push to the side is the very turbulence within the conditions of experience that means that only a hundred years later the Brooklyn Ferry might not even exist or that his countrymen only a century later might be speeding at forty miles an hour over a bridge at the same point, but now too far from the water to see their own reflections and no longer surrounded by gulls, which hover just overhead around boats but seem to neglect cars that pass even closer to their own natural height in the sky as they cross the same water on a bridge. Whitman's countrymen a century later might even be flying in airplanes over the very spot, but now so high in the sky, as they pass, that the gulls are as small as grains of pepper, making what Whitman saw no longer visible.

> I too many and many a time cross'd the river of old,
> Watched the Twelfth-month sea-gulls, saw them high in the air
>   floating with motionless wings, oscillating their bodies,
> Saw how the glistening yellow lit up parts of their bodies and left
>   the rest in strong shadow,
> Saw the slow-wheeling circles and the gradual edging toward the
>   south,
> Saw the reflection of the summer sky in the water,

Had my eyes dazzled by the shimmering track of beams,
Look'd at the fine centrifugal spokes of light round the shape of
    my head in the sunlit water.
                                        "Crossing Brooklyn Ferry," sec. 3

Whitman's belief that all this will be seen by others, fifty years hence or "ever so many hundred years hence" *as they cross*, implies that centuries later he imagines that ferries will exist, that Brooklyn will exist, and that these same moments of experience will compel attention.

Against all logic, Whitman has, at least in part, outwitted any such historical objection. For his details, he has chosen with ingenuity. First of all, like every classical poet he has chosen just those objects within nature that do not change over time, in this case a scene whose elements are light, water, and gulls. But the particular way that gulls circle around a passenger boat, just above the eyes of the passengers from whom they hope to get food, is a historically rooted experience. Nonetheless, the underside of their bodies, seen close up and lit a glistening yellow in small patches with the rest in dark shadow, is an experience available over time.

Whatever the historicity of his first experience, it is the second that is Whitman's masterpiece. With his second experience Whitman has relied on one of those optical illusions that we can imagine would always be noticed: the way all light rays converge on the surface of the water around each observer: "the spokes of light round the shape of my head in the sunlit water." This angelic moment of transfiguration and divinity Whitman returns to at the end of the poem in his exhortation:

Diverge, fine spokes of light, from the shape of my head, or any
    one's head, in the sunlit water!
                                        "Crossing Brooklyn Ferry," sec. 9

That each man or woman at any time, or for all time, will find that the rays of light seem to make this glorious halo on the water for himself alone or herself alone creates an almost mystical image for democratic uniqueness and democratic commonness and interchangeability. It is the greatest single image of Whitman's aesthetics because it eludes what we might call the depression of common experience, the feeling that whatever is there for everyone is unable simultaneously to let me experience my own singularity as thrilling.

If grass is common, then only by metaphor and imagination can it be singularized even for a moment as the "handkerchief of the Lord" ("Song of Myself," sec. 6), and it can only be done by a mind that, in making the metaphor, points out its own uniqueness. When I recognize, in reading the metaphor for grass, that I never thought of it that way before, and never could have thought of it that way without Whitman, this recognition creates a breakdown in the democratic aesthetics because I have to acknowledge that I need another to do my seeing for me. I delegate and then professionalize the act of seeing just as I delegate and create professionals who do surgery or design bridges. But in the moment of wonder at the spokes of light that surround oneself on the water, each person both sees for himself a moment of experience that, even had Whitman never written of it, would have been noticed with pleasure, and in that moment of experience knows himself to be a "center" or unique point in relation to light. But at the same time, as Whitman puts it, he knows himself to be "any one's head." The wonder of uniqueness and the pleasure of commonness are fused. Paradoxically, Whitman's choice of this experience depends on the one side on simple laws of physics, but on the other on a very precise tradition of Christian iconography: the tradition of the halo. To state the wonder of individual identity Whitman locates it inside a rooted, local system known to us in the West from the paintings of Giotto and Fra Angelico. The halo is as provincial a device within Christianized Europe as the ferry itself is within American transportation. But on the other side, the optical illusion of the converging spokes of light retains its freedom from any local meaning.

The moment in which each sees reflected in the water the fact of his individuality transfigured by the beauty of light, yet interchangeable with any other individuality, is an experience that bears out the notion that American aesthetics is intrinsically an aesthetics of abstraction, or even more radically, an aesthetics of the subtraction of differences. This is the point where such an aesthetics restates the central matter of American education: the subtraction of culture rather than its inculcation. Faced with the dozens of immigrant languages and cultures, American education has bleached out those differences in the act of producing "typical" American children.

That a certain civic blankness results is in the interests of transparency. Whitman's great meditation on this problem of imagining America can be found in the poem "The Sleepers." Sleep cancels all differences, all identities, and in this it has a great deal in common with primary education in America. As Whitman puts it:

> I swear they are averaged now—one is no better than the other,
> The night and sleep have liken'd them and restored them.
>
> I swear they are all beautiful,
> Every one that sleeps is beautiful, every thing in the dim light is
>   beautiful,
> The wildest and bloodiest is over, and all is peace.
>
> "The Sleepers", sec. 7

To reach a national harmony Whitman takes a national census of his countrymen as they lie naked and asleep. To picture them all naked would merely have removed the signs of social difference, but to face them only in the unconsciousness of sleep is to abstract from them so as to reach that one point from which they can be imagined to be, at last, equally beautiful. An aesthetic sacrifice, not to mention a sacrifice of personality, activity, experiential differences, makes possible the grounding of a common national world. To imagine the nation through the optics of sleep is to accomplish politically what Descartes had done for matter: abolishing the differences of stone and leaf, mountain and house to reach the abstract fact of simple location, mass, and movement in a certain direction. Yet the extraordinary word that Whitman uses for this process is to say that sleep has "restored" them. In this word he proposes that what we mean by difference is an aberration, like the many interesting, diseased conditions of the body from which we always willingly return to the boredom of health. "The night pervades and enfolds them all," and Whitman can list their differences while observing them all neutralized by sleep.

The married couple sleep calmly in their bed, he with his palm on
    the hip of the wife, and she with her palm on the hip of the hus-
    band,
The sisters sleep lovingly side by side in their bed,
The men sleep lovingly side by side in theirs,
And the mother sleeps with her little child carefully wrapt.

The blind sleep, and the deaf and dumb sleep,
The prisoner sleeps well in the prison, the runaway son sleeps,
The murderer that is to be hung next day, how does he sleep?
And the murder'd person, how does he sleep?

The female that loves unrequited sleeps,
And the male that loves unrequited sleeps,
The head of the money-maker that plotted all day sleeps,
And the enraged and treacherous dispositions, all, all sleep.
                                    "The Sleepers," sec. 1

In evoking for us the sleep of the blind, Whitman begins to
suggest the relief of having identity canceled; as soon as it is erased,
we know it to have been only a burden. To be asleep is no longer
to be blind. Once the eyes of the sighted and the eyes of the blind
are both closed in sleep, human identity prior to the division into
sighted and blind has been restored. In sleep, once all are silent,
none are any longer "dumb."

With this turn we suddenly see that all words of identity are like
the word "blind"—banker, husband, sister—and from each of them
sleep relieves us by equalization. To be asleep is no longer to be
male or female; no longer deaf or a prisoner; no longer a runaway
or unloved. The lifting of the burden of difference makes all difference appear as a burden: to be a money-maker plotting, no less than
to be a murderer set to be hanged the next day. To be enraged or
treacherous, or to have any disposition whatsoever, is to be weighed
down by personality in the face of the lightness of sleep. In his
climax Whitman approaches the political vocabulary which this
common fact of sleep authenticates. He invents a wonderful new
meaning for the word "states" in the term United States. For Whitman these are states of being rather than political entities. Sleep
unites all states, certifying in its abstraction a United States.

The diverse shall be no less diverse, but they shall flow and
    unite—they unite now.

The sleepers are very beautiful as they lie unclothed,
They flow hand in hand over the whole earth from east to west as
    they lie unclothed,
The Asiatic and African are hand in hand, the European and the
    American are hand in hand,
Learn'd and unlearn'd are hand in hand, and male and female are
    hand in hand . . .

"The Sleepers," secs. 7-8

But here he has falsified. Although they lie side by side they do
not lie hand in hand. The false note, as so often happens with
Whitman, mars the remarkable, but for him unendurable, image of
a country that can only be imagined to be one by imagining it
asleep. American abstraction, in the work of Wallace Stevens or
Emerson, or in the great abstract painting of the years following
1945, produced no more powerful map for the real existence of a
common experience. Its price is the negation not only of differences but of consciousness itself. If some are blind then we must
reach the one Archimedean point in which none are any longer
blind. Sleep is that point. The sacrifice of the burden of consciousness will be a feature of the strategy of Melville to which I will
return.

That Whitman can show the existence of just such a basic grammar of experiences for "any one's head" validates just as deeply as a
Bill of Rights or a Jeffersonian farm of "40 acres and a mule" or an
array of everyday products such as Levis, Model-T Fords, and
Monday night football, the possibility of a democratic social space.
Visual as his world is, it is the world of the camera rather than the
painting, because the camera will snap anything and make it count
as a picture. The camera can be held in any hand while the paint-
brush cannot. Pointed toward the sky, the camera "takes" the sky;
aimed at a drop of blood on a shirt, it takes the drop of blood and
some part of the shirt. Every face becomes a portrait once the
camera exists; every random set of things or parts of things becomes
a still-life; every patch of space, a landscape. The camera abolishes

the narrow entranceways of painting through which only certain prestructured faces, scenes, arrangements, and scales of space can enter and present themselves to be seen. Pointed at anything, by anybody, the camera notes it as a picture.

Whitman imagines that he can list conditions of life that are inescapable, and he lists them in the fifth and sixth sections of "Crossing Brooklyn Ferry." His doing so means that a basis of experience over time exists on which a democratic social space can be guaranteed to be enduring. That we "receive identity" from the body is one of those conditions. That we find that "dark patches fall" upon us is another. That we know evil not by knowing others but by knowing ourselves is a third. All together we come to see ourselves playing "the same old role," but the guarantee built into this fact is that all others are transparent to us, including all others in time. If the role is already the "same" and already "old," then it will be, a thousand years from now, no older, no less the same. Whitman saw that what others might realize with depression or despair—that we are within the "same old role"—is an exhilarating fact, and a bond over time. It is for that reason that the fundamental image for this sameness is the moment when the spokes of light transfigure, for each man or woman who notices, his or her own head in the water. That Whitman stages this proof of a democratic coherence of experience over time in terms of a technology—the ferry connecting Brooklyn to Manhattan—that would not survive the next generation opens up a paradox within that aesthetics, and points to its need to be set inside the idea expressed in Emerson's essay "Circles": that the wearing out of reality and its replacement is itself a stable wearing out and therefore subject to a bond across time.

In the 1850s a second, closely related aesthetics of a democratic social space reached its climax and its formulation within Stowe's *Uncle Tom's Cabin*.[3] Whitman's democratic aesthetics had as its alternative the politically potent sentimentality of Stowe's novel, in which the social bond is retested again and again by means of common experiences of suffering. When, in the face of suffering, a spontaneous emotional response occurs, like the tears at a scene of death, at that moment the underlying grass of experience is tested and reaffirmed, even theatricalized. Whitman himself had also, as a detail of his wider argument, built in the key phrase for the political side of sentimentality as it had been developed by Rousseau in the *Discourse on the Origins of Inequality*, the essay that could be called the Constitution for the international politics of sentimentality in the century and a half following Rousseau. Whitman's straightforward summary traps the heart of the elaborate theory worked out by Rousseau and applied by Stowe: "Whoever degrades another degrades me, / And whatever is done or said returns at last to me" ("Song of Myself," sec. 24).

Since I will spell out Stowe's assumptions about pity and suffering later, I mention here only that hers was a strategy equal in power to Whitman's and that each was created in relation to the fact of slavery, the fundamental denial of transparency within American experience. These two aesthetics, both reaching climactic expression in the 1850s, develop, whether in Whitman's unity of replication or Stowe's linked chain of moments of feeling, the inner account of a democratic social space.

Sleep, Silence, Substitution

In the democracy of sleep Whitman's fellow citizens have given up, along with all other differences, the inner experience that we have access to only in speech. Sleepers are silent, but, surprisingly, so are Whitman's dozens or hundreds of carefully pictured trappers and blacksmiths, printers and brides. With only the rarest exceptions, no one speaks in Whitman's poetry other than the poet himself. No one tells his or her own story, or is pictured speaking to another person. Each is locked in place in his or her own poetic one- or two-line frame. When the child asks, *What is the grass?* we have one of the most extraordinary events in all of his work, an unpictured voice that takes us suddenly into the reality of inner life. Someone is wondering about the grass.

Whitman's silent countrymen occur in just those years after Dickens, on his American visit, had heard and recorded the extraordinary, florid American gab, the American line, the sales talk, political thunder, street talk, brag, and verbal fantasy. It was this great verbal making up the world in talk that Mark Twain would catch in Colonel Sellars or Huck Finn, and that Stowe would hear and record in the stories, simple and eloquent, that each slave might tell of her own life, telling as witnesses do. Democratic poetry had arrived in England with Wordsworth's opening out of the actual words, talk, and personal stories of his ordinary countrymen in the *Lyrical Ballads*. Even Whitman's day, fifty years later, was the high moment of the dramatic monologue in poetry, in which Robert Browning's men and women, artists, lovers, and scoundrels unfolded themselves in their own tortured self-relations and self-betrayals.

Why are there no voices in Whitman? He is, next to Thomas Eakins, our best painter of a new world of skills and work. His men are as silent as the rowers on the Schuylkill river that Eakins paints in his version of the "Carol of Occupations" in which surgeons, singers, rowers, boxers, and sculptors spell out the new everyday aristocracy of professionally skilled specialists. This new world of specialization that Eakins and Whitman picture in grave silence replaced the jack-of-all-trades, the handyman, the mixture of fraud and genius that had always made up the American amateur tradition of barbers setting limbs and poets hoeing beans and building houses.

Whitman's world is one where self-identification with work makes up the strong and very widely distributed meaning of professionalism. "The machinist rolls up his sleeves, the policeman travels his beat, the gate-keeper marks who pass . . ." ("Song of Myself," sec. 15). His drivers are fully drivers, his firemen fight fires in our minds forever, his ship captains are fully and completely, no less than the mast, part of the ship. His is not a world of the jack-of-all-trades, the handyman, the Thoreau-type figure who hoes a few rows of beans, builds one and only one house, writes, explores, surveys, makes poetry. Whitman's carpenter is at the board for life; his western trappers are lifers no less than Eakins's surgeons.

As Whitman pictures individuals one by one, we see a world newly fused around professional identity. Each was skilled at a specialty, as the Indian was at hunting or as the Mississippi riverboat pilot was at the wheel. Twain shows these pilots to us as aristocrats, but also as men prim and narrow in their role, just like parsons or gunfighters. In

Whitman we have the proud, variegated aristocracy of skill and talented work as we see it in the publicly visible world of street, shop, and factory. It was in this public world that uniforms became increasingly common: bellboys, surgeons, streetcar conductors, symphony musicians, prostitutes, each in their familiar costumes of labor. The uniforms of the Civil War, blue and gray, were never taken off in the years that followed the defeat of the South. The businessman's dark suit, the baseball player's whites, the gold buttons of train porters, the surgeon's white, the conductor's formal evening coat—these uniforms were the decor of a culture in which the safety and status of profession was eagerly sought and in which the fusion of self and role became a strategy within democratic society. Whitman is the poet for a society in uniform.

Along with the uniform, the photograph, especially the daguerreotype of the 1840s, brought a new kind of silent dignity to ordinary life and activities. Because the first photographs required the subjects to remain still for several moments, they appear to us a century later not only still, but like monumentalized statuary of themselves. The Indians, Civil War soldiers, families in groups, children in their best dresses, are not just silent; their mouths seem clamped shut and their eyes have that immobility of being held open too long. They are the most unrelaxed images in the history of portraiture. Likewise, Whitman's people are not so much glimpsed as captured in the patience of the long duration of early daguerreotypes and photographs. "The squaw wrapt in her yellow-hemm'd cloth is offering moccasins and bead-bags for sale," or "The mate stands braced in the whale-boat, lance and harpoon are ready" ("Song of Myself," sec. 15).

With the modern camera capable of fractions of a second of exposure, we have become used to the smile in photographs, and in fact for us the command "Smile!" is essential to the act of being photographed. But a smile takes place in an instant of experience that could never occur in the first daguerreotypes. Nor could the expression or the accident of mood, nor even the accidental and momentary position of the body, the hands, the angle of the head. These are all features of the tenth of a second, almost instantaneous, time exposures of the modern camera.

When photography came in, it dignified everything it recorded with monumental stillness as a secondary result of the prolonged gathering of light that the plate required. Paradoxically, it was painting that in these same years learned to represent what later photography would call the instant. In Edgar Degas's painting of New Orleans cotton merchants we have what might have been a classic Whitman subject of men seen in the transactions and setting of their professional lives, men dressed in the formal attire of their work. But Degas catches them at an angle, and in a moment of time that we think of as the very essence of a snapshot. Degas was, by our later idea of photography's nature, the only great photographer of the nineteenth century. His dancers and jockeys, his intimately seen women toweling themselves after a bath or sponging one spot on a foot as they stand balanced in a just-for-this-second position in a tub, his laundresses yawning as they iron with elbows held out in a half-second posture: these are the only real photographs (in our sense) in the years between 1860 and 1895, and they were done in pastel or paint.

Whitman, like his great contemporary Mathew Brady in his Civil War photographs, poses his people at rest in postures that endure five or ten minutes at a time. His picture of the wilderness wedding in "Song of Myself" can remind us of either a painting of the West by Frederic Remington or of a solemn daguerreotype.

> I saw the marriage of the trapper in the open air in the far west,
>   the bride was a red girl,
> Her father and his friends sat near cross-legged and dumbly smok-
>   ing, they had moccasins to their feet and large thick blankets
>   hanging from their shoulders,
> On a bank lounged the trapper, he was drest mostly in skins, his
>   luxuriant beard and curls protected his neck, he held his bride
>   by the hand,
> She had long eyelashes, her head was bare, her coarse straight
>   locks descended upon her voluptuous limbs and reach'd to her
>   feet.
>
> sec. 10

What the silence and the motionlessness guard is *their* dignity, or rather Whitman's claims for *their* dignity. This is the reason that the citizens of the daguerreotype are not only the most serious, silent generation in our memories out of all the history of representation before or since, but are also, one and all, dignified, as the later citizens of the snapshot would never be nor wish to be.

Whitman's wedding group is an American version of the Dutch Arnolfini wedding painting by Jan van Eyck in which the work of art functions as a proof, that is, as a wedding certificate. All of the characters in Whitman's extraordinary scene are in poses of rest that can be held for a long time. The fact that the father and his friends are seen smoking is, itself, a claim about stillness and time, since we settle down to smoke, resting immobile for minutes at a time. The groom lounges, holding the hand of his bride. Just married, he is likely to prolong the holding and the position that make it possible for him to stand near her as long as possible.

Whitman's genius here lies in casually describing what the camera would see while bringing our attention to the sexual core of this fact of marriage. He does this by beginning with the blankets covering the shoulders of the Indians and passing to the skins covering the trapper, but then to his beard, and finally to the more intimate curls that protect his neck, before reaching the bride, seen as close up as by someone caressing her. We see her long eyelashes, which could not be seen at the normal distance at which the overall scene is taken. Her head is bare and she seems—in Whitman's description, which does not mention her clothes—to be covered only by her long coarse hair that, like a veil, covers but makes us even more aware of her voluptuous limbs.

This wedding group photo we first seem to see at a distance of thirty feet, so as to take in at one glance the several groupings of actors, all facing front, as though to be photographed. The sequence of intimacy then takes us from the blankets to the skins, to the close-up detail of the curls on the neck of the groom, to the eyelashes, and finally to the tent of hair over the voluptuous limbs that seem, like the bride's head, to be included in the word "bare." This representation occurs within a world where there are poses but no expressions, since the latter are too transient to be held. Our modern instruction—"Smile!"—when we record each other in photographs is part of a modern proof of the instantaneous nature of the self, its variability over the thousands of different photos that we have of each other at every stage of life and relation. Whitman's or Brady's, by contrast, is, like the wedding itself, a world where each self poses only once, yielding one and only one image that is as permanent as the wedding that the picture solemnizes and protects over time.

Each of Whitman's fellow citizens is seen once and once only, in one pose, like the pose of this trapper or like the blacksmiths in an earlier section:

Blacksmiths with grimed and hairy chests environ the anvil,
Each has his main sledge, they are all out, there is a great heat in
    the fire.

"Song of Myself," sec. 12

Or the sign painter who is perched in his concentration "lettering with blue and gold" (sec. 15) or "the clean-hair'd Yankee girl [who] works with her sewing-machine" (sec. 15). Each is silent, and if we imagined them all beginning to speak, a stream of slang and cliché would begin to pour out. They would suddenly become vulgar in the original sense of those who speak in the common tongue. Their silence is their Latin, their language of importance and dignity, like the Latin inscriptions over the doors of ordinary high schools and banks. Whitman has no concept of the vulgar, and that is one of his great accomplishments. Paradoxically, he was dismissed from his job in Washington, D.C., because the Secretary of the Interior discovered that he had written a "Vulgar" book.

Even before Whitman's death, once naturalism or local color, or to put it more directly, once Mark Twain had begun to represent the democratic privilege of speech, the vulgar and the coarse entered, side by side with the colorful. Stephen Crane's *Maggie*, published in Whitman's last year of life, represents an apocalyptic moment of the ordinary poor breaking into speech, into curses and shouts, into the meanness of everyday spite and toughness and that higher inarticulateness which is particularly garrulous and with which all later literature had to wrestle.

Were Whitman's figures to speak, they, too, would pass into the quaint varieties of the sentimental, local color writers—the Uncle

Remus and Sarah Orne Jewett—or into the tough nastiness and banality of Crane and Theodore Dreiser. In the poem "The Sleepers" it was sleep that abolished differences to yield a democratic moment, and more than a moment, one third of every life lived under the actual utopia of sameness. Sleep is our daily return to being just anyone. So, too, in the pictorial and silent daguerreotype, the silence guarantees not just that we will not hear the dozens of accents, regional speech habits and tics, the mixed languages of immigrants and their children, the badges of class or subservience in educated and uneducated ways of speaking, but also that the very worth itself might evaporate in the face of the narrow interests, peeves, envies of spoken inner life, the dissatisfaction, spoiled dreams—that whole sad talk that will be the subject of Sherwood Anderson, Edgar Lee Masters, Dreiser, and Nathanael West. Silence, like sleep, keeps alive the appearance of democratic utopia, a utopia going on behind a pane of glass that filters out the voices and that inner life for which the voice always stands because it speaks of nothing else, whatever it happens to speak of. Americans may speak or feel in many accents, argots, lingoes, foreign tongues, and regional inflections of the language, but they are all—man and woman, black and white, Indian and old soldier—silent in Latin.

Whitman's own voice we recognize as a strange blend of the intimate and the impresario. He stands between us and the multiplicity of the world. He introduces us to the grass, to America, and to ourselves. His voice never leaves us alone with the landscape, the bathing men, the battle of the Alamo, the male and the female. He stands between us and our own groin, pointing it out to us, recommending it to us like a good salesman of products not wholly appreciated.

When an actual distinct voice finally arrives, Whitman places it in italics. "A child said, *What is the grass?*" And this makes us realize that in all the lines of "Song of Myself" the hundreds of our fellow citizens seen in his poem have never spoken.

Impersonation

About his own voice Whitman offers an alternative account: "Through me many long dumb voices . . ." or even more directly,

"Through me forbidden voices, / Voices of sexes and lusts, voices veil'd and I remove the veil" ("Song of Myself," sec. 24). He claims as one of his powers as a poet to speak instead of to listen, to speak for these voices and, finally, to impersonate them. In this he is a democratic poet charged with "Voices of the interminable generations of prisoners and slaves, / Voices of the diseas'd and despairing and of thieves and dwarfs . . ." (sec. 24). Whitman's version of the democratic poet's charge is opposite to and even more egotistical than that of his great contemporary Wordsworth, who recorded himself listening to the stories and to the ordinary language of men and women who made up the discarded and defeated, the crazed and the wanderers of rural society.

Where Whitman sees their suffering he interposes himself at once to say, "I am the man, I suffer'd, I was there." This resonant, brave statement of Whitman's is, when looked at more closely, one of the most morally dubious acts of appropriation ever described or, in fact, boasted of. Wordsworth and Stowe know the clear difference between what "I suffered" and what "She suffered." The poet or writer was not *there*, and it is part of the force of the sentimental tradition that the writer hears the story while remaining distinct in representation, as Wordsworth did in "The Ruined Cottage." Dante remained distinct from all those who spoke their tales to him, sometimes fainting, blanking out in the face of the story, instead of, in the style of Whitman, swelling out his chest to brag of the sufferings that he has taken over from others. The dignity and worth of suffering is completely contained in the full meaning of the words spoken only by the voice of the victim: I suffered, I was there, this happened to me. But Whitman will draw the line even more sharply.

> I do not ask the wounded person how he feels, I myself become
>   the wounded person,
> My hurts turn livid upon me as I lean on a cane and observe.
> "Song of Myself," sec. 33

Whitman passes into the victim, merges, and then returns to himself in the final word "observe." He appears everywhere. "I am an old artillerist, I tell of my fort's bombardment, I am there again" (sec. 33). Whitman himself claims that the act of putting himself in the place of another is half generosity and half rivalry that will not share the air with any other voice. He calls his poem "my omnivorous lines" (sec. 42), and the image of eating rather than observing is the best one for his poetic act. He breaks down in the stomach of his poetry the variegated things of the world, turns them into his blood, muscle, and brain to make up himself from their substance. His is intestinal poetry, pulverizing, mixing, lifting out the nutrients from a devoured world.

The most striking moment of thrusting himself forward to take over the acts of another is the sexual moment, not the moment of suffering that had been for Stowe and Wordsworth the key moment of representation.

> I turn the bridegroom out of bed and stay with the bride myself,
> I tighten her all night to my thighs and lips.
>
> "Song of Myself," sec. 33

In this passage the rivalry and the easily imagined rage of the bridegroom at being represented—displaced and substituted for, thrust aside—on the body of his bride is underlined by the first act of turning the bridegroom out of the bed. Whitman does not turn him out of the room, only out of the bed, and we have to imagine him to be, just as we are, present to watch the all-night scene that follows. Whitman's representation does not have him merge with the bridegroom by imagining their two bodies pressed together into the bride. Instead he turns him out, thrusts him aside in the very act that defines the man as a bridegroom. Where rivalry and not empathy takes over, Whitman puts out the fire instead of the fireman. He fires the cannon instead of the soldier. It is he who drives the locomotive or impregnates the bride as her husband stands idly at the bedside watching.

To speak for is one of the political meanings of representation. The lawyer acts in court for his client. The congressman votes for his half million constituents. But in Whitman's case we see that speaking for others in the act of representing them does not allow them to speak through him, as Dante's souls in Purgatory speak through him when he represents them and retells their stories in their own words. Whitman speaks instead of the artillerist, the wounded man, and when he drives the bridegroom out of bed we see that he not only speaks instead of all others, but he acts in their places as well, because there is ultimately no line between speaking and acting. As Whitman fires the cannon, drives the train, and hoes the field, he turns all of his countrymen out of bed, shoves them off their drivers' seats, off their crutches, and turns them into an audience of idle observers of his enthusiastic substitution of himself for them. What the bridegroom sees, standing all night by the bed, is that he is not a bridegroom at all, but a cuckold. To be displaced and represented in this act is to be changed forever from what he took himself to be in that moment when he exchanged vows with his new bride.

In these lines Whitman has unveiled the paradox of artistic representation (to be present, visible, counted in) in its relation to political representation (to stand in the place of someone else) under conditions where only by being unrepresented, that is, present in person, carrying out one's own identity, can full being be secured. To be a bridegroom cannot undergo representation. He must be there in the bed in person, and it may be that he cannot even be represented there in the sense of being described, pictured, or written about in the act of lovemaking with his bride. All picturing or description requires an imagined observer present in the room, a third person present. If the bride and bridegroom were to imagine a third person present, they could no longer act as bride and bridegroom. Even in this purely artistic sense, they cannot be represented without being violated. If they were to know that they were being, for example, filmed or photographed and that the images might be seen later by others, their very acts would be not just changed but prevented. The moment of the bride and the bridegroom cannot take place under either meaning of representation.

This paradox Whitman notices when he says that he cannot tell of what happened at the Alamo. "I tell not the fall of Alamo, / Not one escaped to tell the fall of Alamo, / The hundred and fifty are dumb yet at Alamo" ("Song of Myself," sec. 34). If no one escaped there can be no story, and if there is a story there can not have been a *total* massacre. The story cannot exist or the massacre cannot exist.

Here is the full and proper meaning of dumbness and the unsayable and even unrepresentable experience.

This extreme condition is precisely the case with the many other stories where Whitman steps in to represent and replace. Whitman will not overstep the fact of death. This he allows to be the only dumb experience. The silence of Whitman's many democratically pictured fellow countrymen can now take on its full meaning. Short of the barrier of death, the heart of his representation is the strong, violent act of interposition and replacement.

It is in the sexual experiences of "Song of Myself" that the fused and displaced alternatives of the poetic act appear most richly. The first experience is presented as Whitman's own, and it makes up one of the great moments of classical personal narration within his poetry, and one of the moments in which proud avowal can be felt in its difference from boast or appropriation.

> I mind how once we lay such a transparent summer morning,
> How you settled your head athwart my hips and gently turn'd
> over upon me,
> And parted the shirt from my bosom-bone, and plunged your
> tongue to my bare-stript heart,
> And reach'd till you felt my beard, and reach'd till you held my
> feet.
>
> "Song of Myself," sec. 5

The scene of sexual ecstasy, along with the "peace . . . that pass[es] all the argument of the earth," ends with measuring a man, one hand on his feet, the other on his face, the measurer's head and mouth at his sex. The scene in its schematic diagram sets out a modern, a sexual humanism that is a variation of the great humanist pride of Leonardo's naked man in a circle, his arms and legs forming the spokes of the perfect wheel. Whitman, in this scene, is both the actor and the older self who remembers this moment. "I mind," he begins, meaning, "I remember." Classic narrative always preserves this clear matrix: *you* who hear, *I* who speak and remember, *those* whose story I tell.

To set up these barriers of classic narrative practice only makes clear the very different goals and triumphs of Whitman's ordinary practice. In the eleventh section of "Song of Myself" there is one fully rendered scene that occupies the entire numbered passage. "Twenty-eight young men bathe by the shore," and he repeats three times this exact number to underline the precision and the wealth of bodies. At first we see all the narrative positions clearly, even pedantically. A woman, finely dressed, behind the blinds of her house at the shore, secretly watches the naked young men while the ironic poet observes her in the act of spying and chides her. "Where are you off to, lady? for I see you, / You splash in the water there, yet stay stock still in your room" (sec. 11). The question that he imagines asking her, posed as if by a clever detective who has caught her in an act that she herself, but not he, regards as shameful, is the question of the imagination itself that stays physically in the room, but in fantasy is already in the water with the naked young men. The speaking poet has his own psychology of banter and finger-wagging that plays off against her sexual arousal, conceal-ment, and shame. In the poem, however, she is clearly an artifice, a screen that converts to a heterosexual transgression the actual fan-tasy of Whitman himself, a transgression of a quite different order.

In the sexual act that follows, the pronoun disappears and it is either *he* (Whitman) or *she* (the rich lady) or *we* (the readers) who swim in the waters of sexual play while still remaining hidden, but now beneath the water, rather than behind the curtained window of the house.

> The beards of the young men glisten'd with wet, it ran from their
>   long hair,
> Little streams pass'd all over their bodies.
>
> *An unseen hand* also pass'd over their bodies,
> It descended tremblingly from their temples and ribs.
>
> The young men float on their backs, their white bellies bulge to
>   the sun, *they do not ask who seizes fast to them,*
> They do not know who puffs and declines with pendant and bend-
>   ing arch,
> *They do not think* whom they souse with spray.
> > "Song of Myself." sec. 11: emphasis added

By reversing the point of view to that of the young men who float with their eyes closed in the water as they are caressed to orgasm,

Whitman can keep us aware of the open question of just *who* is doing this. He emphatically repeats: they do not ask who; they do not know who; they do not think whom they douse with their seed.

Here we have not classic narrative, but classic Whitman narrative. His most critical narrative term is the word "merge," and here sexual merging in the act of love is, if anything, secondary to the merging of all possible lovers of the young men: the rich woman, the poet, the reader. Because they do not know or care who is loving them, it can be anyone or, best of all, everyone at once. Because there are twenty-eight of them, neither the woman nor the poet chooses one out of the group to focus erotic attention on, taking him aside to make love just to this special one. The twenty-eight men make up the perfect partner term to the "we" that ends up represented by that classic actor of mystery stories: an unseen hand.

That Whitman has to take over for a moment the language of crime stories with his phrase "an unseen hand" is his one concession to the moral in this extraordinary scene, the democratic Eros in which, in a word, *we* make love to *them*, and where both the *we* and the *them* are unlimited but simultaneous. Whitman does not intend a scene of orgy or promiscuity. The scene is the essence of the amorous poetics that Whitman set out to write, and it has at its heart an act of abstraction from particular identity that takes one familiar form in the language of numbers (twenty-eight) and one novel form in the creation and then the erosion of distinct personalities (the reader, the ironic voyeur poet, the lusty, mature, but lonesome woman hidden behind the blinds of her house). These identities fade in making love, first into the synecdoche (an unseen hand) and then into the passive voice once the point of view has switched from the lovers to the young men, lying on their backs in the water, receiving the caresses. In that passive voice, the whole representation of our own distance or participation is bleached out in the interrogative words "who," "who," and finally, recipient of the climax, "whom."

Like the sleep of the sleepers that *restores* all who sleep to genuine, because undifferentiated, democratic identity, or the silence of the pictures and scenes that locates all Whitman's voiceless countrymen in the Latin of dignity, this erotic "who" of the unknown actor is at once an abstraction and a capacious enlargement of all, at once, to a full sexual identity, outside shame (which we feel through the woman), outside ironic voyeurism (which we see in the poet's chafing questions as he watches her watch the bathers), and outside distance and removal (felt, naturally, by readers and observers of these two earlier, nested observers, the poet and the woman).

With the bridegroom, the poetics of sacrificing Whitman's countrymen to himself depends on rivalry and interposition. Whitman does this as well, in one of the most shocking moments of *Leaves of Grass* when in "I Sing the Body Electric" he speaks of often going to slave auctions to watch the sale and pushes aside the auctioneer—"I help the auctioneer, the sloven does not half know his business"—and then begins to speak for him, addressing his readers as though they were the buyers of slaves: "Gentlemen look on this wonder, / Whatever the bids of the bidders they cannot be high enough for it . . ." ("I Sing the Body Electric," sec. 7). He sells his readers first a male and then a female slave. The better he sings the praises of their naked bodies, the higher their price, the more certain their slavery.

In the erotic picture of the twenty-eight young men, the interposition and displacement has been surpassed in just the moment that the possessive choices of desire have been. To desire is commonly to single out, to create a relation to just this chosen one, and then to possess and defend possession against any rival. Whitman in this remarkable moment within "Song of Myself" delivers not only the sexual, but even the narrative components of a democratic transcendence of the particularity of desire. As he says late in the poem, "It is time to explain myself—let us stand up" (sec. 44), in which only the "us" can really explain "myself."

Substitution of voice and act is finally taken to its last extreme when near the end Whitman claims, "It is you talking just as much as myself, I act as the tongue of you, / Tied in your mouth, in mine it begins to be loosen'd" (sec. 47). Until the final words it seems he might be asking us to picture his tongue tied in our mouths, but then the later clause restates the words as no more than "tongue-tied" in you, free in me. This momentary picture of another tongue

87

present so as to speak when we open our lips takes us to the physicality of displaced voices, and it has to be contrasted with the strongly present alternative of supportive, side-by-side amatory tenderness: "My face rubs to the hunter's face when he lies down alone in his blanket" (sec. 47). In this there is no violence of displacement or silencing, but a loving second presence that as Whitman promises, will be "with you always."

The two alternatives of substitution and amatory companionship mark out the equally present effects of the strong poetic nearness that we feel in Whitman. We never simply hear "a man speaking to men" because he sets out to interfere with us, even to invade us, in acts that go far beyond mere speaking and being spoken to. He has always a wider Lucretian purpose. The grass itself is pictured as the grass of graves. It exists from the transfigured strength of the corpses, and it replaces or displaces them. It is them: their carbon and minerals, water and oxygen. They must die for there to be grass. Whitman's countrymen must also pass away for there to be not grass, but *Leaves of Grass*. Whitman's own leaves (or pages) of grass, are lines said on the graves of others. All of those he pictured have now died. His book is the grass on the graves of his countrymen. They died to make this green. They passed into the true silence of death, that he might now, a century and a half later, remain behind to speak for them all.

PART TWO

Defecting from
American Abstraction

chapter three

Transparency and Obscurity: Melville's *Benito Cereno*

Stowe and Melville: Sentiment and Damage

The sentimental novel, of which Stowe's *Uncle Tom's Cabin* is a primary example, depends upon experimental, even dangerous extensions of the self of the reader. At its center is the experimental extension of normality—of normal states of primary feeling—to people from whom they have been socially withheld by means of a concept of "difference." The political content of sentimentality is democratic in that it experiments with the extension of full and complete humanity to classes of figures from whom it has been socially withheld. The typical objects of sentimental compassion are the prisoner, the madman, the child, the very old, the slave, and the animal. All earn inclusion within the social space by means of the reality of their suffering and our own spontaneous response to that suffering.

Sentimentality, by its experimental extension of humanity to prisoners, slaves, or children exactly reverses the process of slavery itself, which has at its core the withdrawal of human status from a part of society. Within a sentimental narrative like *Uncle Tom's Cabin* the act of extension occurs in two ways: first, by means of dramatic scenes that are variations of the core scene of sentimental feeling, a scene of parting or forced separation, the ultimate form of which is the deathbed scene; and, second, by means of brief, almost Wordsworthian life histories told years later by the victim herself or himself, a victim for whom this story has become the single content of life itself.

The many disconnected scenes and brief stories make up a narrative structure of glimpses. They sample slavery and represent it by some few dozen patches of experience. They have, therefore, a narrative authority like that of a newspaper, which samples daily reality by means of bits of experience. Stowe's narrative of patches and glimpses records also her spatial structure, in which we come to know one farm in Kentucky glimpsed for a day or two, a Quaker settlement in Ohio seen for a few hours, a patch of Canada, a single plantation, Simon Legree's, in the Deep South of cotton farming.

The force of Stowe's novel is to detail a world torn into pieces—islands of social experience—and then to propose sentimental feeling as the one universalizing, radical method for reconstructing the social world, repairing it, and producing a composition that settles it once again into a democratic social space.

In Melville's *Benito Cereno* an entirely different problem is presented. We can see this from the outset in his choice of setting. A ship is not only the classic image of the political totality—the ship of state—it is also a world that is inherently undividable, short of shipwreck and sinking. Both spatial damage and spatial repair within narrative are forced into a different route. Stowe's world has behind it the challenge of Jeffersonian uniformity, the social model for American family agriculture. The independent, modest, family farm is the social cell damaged and, in her implied utopia, still to be built universally within America. Melville's ship in *Benito Cereno* is, like the Pequod in *Moby Dick*, a model of an industrial, capitalist society. The ship is a factory world as well as a *polis*. Melville's is the model of damage and composition for a successor to the America of family and homestead. His is the repair of a space that bracketed the Civil War in time, while ultimately posing an entirely different, and nonagricultural, nonfamily-based challenge to democratic uniformity. Melville's model is ultimately our own spatial complication in ways that Stowe's is not. This has more to do with the passing of family life as the core of social experience than with the disappearance of the Jeffersonian farm as the point of reference for social experience as a whole. Melville's is one pattern language, professionalism and mass culture being the other, for our own space.

Work and Ritual

In Melville's story, a slave ship adrift at sea is boarded by the naive Captain Delano, whose innocence of just what is going on within the ship allows him to survive and permits the ship to be recaptured from the slaves who had taken power. This brief summary makes clear that the "composition" that takes place is a return to slavery for the blacks, and the repair of a social space of slavery that had undergone mystification, but not precisely revolution, through an uprising of the slaves.

The ship that Delano finds adrift is a near derelict; neglected, shabby, and seemingly unable to steer or to protect itself. On board, nobody is doing the ordinary daily tasks that make up the life of a well-run ship. All novels of shipboard life agree about one thing: the ship is a beehive of activity in which men dart to and fro; the air is filled with shouted orders; work and the sounds of work are everywhere.

Melville's ship, like Samuel Taylor Coleridge's in "The Rime of the Ancient Mariner" seems, by contrast, rigid, impotent, frozen in a posture of waiting and drifting. The acts that we see have that stillness and emphatic quality that are the signs of communication rather than labor. In fact, no work is being done. At the same time, there is a frantic busyness. Groups of silent men polish hatchets; others seem to have turned the shipboard duty of standing watch into watching each other instead of the sea; others pick oakum. Figures glide from place to place, appearing from seclusion, then turning back into the dark like figures met by Dante in Purgatory.

These gestures and acts all have the look of work. They are day-long, regular, simple, repetitive acts almost like those in a factory where the final product is not quite clear to the onlooker. The ship itself is neglected, disordered, with little normal maintenance in process. Its sails are torn. If the hatchet cleaning, the shaving of the captain, and the rope picking are not work, what are they? The answer, I think, is that the ship is organized by rituals rather than tasks. Tasks—the small units of work—aim at an outcome that can be counted up as so many clean hatchets per day or per hour; a ship newly painted; a captain freshly shaved. In ritual, the goal is the participial act itself: cleaning, shaving; running, watching. By stripping the social life of the ship of its work function, Melville has made it clear that all of its actions refer to society itself. They are all manifestations of its self-regulation.

In its rituals every state is a police state. In Jürgen Habermas's important phrase, rituals are part of the steering function of social life, its self-adjustment or self-regulation.[1] In ordinary social life the acknowledgment of the underlying realities of power and relation occurs in an undertone. These realities are more likely an aspect of form than of content. But in ritual, what is ordinarily present only as form appears as content and is directly available for perception and consciousness. The adjustment of social realities, including the repair of or reinsistence on the realities of power and relationship is, in our ordinary lives, occasional. A formal family dinner is an occasional display, acknowledgment, and adjustment, by means of ritual, of the inner life of the family. Usually these social facts are buried within ongoing tasks during which consciousness is directed toward results and not toward the social reality itself.

Melville has made his ship, and with it his slave society, a world that we would have to describe as one with no output whatsoever. All of its energy is needed for self-regulation. The ship is a utopia of self-consciousness, a police state in which every daily act is distorted toward consciousness of the order of social life as a whole—toward what Georg Lukács and Jean-Paul Sartre have called the "totality," but here the totality is present as a specter that haunts reality and can never be forgotten. With this consciousness of the order of social life as a whole, goes submission to it, as when the greeting "Heil Hitler!" was imposed on every daily transaction of life in German society in the 1930's, so that each social act, whether buying a newspaper, opening a meeting, or greeting a customer in a bakery, became a restatement of a public submission to a new order.

The more empty of output, the more the state is capable of self-maintenance as its only product. Its only output is its own social life. The events on Melville's ship are exactly like the contents of a dream because dreams are the self-adjusting, self-describing, and self-regulating condition of the mind: thought without output; the mind turned inward toward the steering mechanism of the psyche.

One important aspect of this contrast between work and ritual, between output and self-regulation, is that all societies are transparent to one another in so far as they are organized toward output. This is so because, no matter how they produce the food, clothing, dishes, and spoons, the processes can be read backward from the results. The spear or the tank, the boomerang or the machine gun, can be decoded back to the steps and to the social organization that produced it. To do this is the task of archaeology, which from the simplest metal objects or pottery can infer the work structure, type of industry, and social life of a society, as well as its changes over time. But insofar as social life is organized for self-regulation, it becomes opaque to outsiders. Work promotes, just as ritual blocks, social transparency.

Where there is opacity, we find interpretation. The damaged space of social interpretation in *Benito Cereno* is only made more difficult to understand by the good-natured innocence of Captain Delano. It is the nature of the self-conscious ritualizations of social life to be riddle-like and encoded. Paradoxically, here we have society naked, free of the clothing of output. Once naked of output, society appears opaque to outsiders and most cryptic, as the mind of another person is in the dream state. But it is in just this state that the society is most unambiguous and insistent, even urgent, for its own members. In exactly those rituals of self-regulation that appear codelike to outsiders, each and every member of the group is absolutely clear about social life as a whole and, in particular, about the relations of power and weakness, danger and safety.

One reason for this riddle-like structure is that one of the key facts acted out in the self-adjustment of society is the difference between members and strangers, the inside and the outside. The line of membership is drawn and reaffirmed by this daily, coded set of acts, which some understand and others do not. The second group learns in this way where it does not belong.

The Ritual of Whispering

In *Benito Cereno* the simplest ritual is the one that takes place a number of times in the middle of a conversation between Delano and Cereno when the latter's servant, Babo, is present, but apparently present only to attend to his master's needs. Suddenly, Cereno and his servant go off to the side to whisper together. They then return to the conversation. Whispering is the simplest ritual for the mystification of speech because it draws the fundamental social line between those who are involved in the speech and those who are pointedly and deliberately excluded from it. To whisper is to set up the signs of an inner, counter world against the larger world and to indicate *loudly* the social fact of inside and outside, included and excluded, while silencing the output or content of the voices. Here in whispered conversation we can see once again the trade-off between output and self-regulation. Whispering, in other words, is always loud as to self-regulation, but empty as to content.

Self-regulation, in summary, occurs as enigmatic, riddle-like, opaque details of social life, because the first act of self-regulation is not the question of power but the far more primitive question of membership, of inside and outside. Melville's slave society, as a society without work or output, is represented as a world of full-time self-adjustment, self-regulation, and self-manifestation, but only to itself and not to others. Those others find themselves to be "observers" who are forced to understand themselves to be outsiders. It is the essence of a police state, but also of a revolutionary society, that the sudden and recent transformation of social life needs to be printed and reprinted in the minds of all members by means of a neglect of output in favor of dramatization of the new social realities.

For Melville one of the measures of society is the degree of intelligibility or, more accurately, of transparency. This, we can now see, is an exact record of the balance between work and self-regulation, between output and ritual. A newly revolutionary state or, as

Melville generalizes it, a slave society, even one in which no reversal of power has taken place, reduces output and work so radically in its need for self-regulation that it becomes self-obsessed for insiders and, simultaneously, opaque to outsiders. Like a seriously damaged neurotic's behavior, the society's every expenditure is self-obsessed and directed to self-maintenance.

A social life of tremendous output—late-nineteenth-century American capitalism, for example—would be a social life of utter transparency. The flood of goods delivers society over to visibility. A social life of no output—a monastery, for example—would have its entire daily life enigmatic to outsiders because that life is entirely engaged in self-manifestation and self-regulation. Throughout his story, Melville's running analogy or metaphor for Cereno's ship is that of a monastery in which Cereno himself is a monk along with the many blacks who make up the monastic community. A twenty-four-hour day of self-manifestation and self-steering yields an opaque world as well as one with the sharpest possible line between insiders and outsiders.

Output and Transparency

Even if it is obvious why a society in its rituals is able to draw a line between insiders and outsiders, restating both the solidarity of those within and the exclusion of those who find the ritual mysterious, the contrary claim that insofar as a society is given over to output it will be transparent may not seem equally obvious. Is this transparency the same as the transparency that was earlier described as a consequence of democratic uniformity, whether in the way of life of a nation of Jeffersonian family farms or that of a modern suburb? In my opinion the two are distinct.

It is useful first to consider again Whitman's line "If these thoughts are not your thoughts as well as my own, then they are nothing, or next to nothing." Or Thoreau's belief that if all false and wasteful details of ordinary life were stripped away, he could find the *one* correct size for an elemental house, the one amount of food needed for a year, the one division of a man's time that would be spiritually ideal, and his belief that a most important feature of his experiment at Walden Pond would be that it would not be special or unique to him, but could be lived by anyone and therefore, potentially, by everyone, once they woke from the half-sleep in which daily life is usually conducted. Whitman's and Thoreau's aesthetics depend on the existence of a universal essence that could ground a democratic social existence. Similarly, in sentimentality a shared core of experience was located in moments of feeling that, as Rousseau had argued, made of pity or compassion a species-preserving emotion, as powerful in its way as the drive for self-preservation, which had dominated political thought since Hobbes and Spinoza.

In sentimentality an aesthetics with a universal core of feeling was generated around the response to suffering. In philosophy the passions, including pity, have traditionally been important precisely by virtue of their status as the one part of inner life that is transparent. Because a passion takes place simultaneously in the body and in the mind or soul, it is visible to others. Grief and the body's sign of grief, tears; embarrassment and the visible blush; anger and the reddening of the face, the tightening of the muscles: each of the passions has a physiological aspect, which means that, unlike thought, feeling, or belief, every passion appears on the body by means of universal signs recognized at once by all others. This universality is independent of culture. The signs of rage, fear, grief, or surprise are the same over time and over every known culture, even though each culture refines and complicates the passions in its own way. The passions are transparent. The aesthetics of sentimentality, which had its central moment in the scene of loss and especially in the deathbed scene of final loss, drew on this fact about the passions to promote a universalized base for experience through the cultivation and open manifestation of the passions, especially the mutual, social passion of pity. Pity is the one passion whose content is the experience of others. That is why Rousseau called it a species-preserving feeling, and in the term itself we can see that he intends it as an antidote to the equally universal fact of self-preservation.

Each of these aesthetics and ways of life—the Jeffersonian farm, Thoreau's self-sufficient cottage life, the twentieth-century suburb, Whitman's universalism, and Stowe's sentimentality—has as its enemy privacy and individuality. Insofar as the development and protection of an ever increasing realm of private experience and of individuality are taken to be key features of modern bourgeois experience, democratic social space and its aesthetics are deeply hostile to bourgeois civilization.

The transparency that results from organizing society and daily life around output rather than ritual is of a related but distinct kind. Society, in its output, is an economy; but in its rituals, it is a religion. If we watch a man sitting silently at the side of a stream, holding what looks like a long stick from which a thin string falls into the water, we cannot place his actions clearly into any realm until we see the line move, the man stand and catch his fish, then light a fire, cook it, and turn to eating it. Similarly, a man sharpening a hatchet by rubbing it against another becomes transparent at the moment when he takes the hatchet, places a stick on the ground, and cuts it in two.

A tool exists at the site of a repeated social action. Its weight, size, and materials are all organized around the action. If the act were not a common or a necessary one, there would not be a specific tool in existence since the refinement of tools is simply a legible guide to the specific actions that are common enough to call differentiation into being. That there are not two or eight but three and only three common tools for eating in most Western societies (knife, fork, and spoon), one of which is a fairly recent introduction, depends on and makes transparent the commonly repeated types of food, along with the actions of cutting and lifting to the mouth that those tools outline and service.

If I watch an Indian make a canoe and then see him put it into a fast-moving stream, and, using a paddle, fight his way across, aiming his boat upstream so as to end up (once the current is figured in) at a point exactly opposite on the other bank, his actions are transparent to me, just as they would be if, for a smaller stream, I watched him cut down a tree so as to make it fall across the banks, and proceed to walk across. By the linked chains of output and action all social groups are transparent to one another because they are reflecting a common underlying natural world to which they stand in relation, and a common set of human needs. In watching a potter make a small cup or bowl from which liquid can be drunk, I find the social act to be transparent because, for example, baked clay rather than straw is the material, and the size of the object is based on the amount that constitutes the act of taking a drink, which is, in turn, based on how much a human body needs regularly to replenish itself. The size is also related to the hands that must be able to grasp and lift the container and to the lips against which it will rest in the act of drinking.

Because there is a negotiation built into all objects and tools—all output—between the facts of the natural world and the facts of the body, there is transparency. Any object, produced by any culture, can be recognized as a boat because to be a boat requires acknowledgment, in its design, of the facts of water, currents, waves, and motion through water in relation to other facts of the human body or bodies that will sit in the boat. Just as every "boat" can be recognized as a boat, no matter what society has produced it, so can all societies, as more and more of their time is organized around output, be seen as more and more transparent to one another. Where society is an economy rather than a religion, it is engaged in a necessary transparency because in the making of useful things the realm of freedom is constricted by, on the one side, the facts of nature that tell us that baked clay will hold liquid while straw in the same shape will not, and on the other side, by the facts of the human body and its needs. Insofar as society is an economy, it maneuvers in a far narrower realm of possibilities than it would if it could be open to the free invention of the symbolic realm in which it elaborates the ritual acts for its self-policing. Ritual is opaque because it is unconstrained in just those places where output is constrained: that is, by the set of boundary conditions that make all boats recognizable as boats. All punishments are not equally recognizable as punishments, although many certainly are.

I have characterized this transparency of work and output, by contrast to the opacity of ritual and self-regulation, at some length because it seems to me to provide the key to the achievement of a democratic social space in nineteenth- and twentieth-century America. Because American society after the Civil War became, above all, an economy rather than a culture, it became increasingly transparent. Neither subjects nor citizens, Americans were above all else workers and consumers who produced and enjoyed a certain way of life. The central fact of the economy became the production and widest possible distribution of common economic goods, from food, clothing, and housing to television programs, domestic appliances, and automobiles. The movies of Charlie Chaplin or the books and lectures of Mark Twain were distributed throughout the culture as universally as Coca-Cola. Because those goods spilled out over a coast-to-coast market, the society developed a common culture in spite of the complex and varied geography, which the combination of mass production and good transportation unified, and in spite of the ever increasing diversity of an immigrant population, who made up a society of volunteer members.

Within the flood of production, certain objects took on the power to focus and identify American culture to itself in a way that in the past had been done only by leaders or other heroic individuals. For example, the period from 1880 to 1900 might best be described as the cultural era of the bicycle and the Kodak camera. In the 1890s the bicycle craze signaled the first national love affair with an object. For such a fad to be possible there had to be a media system in place to blanket the society with both news and the newest things. As David Hounshell has shown in his book *From the American System to Mass Production, 1800–1932*, the bicycle was the first universal object requiring advanced manufacturing techniques that was not a tool.[2] Following in the line of such earlier breakthrough products as the sewing machine, the reaper, and the Colt revolver, the bicycle placed at the center of advanced manufacturing techniques an object of recreation. Later objects, from the Model T passenger car to the computer, would exploit the ambiguous realm between work and pleasure that the sewing machine and bicycle had opened up.

In the same years, the Kodak camera in its simplicity and cheapness made possible the family album, one of the few religious objects of ordinary American life. From the 1890s on, successive generations might best be designated by the powerful, universal objects that swept the culture as the Kodak camera and bicycle had between 1880 and 1900. The Model T, movies, and the telephone set their stamp on the generation of 1910 as the radio and the phonograph would on the generation after 1930. The television, the suburban home (with lawn), and the family car frame the generation of the 1950s. The computer, which plays some of the same part as a cultural focus for the generation of the 1970s, has more in common with the sewing machine or the reaper—a thinly disguised work object that only at first seems to belong to the realm of pleasure.

The farmer in Levis on his John Deere tractor or his grandson staring at the screen of his Macintosh computer both were part of a socialization by means of things rather than by means of the traditional agents: education, culture, and what we today call ideology. As America became increasingly what James MacGregor Burns has called "the Workshop of Democracy," it became less and less what Melville's ship of state is: the monastery of a ritualized social life.[3]

One of the strongest implications of Melville's story is that it is not slavery in itself, with its absolute power of one man over another, its cruelty, its separation of families, that is intolerable within the ship. Every one of these features characterizes normal shipboard life, where the absolute tyranny of the captain, the tradition of beatings and torture-like punishments, and the separation of men from their families is the norm. By representing slavery at sea, Melville simply reduplicates the actual conditions of shipboard life. The ordinary conditions of any ship make invisible, so to speak, those very aspects of slavery that for Stowe in *Uncle Tom's Cabin* were its darkest essence.

It is the breakdown of slavery rather than its working life that is Melville's subject. Slavery itself, since it is an economic system, is no less transparent than factory life or the working life of a maker of pottery. Stowe's novel depends on this transparency of slavery as an economic system, and she counts on its inevitable self-publication to create the evidence that will lead to its abolition. What Melville is characterizing in advance of the Civil War itself is the aftermath and residue of slavery. He was predicting the peculiar listlessness and paralysis that would ensue in American society once slavery was past, no matter whether revolt or emancipation had brought about its end. Melville's is the account or prophecy of the permanent damage to American transparency once it had no other choice than to view itself as a post–slave-owning society. For Melville there is no alternative to this history of a society whose members will be stamped forever as ex-masters and ex-slaves. More important, he defined the extent to which, because of slavery, America was doomed to pass from a society that was in its essence an economy to one that was a mystified culture: to pass, in other words, from ship to monastery while retaining the ongoing simulation of shipboard life. What Melville represents is the simple fact that there might be no fundamental sense to the belief that slavery could be, in the strong sense, "abolished."

Unintelligibility and Interpretation

If output implies transparency, then unintelligibility is the first sign of a damaged social space, one torn into inside and outside, members and observers. The replacement of output or work by self-policing and the self-manifestation of society as a whole are the clear signs of this condition. The image of two men who go aside to whisper within sight of a third man who hears that they whisper but not what they whisper is Melville's image for the social life of this world. The function of unintelligibility is to police the borders of the social world by marking visibly the moments of exclusion.

Wherever social life is unintelligible, as it is in *Benito Cereno*, we are thrown back onto the interpreter. In fact, most discussions of Melville's story concern themselves with the good-hearted innocence or stupidity of Captain Delano, whose visit to the ship creates the narrative. It is through him that we see or do not see the life of the ship. Delano survives only because he does not come to understand that the ship has been taken over by the slaves. Exactly his innocence, his unwillingness to be suspicious, his optimism—all of which make him unable to see—save his life. He would be killed at once if it were thought that he suspected. Likewise, he would be killed if he interfered.

But it is not to these psychological aspects of the point of view, the narrator, or the moral nature of his survival that I want to call attention. I have argued, first, that because society turns from output to self-regulation, from work to ritual, it becomes unintelligible, creating a damaged space for perception and knowledge. This is the case because the first goal of ritualization is to mark the line between inside and outside in order to affirm membership and exclusion. Second, it is the unintelligibility that follows from this ritualization that first creates the observer: he who watches others whisper and speculates about the meaning of what he sees withheld from him. Third, it is at this point that we are for the first time forced to become precise in our description of the individuality of the observer. Is he too cautious? Is he so pessimistic that he always imagines that situations are worse than they are? Is he projecting rather than seeing? Does he always imagine that others are acting as he himself would? It is social unintelligibility that creates individuality and a necessary fascination, on our part, with the unique traits of perception and response that might be deforming the interpretation that makes up our only access to this world.

These features of individuality become of value as features of an outsider who has been given his position by means of the unintelligibility of the world. A world strongly marked by output—late-nineteenth-century capitalism, for example—does not raise the question of observation, or the question of individual differences, that would lead to strong concern with the nuances of individualism. Because it is within the sphere of differing interpretations that uniqueness becomes clear, the transparent social life of work and output is free of uniqueness. It is bland in the Emersonian sense of universal and blank, as is personality in Whitman or Dreiser. Individuality is itself the product of social damage. It is opposed to Whitman's "loose drift of character, the inkling through random types." The random, the typical, the drifting, and the loose make up in combination almost a program for an antithetical relation to individualism.

Finally, the ritualization of the social surface raises epistemological questions. How can I know what is going on? Is there any unencoded social experience? Can this be known only by a certain type of outsider or only by means of certain methods? Exclusion and unintelligibility generate at once the special type of individualism that we think of as "self-consciousness" and, in particular, the special kind of self-consciousness that has at its center the problems of knowledge, doubt, and skepticism. These classic epistemological questions always arise where knowledge cannot be understood collectively, but is regarded as the problem of a single, isolated individual who is his own sole resource. Thus the problems of knowledge, individuality of point of view, and survival in Melville's story are secondary outcomes of the opaque ritualization of society within slavery.

Either Master or Slave

In *Uncle Tom's Cabin* Stowe had confidently reconstructed her damaged world through the universal inner life of feelings that the sentimental tradition drew on. Above all, the universality of the experience of separation through loss or death, and the spontaneous humanity of pity in the face of suffering, provided a mechanism for the testing and subsequent assertion of a universal, nonracial humanity. The function of art within this tradition of sentiment is to retell the stories of the slaves themselves and by this story-telling to spin a web of truth across which feelings might travel to repair the social world. This was the essence of Stowe's composition: relentless accumulation of brief stories that bear witness to the individual life experiences of the slave and to the spontaneous universality of such key passions as fear, pity, and the love of a parent for a child.

Each older slave, like a Wordsworthian figure, retains both humanity and the power to speak. It is one of the key sentimental assumptions that suffering does not brutalize; nor does it silence its victims or lead them to save themselves by repressing what they have undergone. Instead, suffering leaves them in ruins with their own story remaining as their only property. All else has been taken from them, starting with whatever Lockean property they once had in their own selves. Their only power is to speak, to remember, and to invite sympathy by means of stories that, if heard, will provoke a state of social crisis. Within Stowe's novel the slave stories sicken and finally kill Little Eva. Stowe's own book, as Abraham Lincoln said, brought on the Civil War. These stories lead to political change or to death. Stowe's novel is frankly a scrapbook of true stories. It is at once the *Canterbury Tales*, the *Decameron*, and the *Thousand and One Nights* of American slavery.

What is socially scattered can undergo a composition by reassembly. Stowe herself assembles stories. That is her function as an author. Within her novel, one of her two main slave families is literally reunited in Ohio, brought safely to Canada, and returned to Africa. The plot, like the author, reassembles. Melville, in *Benito Cereno*, faces an entirely different problem. The ship of state has simultaneous and overlapping worlds: a world of white command and a world of black, revolutionary power. Only the whites know how to sail the ship or preserve the freedom and lives of the blacks when other ships are encountered. Thus it is not a solution for the blacks to kill the remaining Spanish sailors, including Benito Cereno. Their power will vanish if they assert it openly. On board the ship, life itself, for both blacks and whites, depends on keeping alive the superimposed social life of a crowded, overlapping world.

The syntax invented by Melville as a rhetoric and a logic for this superimposed world is based on the "either-or" structure. Hundreds of sentences within the story have the same form, which we can see in its opening descriptive paragraph. *"Whether* the ship had a figure-head *or* only a plain beak, was not quite certain, owing to canvas wrapped about that part *either* to protect it *or* else decently to hide its decay."[4] This early sentence manages to build in two distinct branching paths for explanation, four alternatives in all.

When the ship is first seen it is conspicuously without a flag, and therefore most likely a pirate ship. But then it seems to be drifting toward a reef. So instead of being a threatening fact, the absence of a flag might be part of its helplessness. The simple fact of being without a flag is *either* the sign of a cunning rapacious power *or* a mark of impotence and victimization. Captain Delano assumes that the ship is weak and in need of help. He is, therefore, generous *or*, perhaps, stupid. Once on board the ship, he finds that Benito Cereno seems listless. He avoids giving the many small orders that make up the daily life of the ship. Thus *either* he is weak and powerless *or* he is an example of that kind of rigid and icy captain who demonstrates that he is totally in command by the way that he "obliterates alike the manifestation of sway with every trace of sociability, transforming the man into [*either*] a block *or* rather into a loaded cannon, which, until there is call for thunder, has nothing to say" p. 246).

When he first sums up Cereno, Captain Delano says that he is a case of *either* "innocent lunacy" *or* "wicked imposture." In each of the examples that I have quoted the either/or structure is not the familiar, Aristotelian structure of logical exclusion. Rather, it is an entirely modern rhetorical trope of masking and hollowing out from within. For example, if we say, "Either Delano is kind or he is stupid," the second term "stupid" preserves the first while reconstructing it from within by implying that his kindness might best be understood as a form of stupidity. Similarly, Cereno's refusal to give orders is not an alternative to power, but a masked and therefore more essential variation of power whose symbol is the loaded cannon.

In the logical use of either/or when we say that the paper is "either black or white," the second term "white" can not be a more essential version of the first term "black." In logic the either/or is exclusive: "either a man or a woman." Melville's, however, is an inclusive alternative in which the second term, so to speak, surrounds and saturates the first as an illness does the body or as the unconscious does the conscious mind. Our everyday use of either/or makes possible an essential technique within logic that depends on the Law of the Excluded Middle. Once we assert, "Either A or B," we know that (1) either one or the other is the case; but also that (2) that not both are; and (3) that not neither is. We know at once three distinct things about the situation. For example, if a friend misses an appointment with me and I say, "Either he made a mistake or he has deliberately insulted me," then I have already ruled out all other possibilities. This is the strong power of the either/or. It represents a state of near finality, because the logical form commits me to the fact that it must be one or the other and cannot be neither of them. No further possibilities need be considered.

The first result of the Aristotelian either/or is to shrink the domain of possibility to a clear, finite set, and to invite an act of choice. In the example of the friend who missed the appointment, once I learn that he made a mistake I can feel relieved because I know also that I have not been insulted. This is an aftermath and quite distinct fact that follows once we learn which is the case. We also learn that one explanation is true, and therefore not the other. Sometimes, as in this case, that negative fact—that it was not an insult—is more important than the positive one. This negative certainty follows from the other consequence of the either/or structure: that it cannot be both.

In the twentieth century, as a result of Sigmund Freud, our sense of the complexity of the either/or structure goes much further. If I visit a friend who has a new rug on the floor, praise the rug lavishly, and then accidentally spill a glass of wine on the rug, ruining it, we can say, "Either the spill was an accident or I wanted to spill the wine while disguising my malice within an accident." The force of Freud's *Psychopathology of Everyday Life* lies in the way that it forces us to regard just such situations of alternative possibilities within daily life. Here the Law of the Excluded Middle—*tertium non datur*—no longer holds. As a result, negation no longer gives me any information.

In logic the most powerful result of the either/or is the constructive part played by negation or denial. If we know that "either an object is black or white" and "it is not white," then we know with certainty that "it is black." This device lies at the heart of what is known in mathematics as indirect proof. Even in the absence of any positive way of knowing that it is black, we can be certain if we can negate its alternative. In the logical either/or, denial or negation becomes a decisive step, equal in importance to assertion. If we describe this in temporal terms we have the following: (1) a shrinking of the unlimited field of abstract possibility down to a finite set; (2) an act of denial; (3) clarity and certainty.

In Freud's or Melville's use of this structure, where the first term is preserved and regrounded in the second possibility, a denial or a negation only increases the uncertainty. If I were to say, after spilling the wine on the rug, "I can assure you that I did not mean to ruin your rug," then, like the famous denial "I am not a thief!" I have only made the ambiguity more obvious by calling attention to it, pointing to it and underlining it. I cannot resolve it. The longer and more strenuously I go on denying, the more troubled the situation becomes. If I send a five- or ten-page letter the next day explaining the long history of my affection for my friend and the many reasons why it is impossible that he could think that I might have intended to ruin his prize rug, I will only increase his suspicions.

Denial functions here exactly as the ritual of whispering does in *Benito Cereno*. The whispering calls attention to the fact of something not being said out loud. It marks out its incomplete concealment. In Melville's story, the slave Babo is either Captain Cereno's officious servant or his master. He is either saving him again and again or he is weakening him. In each case the second alternative preserves, deepens, and regrounds the first while insulating both terms from denial. A cunning trap is set for negation, which is made impotent, even amusing. It is what we might call the sterilization of negation that is the fundamental goal of the either/or structure as Melville or Freud uses it. A social life is created that both locally, in the small interpretive details of experience, and as a whole is not subject to denial, because it has sterilized negation in advance. Like all perfect systems it cannot be overthrown because it has made all that lies outside itself part of its own inside.

For Melville this either/or that is protected from denial is the syntax of the superimposed space of American slavery. It is the political space of what we call occupation rather than conquest. Each gesture and every single fact have a double location, which can only be experienced by means of what appears to the eye and to the mind as an either/or.

It is in describing the relations between Captain Cereno and the slave Babo, his body servant, that the core of Melville's either/or structure is worked out. The everyday gestures of help, aid, solicitude, and caring are, even in ordinary life, subject to paradox. Even in ordinary life to hold some one's hand is also to imprison it; to shake hands is also to seize hands; to embrace is to restrain and immobilize. To help someone who is weak also makes that person weaker. If we picture for a moment a man surrounded by servants who attend to his every need to the point that they make his coffee, lift the cup to his lips when he wants to drink, dress him, remember his appointments, and make his apologies, then we could say that they are destroying him in the act of serving him. They sterilize him by means of their care. Soon his arms are too weak to lift his own cup. He no longer remembers how to dial a telephone and does not remember the numbers anyway. This is the process of slavery and its resulting enfeeblement of the master that is well known from Hegel's *Phenomenology of Mind*.

Melville's description of this process of enfeeblement captures the process in its final stages. "Here there was a sudden fainting attack of [Cereno's] cough, brought on, no doubt, by his mental distress. His servant sustained him, and drawing a cordial from his pocket, placed it to his lips. He a little revived. But unwilling to leave him unsupported while yet imperfectly restored, the black man with one arm still encircled his master, at the same time keeping his eye fixed on his face, as if to watch for the first sign of [*either*] complete restoration, *or* relapse, as the event might prove"(p. 248; my emphasis). The literal either/or of the final line brings out into the open the larger, pervasive problematic of care and weakening.

Just as we would want to look at the details of the gestures of love, such as holding someone, as gestures within an either/or structure of love or domination, so Melville, in the superimposed spatial world of slavery, requires such a structure. Captain Cereno is heading either for restoration or for collapse; his servant either supports or restrains him. Around Cereno's neck hangs a key to the chains worn by the slave Atufal. The key is naturally a sign of the power to free, but worn around the neck, it imprisons, in perhaps a deeper way, the man who wears it. It is the royal slave Atufal, literally in chains, who is free to speak or not to speak. So long as he will not speak, the captain must wear the key. Where the power to free or to keep under restriction actually lies within this ritual is undecidable.

The Riddle

In larger narrative terms the syntax of either/or could be called a riddle structure, but one seen from the other side of the temporal process of solution. Like the key around the neck of the captain, the many physical details of *Benito Cereno* are riddle-like in structure. The intricate knot held up in front of Captain Delano by one of the sailors is a meta-riddle, a riddle about riddles, or one that tells him that all other events are riddle-like. The blacks sharpening hatchets, or the dreamlike shaving scene where, draped in his own flag, Cereno offers his neck to the black bending over him, razor in hand: these are the typical semantic units of the story. Each is both a ritual and a riddle. Epistemologically, a riddle postpones as long as possible the collapse of the possible into the much neater actual. In the moment of learning the answer to a riddle we say, "Aha!" both pleased and relieved that a chaotic world has shrunk into a familiar one. The riddle creates a temporary open space of chaotic, multiple possibilities. It is the form of an as-yet unstated certainty. Its essence lies in the pause, the brief gap between with-held and delivered certainty. The riddle mystifies, but only briefly, the familiar, and then restores it. In this it is a natural form for political occupation, which temporarily occults the ordinary. Melville's story concerns not an achieved revolution in which the blacks openly take power, but rather a half-way revolution in which the appearance and therefore much of the reality of white power must be maintained. What has occurred is a mystification of the conditions of power, not their inversion. That is why Melville's story can ultimately address the mystifications present within all slavery that are transposed from form into content by this ritual-ized, temporary stage of complexity.

The riddle is the opposite of the enigmatic, because it is the narrative form for a surplus of sharply defined clarities, not at all the form of the indefinite or the indeterminate. Babo is clearly a slave and an attentive servant. His every gesture is sharply drawn and unmistakable, but, as we know, too much clarity is the mark, not of fact, but of performance. At the same time, he is clearly master. It is he who breaks off conversations or announces new rituals such as the shaving.

As long as the riddle continues and the either/or remains un-damaged, life itself can continue in the world of the ship. It is only because Captain Delano does not, like Oedipus, push forward to solve all riddles that he survives. Only because he does not see that Babo is the master, that the slaves have taken over the ship, do the slaves allow the two white captains to live. By postponing or suspending knowledge, Delano actually saves his own life, frees Cereno, and makes possible the recapture of the slaves and the reconstruction of social reality. Melville's story, unlike Stowe's novel, leads to the repair of slavery. The northern captain preserves the ship as a slave ship. In retaking the ship by force, the white sailors try not to kill the blacks because they are valuable slave property. They must be retaken in the social context of slavery: not killed or injured so as to be unsalable. If Delano were reconstructing a northern world, the act of retaking the ship would be guided by exactly the opposite strategy. He would try to minimize injury to his own sailors and would therefore willingly kill as many of the black rebels as might be necessary to bring about their surrender.

The riddle delays recognition until the original state can be composed. But the riddle structure itself, along with the inclusive either/or of undecided possibility made safe from the danger of denial or negation, defines Melville's syntax for the composition of a slave world by means of the reassertion of white mastery over blacks.

Knowing or Fainting

Slavery, whether on Benito Cereno's ship or on Simon Legree's plantation, must inevitably be a system in which the blacks outnumber the whites. And it is a world in which whites will, like Benito Cereno or Stowe's Augustine St. Clair, the father of Little Eva, become effete or enfeebled by the cunning, disempowering daily care of their slaves. This Hegelian paradox, as well as the question of numbers, points to the fact that slavery will always lead to a riddle of power. What appears to be exceptional in Melville's case—that the slaves have taken over, but have for reasons of their own survival concealed that fact from the white masters—is only on the surface the opposite of the everyday situation. By this exception of revolt, Melville has forced the inner state out into the open. He has converted the latent into the overt.

Stowe's politicized sentimentality and her transcription of the stories told by the slaves themselves were the universalizing means by which the torn space of slavery could be pushed toward crisis and then reassembled on a democratic social basis. The universality of the feeling of grief in the face of death or separation stands as the first step toward a political and democratic universality of actual social life. Sentimentality and story-telling are both forms guaranteeing the knowability of social space. They insist on knowledge, as all realism does, as the ground for a common life. Social transparency and, with it, intelligibility are predicated on the web of slave stories that, once known, will kill off the masters, leaving behind only men and women, some black, some white.

Knowing and intelligibility play the same role, but in reverse, in Melville. It is the preservation of the riddle, the lack of resolution in Captain Delano, his not knowing and not seeing, that save his life and save slavery, which, by the end of the story, has been repaired. The essence of any slave society lies in the instability that comes from the riddle of power in a slave society. Although technically powerless, the slaves are strong and numerous. They are highly skilled. They have become the masters of nature by means of their work. The masters, although technically all powerful, are enfeebled by a life of delicacy and consumption. They are as helpless as invalids whose every need is supplied by a series of nurselike attendants. Outnumbered, having no power over nature, they still remain the masters.

Only not knowing, or not simplifying, the structure will preserve it. In Melville's story, the one action that we see Benito Cereno perform spontaneously again and again is the act of fainting. He passes out into the arms of his servant, who holds him and nurses him back to consciousness. Fainting is to the body what censorship is to the mind or to the state. It is the creation of a gap or a blank. Rather than go on seeing, Cereno passes out.

Structurally, fainting is an act opposite to solving the riddle. When the double reality in which he must simultaneously be captain and prisoner, all powerful and at the same time in dread of instant death, becomes unendurable, Cereno can either cut the knot and bring on the simplification of reality that would reduce his own roles to one unified role, or he can take on the maximum epistemological denial and create a blank space by fainting. Naturally, he chooses to faint rather than to die.

As long as the riddle is maintained, it leaves on either side of its tension and anxiety two solutions: (1) the abolition of complexity by the solution of the riddle; or (2) the abolition of consciousness, for which fainting is the small-scale, occasional ritual. In between these two is balanced the delay of recognition on which both the riddle and the preservation of life itself are based.

The Room of Slavery: From Jefferson's to Jasper Johns's Map of America

Benito Cereno's own room on the ship miniaturizes the social space of the ship as a whole. It is here that, draped with the Spanish flag, he is shaved by Babo. More or less an attic, the room is, like all attics, a place of storage. In feeling it seems like a museum for objects no longer in use, a place of junk and memory. In the cuddy, partitions have been taken down to make one large room. Formerly the officers had lived in individual rooms here before they were killed. It is a room marked by the revolution, its very openness a sign of the canceling of some previous power. "On one side was a claw-footed old table lashed to the deck; a thumbed missal; on it, and over it a small, meagre crucifix attached to the bulk-head. Under the table lay a dented cutlass or two, with a hacked harpoon, among some melancholy old rigging, like a heap of poor friars' girdles"(p. 277). A flag-locker with heaps of cloth spilling out, a bed that looks like the very debris of troubled sleep, an opening in the bulkhead for cannons, but no cannons to be seen: this is a confused and mostly no longer functional space. Delano looks over this room, as littered as the street of a slum or the rag and bone shop in a Dickens novel:

> "You sleep here, Don Benito?"
> "Yes, Señor, since we got into mild weather."
> "This seems a sort of dormitory, sitting room, sail-loft, chapel, armory, and private closet all together, Don Benito," added Captain

Delano, looking round.

"Yes, Señor, events have not been favorable to much order in my arrangements." (p. 278)

This room reflects the political world of which it is a part. It contains too many overlapping facts. When we see it in use, it is a rather sinister barber shop where the captain is shaved, draped in his flag. The room suffers from simultaneity. It is here that a new world, its barriers torn down, has been created after the death of the officers. The ritual that we see here displays the threatening servitude of the slave who might cut the captain's throat at any moment, but who nonetheless is assigned the duty of passing the razor across his master's throat.

Built over an abolished world, the new world is a multiple space of anxiety and misery. Here the captain sleeps, but not well; here he prays, but all is hopeless; here the ceremonial shaving occurs that mixes humiliation, grooming, and danger; finally, here the useless weapons and desecrated flags remain as tokens of the feudal world of gentlemen, but now they are piled up as junk among which, at last, the white captain has to settle down to live.

Harriet Beecher Stowe made of Uncle Tom's cabin both the title and the central symbolic place of her novel. The cabin is the family home in which Tom never again will live. In the novel it is replaced by the Quaker farmhouse, where, around the kitchen table and as if in a dream, the American family, black and white, sit down to eat. Against these two homes, cabin and farmhouse, stands the plantation of Simon Legree with its manor house and slave quarters. Taken together, these distinct dwellings begin an architectural map for a society of slavery. They have moved apart like scraps of what was once a single space. Stowe's claim is that, although separated by thousands of miles, they are all really rooms of one national house through whose corridors narration and feeling can flow.

Melville's captain's room is the prolongation of a wilderness of "or" choices that never will collapse into just one thing—dormitory or sitting room or sail-loft or chapel or private closet or barber shop or execution chamber. In this resistance to simplification, it is the opposite not only of transparency, but of riddle, which is only a deferred transparency. It is the opposite as well of the traditional "either-or" and of the promiscuous, all-embracing "and" that is the mechanism of Whitman's poetry.

The captain's room is a scene of historical melancholy. The more history, the more broken the space. Here there are no longer any tools, only relics of one system or another. The complexity provokes a depression, even a national willingness to faint rather than to think, just because such a room is the very image of history as aftermath. The temporal question in the air throughout Melville's story is this: The mysterious ship is as it is because its state is an aftermath; but an aftermath of what? By the end we learn that this question hardly matters.

Superficially, the ship is the aftermath of a solution to slavery by means of a black uprising, but it is in fact a picture of any aftermath whatsoever to slavery, even Lincoln's Emancipation Proclamation or the solutions imagined by the earliest abolitionists. The room describes a world in which there is no longer any leverage, a state of sickness that no longer has any way back to health. Slaves that have revolted and have held power for even a few days can never be simply captured or returned to slavery. Having tasted revolt, they are no longer slaves because they are men and women on whom no master can afford to turn his back for a minute. But this is only half of the story. Men who were once slaves, even if certified free, would never be more than ex-slaves. The new category is needed because the aftermath of slavery cannot be called "free" any more than the recaptured rebel can any longer be trusted to resume slavery.

To live as a nation in the captain's room is to live within a storehouse of irreversible mistakes, a history of damage. Whitman, whose social space was always focused toward a constructible future in which the broadaxes of the settlers would make what he called "shapes"—boards, door frames, houses, villages, states—was also forced, as the Civil War approached, to consider what it might mean for a democratic society to have not only promise and a buildable future, but also an irrevocable residue of mistake. In "As I Ebb'd with the Ocean of Life" he pictures himself walking along the seashore, looking down rather than out. At his feet he sees "Chaff, straw, splinters of wood, weeds, and the sea-gluten, / Scum, scales from shining rocks, leaves of salt lettuce, left by the tide."[5] Instead of wood lasting as the house, perhaps it is only the shavings and splinters that last, so that the boards of the house are only held off for a short while from becoming as much splinters and shavings as the scraps around the carpenter's bench. If not leaves of grass, then leaves of salt lettuce in a junk heap at the shoreline, down near his feet; himself part of the random heap that circumstance has brought together here and now at this part of the shore.

Whitman finds himself "seiz'd by the spirit that trails in the lines underfoot" (sec. 1). The lines of poetry at his feet write out the poems of sediment and debris. In this one poem Whitman located himself where all of Wallace Stevens's poetry would be written two generations later, on the municipal dump where the traces and scraps of various aesthetics and formerly valid ways of feeling end up. Both Melville in *Benito Cereno* and Whitman in "As I Ebb'd with the Ocean of Life" built the damaged space of history into democratic aesthetics. They started with an American map that had the simple repeatability of Jefferson's 640-acre square, a unit of action and property, but later found themselves surrendering transparency for the open-ended, paralytic "or" of historical damage. Captain Cereno is shaved draped with his own flag. By being simultaneously shaving cloth and flag, the object is not enriched by multiplicity, but ontologically paralyzed.

The wonderful square map of Jefferson's land ordinance of 1785 was an aesthetics of democratic prospects, much as was Whitman's *Song of Myself* or Henry Ford's cheap black Model T. Two hundred years after Jefferson created his map of one-mile-square sections, Jasper Johns executed a set of paintings of the American map that restate the alternative aesthetics of aftermath that Melville embodied in the captain's room and Whitman in the debris at the edge of land and sea. Johns painted what looks like the schoolroom map from which every child has to memorize the names and locations of the fifty states. Somewhere in every American memory is a scene made up of a box of crayons, a blank copy of the map of the states, and a second- or third-grade classroom. This icon of childhood memory already overlies the sober political facts of boundaries and names of what, for American viewers of Johns's paintings, makes up their own country. But Johns has painted (not colored in) the map with the highly personal, free brush strokes of the Abstract Expressionist painting style. No color stays put within the borders of one state. Clearly, he refused to be subject to the reprimands that any child would hear whose orange crayon wandered past the edge of Utah into Colorado, or who wanted to color Texas half red, half blue.

Every inch of the canvas is trying simultaneously to be map and painting, and to look at it is to pass back and forth between two similar but distinct acts of seeing. To read a map involves a set of mental activities entirely different from those involved in the act of looking at a painting, and Johns's work forces those differences into consciousness by making both acts necessary and insufficient at the same time. Behind these two competing ontological facts of map and painting is the third competing fact of a personal memory of crayons and the schoolroom, the struggle to learn the forty-eight or fifty names. To reminisce while in the presence of a souvenir is itself a third distinct temptation alongside the possibilities of map-reading and aesthetic enjoyment of the object as a painting.

What we might once have called aesthetic richness or complexity in Johns's paintings no less than Captain Cereno's flag/shaving cloth is clearly, at least in part, aesthetic damage in which we trade in transparency for the "or" that sterilizes not only decision and negation, but something ontological within the object. What is left is not an interesting series of epistemological questions about how we might know this or that or how we might distinguish, within the experience, layers of attention separately addressed to flag and shaving cloth or to map and memory and painting. What such objects record, just as the term "ex-slave" does, is an ontological damage to Cereno's room, to the flag become a shaving cloth, to Jasper Johns's painted-over map.

Both Jefferson's map and Johns's map are part of an experiment with abstraction. Every map presses down onto a physical terrain that it in part orders and in part effaces. Walt Whitman's display of his countrymen asleep is, to that extent, a map that suspends all the ordinary information that makes up identity to locate the overall mechanism that can, at whatever price, bring them all simultaneously to the same plane of representation. The paradox of American aesthetics lies in the fact that it is precisely when it is most engaged in the problem of abstraction that it is most historical and cogent. Emerson, Thoreau, Whitman, and Stevens have always been charged with a vaporous quest for the All that in its indefiniteness stands back from the thick description of realism. After 1945 it was by means of a maplike style of overall Abstract Expressionism that American painting became a no longer provincial practice. American emptiness and American fullness are one and the same; both trace out the consequences of a democratic social space captured from and damaged by the map of abstraction.

chapter four

Hierarchical Social Space:
Twain, James, and Howells

Melville's *Benito Cereno* explored the important claim that a democratic society damaged by slavery would not simply heal following the legal end of slavery. In the aftermath of slavery a riddle-like surface of everyday life would challenge transparency just as slavery itself had. Like an invaded and occupied nation or one that had undergone an incomplete revolution, an insecure coup, or a reconstruction of moral and behavioral life in which generations-long habits remained just beneath the surface, the aftermath would find itself within a damaged social space. Melville's strange and troubled image turned out to be correct. American abstraction and democratic social space on which it depended were forced to endure a permanent and richly coded deformation. Slavery in the American South gave way after the Civil War to what we might call race relations throughout the nation as a permanent fact. The preoccupying history of race relations down to the present made it a tempting model for a wide range of socially complex situations, including the relations between citizens and new immigrants and even those between men and women. In my fifth and sixth chapters on regionalism I will explore the hold of this model created in the aftermath of slavery, the model of black-white relations and the identity politics within literature and representation that resulted.

Even if slavery had been capable of genuine abolition in the deep as well as the legal sense, American society in the years following the Civil War displayed a second challenge to abstraction and to the democratic social space in which abstraction thrived. We might at the social level identify this new social space with the rising prestige of the professions—medicine, law, engineering, business—or with the rise of the modern publicity system that created in every field the star system and its partner term, the fans, the crowd of admirers who regard themselves as just ordinary people. The rise of brand-name products created the same gulf between mere objects and the magical goods that everyone knew and everyone wanted. A hierarchical social space of magical personalities, crowd-pleasing speakers, and larger-than-life events came into existence within the machinery of fame and stardom that was first seen in the popular press, but came to seem, in the end, a natural result of a media culture. The surprising link between this new machinery of stardom and the articulation of a domain of treasured intimacy and privacy is the subject of this chapter. Inwardly treasured privacy, usually felt to be under threat, and the glare of magnified stardom are partner terms defining the second damaged form of democratic social space: the space of hierarchy.

High Visibility

High visibility, like most light, comes in a variety of colors. To be notorious or to be infamous may be no more than shortcuts to that final moral neutrality of fame, and as such, more efficient uses of the machinery of fame. As many muckraking journalists at the turn of the century knew very well, a by-product of making someone else notorious was making themselves famous. The owners of the papers in which the great civic exposés of the 1880s and 1890s appeared, Dana, Pulitzer, and Hearst, could also see that once the newspaper fills its front page with the fame-making and notoriety-making process, the newspaper itself becomes news, and its daily appearance, shouted from street to street, becomes the most exciting daily event in the lives of many of its readers.

By means of the Armory show of 1913, modern art became notorious in America long before it was in any ordinary sense well known. Scandal is not the most refined form of publicity, but it does conveniently insert a fact, a name, a product solidly into the space of appearance. The remark of Roscoe Thayer that the most representative man of the third quarter of the nineteenth century was P. T. Barnum should remind us that the public in the years following the Civil War was giddy, intoxicated with the newly available energies for the magnification of personality that had been discovered in the economic and political realms.[1] The ability of the mass circulation newspapers to create ever new overnight sensations, or faces instantly recognizable to millions of people, permitted them to focus everybody's attention on, say, the Philippines, a shipwreck, a baseball star, or a political scandal, and then to rotate this attention from one event to another, from one personality to another.

In the same period, ideas, or "movements" as they significantly came to be called, had available the amplification of voice and message offered by the personal appearance of a charismatic lecturer on a platform before a crowd. The platform had taken on a new importance thanks in part to the successful use of emotional oratory and staged events by the abolitionist movement and then by the temperance movement with its dramatic oratory, its repentant drinkers, and its ceremonial signing of the pledge. In late 1875, the religious revivalist meetings of Dwight Lyman Moody and Ira D. Sankey in Philadelphia that assembled crowds of thousands night after night for two months convinced the merchant John Wanamaker that, by means of carefully crafted events, city-wide crowds could be brought together, for example, to patronize a dry-goods store. His biographer has written, "No memory of his crowded life was more precious to the great merchant than this revival. No event had a more far-reaching effect upon his business and religious activities, always closely related."[2]

John Wanamaker's store set the pattern in America for the successful use of newspaper advertising, periodic sales events, high-cultural entertainment, the theatricalization of Christmas, and the enormous crowds of shoppers and the carefully staged display of merchandise that made the department store the most important and exciting theatrical space in every major American city in the final decades of the nineteenth century. Not even Edwin Booth's Hamlet could draw crowds and excite public attention like a Wanamaker white sale or the unveiling of Macy's Christmas windows.

The platform from which moral or political emotion sensationalized ideas, just as the newspaper did events or the department store did merchandise, had also made possible the appearance of an author before the no longer invisible audience. Now the public might have him "in person" while he would enjoy the visceral attention and emotion that his words might, ordinarily in private, evoke. In 1867 Charles Dickens earned more than $100,000 for a series of crowded readings that made author, book, and audience—"live and in person"—performances that would pose the challenge of celebrity to American authors of the next generation, a challenge that was the despair of Henry James as well as, finally, the source of one of his richest topics. The space of performance invited the writer or artist to imagine, at once, a high cultural form of celebrity and a personal hold on his audience. Mark Twain, with his lecture style and his appearance carefully chosen to create an iconographic display of his role as performer, actor, and artist all in one, was the writer who grasped and managed the intoxication of the magnified and performed self. For thirty years, from the time of his first lecture tour in the late 1860s to his world tour of 1895–96, Twain was the first major American writer to become a "star," a position approximated after Twain only by Hemingway.[3] On a plane beyond Dickens or Twain, Emerson had, in the previous generation, created American philosophy in public as the performance of philosophy and thought before the lecture hall crowd.

The Performance of Mastery: Eakins's Two Clinics

The space of performance is itself the subject of the most important and in some cases most notorious paintings done in America between 1870 and 1900, those of Thomas Eakins. Many of Eakins's greatest paintings depict the performance of a skilled master before an audience—an opera singer on a stage, a rower before the crowd that we assume lines the banks of the river, a boxer in a ring surrounded by fans, or a professor of surgery before an audience of students. In *The Gross Clinic*, certainly one of the very greatest of nineteenth-century works and, arguably, the single most important American painting between the Civil War and the First World War, what is performed is surgery, and the surgeon is seen as a noble celebrity in a world of acclaim that we see made visible in the internal audience of students and professional observers.

Surgery differs from Eakins's other subjects such as boxing or rowing because it is normally a socially invisible act that for most people holds an aura of mystery and fear. Eakins brings surgery into public view by means of this painting in the same way that realist and naturalist novelists or the journalistic muckrakers would bring into the light of public scrutiny the normally invisible and often deliberately concealed affairs of political and economic life. To be prepared to look at this act of surgery was the mark of a society that had set out to face everything. Narrative realism; the new photography as used, for example, by Jacob Riis in the slums of New York; the newspaper exposé—all had mastered the techniques of seizing attention by means of daring and shock and then sustaining attention by narratives that seemed to permit the public to educate itself about the realities of its own life and times. As Eakins's medical paintings illustrate, that process of gaining attention cannot be achieved merely by the appearance of what had until then been invisible. What is required is the highest pitch of appearance: not surgery, but the performance of surgery as though on a stage with a spot-lit star, a supporting cast, a visible audience, and the melodramatic clues of knife and blood, a horizontal, unconscious body, and its proud, vertical assailant. When surgery not only is permitted to appear, but is depicted as performance, the viewer of the painting is asked to regard himself or herself as part of an audience and to become aware of, even morbidly self-conscious about, both the details of surgery and the details of observation, of attention, of the respect that creates the star-system of professional experts, and of the great civic drama of the one and the many, the leader and the people.

Dr. Gross himself is illuminated as if he were the star of this medical theater, isolated, erect like a soloist or conductor. The students whom we see are half of a symmetrical audience. We viewers of the painting are the other half of the circle, but we are witnesses to two superimposed demonstrations of mastery: that of the surgeon, Dr. Gross, and that of the painter, Thomas Eakins, both of whom work with an extended hand holding scalpel or brush covered with the brightest of crimsons, blood or paint.[4] We, as the audience for two performers, also have before us an audience—the students—who instruct us in the intensity of attention that should be given to the scene, to surgery, and to painting. As Gross instructs them in surgery, they instruct us, by their variety of expressions and postures, in the art of observing and witnessing, learning from skill and repaying it with the reverence and attention that it has earned. What we learn from them we apply to the (to us) equally visible skill of the painter, Eakins, who, although no longer standing there in front of the finished painting, is still visible in his surrogate, Dr. Gross.

Between *The Gross Clinic* of 1875 and *The Agnew Clinic* of 1889 Eakins, returning to surgery as his metaphor for the performance of the artist, increased his emphasis on the audience that we can see behind the surgeon, his patient, and his assistants. Now almost a wallpaper of faces, the thirty or so observers spell out the painter's instructions to his own observers. The colorless technique with which the audience is painted increases our feeling that this is a scene in a theater because the audience seems like one of those painted drop scenes of landscape or train station that so crudely set out the frame of reality in a play. At the same time, the audience of students is rendered in so different a technique that they seem to be only half real, as though full personal being were denied to spectators. Their uniformity, their sameness in shadow, makes of them a mass rather than an audience, almost a science fiction cartoon of efficient and decent mass men.

The striking ontological distinctions made in Eakins's painting between, first, the thing-like existence of the anesthetized, faceless, uncovered body and, second, the massified realm of spectatorship thrown into shadow almost as a visual equivalent for the anesthesia, and, finally, the full and singular humanity of the performer are distinctions with profound implications for the larger social world.

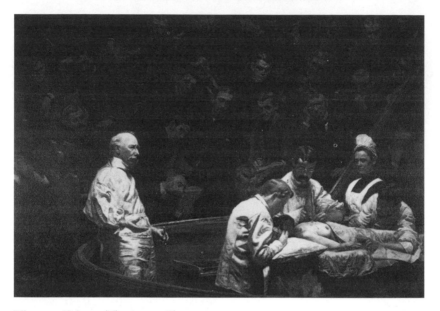

Thomas Eakins, *The Agnew Clinic*, 1889. (Courtesy of the University of Pennsylvania School of Medicine. Photograph courtesy of the University of Pennsylvania Archives.)

These ontological levels are given in several other structural ways in the social design of the painting. In *The Agnew Clinic* we see a three-part progression: the nakedness of the patient; the business suits or social dress of everyday street life of the audience of students; and the white uniforms of the doctor and his assistants. Uniforms here, like costumes in a theater, are part of a higher reality than the social, which is, in its turn, higher in reality than the nakedness of the patient. The patient is unconscious; the audience is alert and attentive; but the doctor and his assistants act and move freely in space—once again a third level beyond spectatorship, just as observation and attention are beyond the sleep of ether. The patient is faceless. The audience is a screen of faces seen frontally. The doctor, however, is in profile; only half of his face can be seen, and his hands are given equal standing with his face as centers that draw our attention. His hands are, literally, the other side of his face, his humanity. His assistants are seen from a variety of incomplete angles that deprive us of their facial expressions while reminding us of their activity. Finally, the patient lies down in the position of death or sleep or receptivity; the audience sits; the doctors stand, many of them bent over the patient. Only the star performer, Dr. Agnew (or Dr. Gross), is given that final position of full human-ity—*Homo erectus*—here defined as the ontological opposite to un-conscious, horizontal nakedness.[5]

These spiritual distinctions made in technique, in posture, in hu-man presence are clearly deliberate, even pedantic. We see here a reality that is hierarchical, no longer democratic. It is one of the many images by which the late nineteenth century seemed to be memorizing a new social aggregation for which professionalism, expertise, and performance offered key models. Eakins's paintings remind us of those many civic symphony orchestras, among them the Boston Symphony and the New York Philharmonic, that came to be a key image and ritual of society in late-nineteenth-century American cities. The symphony is made up of the conductor—stand-ing just as Eakins's doctor does; the soloist—parallel to Eakins's pa-tient; the musicians—the group of assistants and experts; and, finally, the audience of observers and listeners. This configuration also de-scribes the corporation, with its great founder or leader, its managers, the product, and the great audience of consumers. The social fracture of reality into layers marked by diminishing degrees of reality Eakins so richly renders in his clinic paintings makes available, as though for practice and memorization, the elements of a new order.

In *The Agnew Clinic* Dr. Agnew's right hand is raised and flat, extended toward our half of the audience in the familiar religious gesture of Renaissance painting: Behold! What we behold in Eak-ins's pair of paintings is both surgery and the teaching of surgery. The audience is not a mob of the curious, but those who watch in order to learn to perform themselves at a later time. Eakins too is a teacher of artists, as head of the Philadelphia Academy. One reason to expose in public not only surgery but the teaching of surgery is to insist that the audience for art is not the audience that gapes and stares at wonders or sensations but the alert, serious bank of stu-dents whose intelligence and learned respect for the skilled hand translates back into veneration for the gray-haired master who commands the performance.

The crafts of rowing, boxing, and surgery that Eakins portrayed as performances were all highly visible physical skills: the boxer's jab, the rower's stroke and turn, the surgeon's cut—each made visible to the trained eye under the pressure of a race, a boxing match, or a life or death surgical act, the pose of assurance and economy that would triumph in circumstances where even the smallest clumsiness would invite defeat. It is obvious that Eakins considers these to be metaphors for the heroism of the painter who applies his careful strokes to the canvas as the rower does to the river or the doctor to the patient. In American painting from Eakins to Jackson Pollock, there has been present in the paintings themselves an unusual awareness of the dangerous and elegant skills of the artist risking himself in full view before his audience. Hemingway's life-long analogy between writing and bull-fighting was another version of this life-or-death account of the performance of art.

Within the two clinic paintings that exhibit the arts of surgery, teaching, painting, and observing, we find one final and startling exhibition: the exhibition of privacy. The naked and surgically opened part of the body, a breast in *The Agnew Clinic*, offers, as the ultimate material of the crowded and surrounded public stage, the most intimate and private physical self. Surgery, by making for a moment the inside of the body appear in a visible space, has in its power a greater nakedness than that of the merely social nude. It is the cut flesh that makes painting and performance notorious.

In *The Agnew Clinic* the female breast is desecrated both by surgery and by the imputation of disease that surgery implies and then by painting that exposes not only the breast but the body within the breast. What Eakins has done is to graft his own performance as a painter onto the double energy of a newly composite public space, one that saw complex undercurrents that linked fame and exposé. The heroic celebrity of the surgeon transmits half of this composite energy. The surgeon and with him the painter are seen as stars subject to an extraordinarily reverent treatment that magnifies the greatness of the skilled practitioner. But alongside the energy of enchantment and professional mystification occurs the demystification of the body, of privacy, the de-idealization of breast and groin. The energies of mystification and demystification, of star-making and muckraking, of celebrity and exposé are simultaneous and draw their energy from one another. The collision of fame and privacy that takes place in Eakins's paintings of medical performance places American art on a paradoxical and very knowing moral plane.

The naked body that would in any painting catch the eye at once is made shocking and conspicuous by the surgeon's bloody hand and scalpel. In the delirious years of the sensational press, Eakins had produced the first great American paintings whose psychology was grounded in the avant-garde tactic of shock. Appropriately enough, Eakins's first masterpiece that had so deeply meditated on the appearance in public of the most private and the most famous (of the body and the surgeon and the painter himself) itself first appeared at the Philadelphia Centennial Exposition of 1876, the same year that saw the appearance of John Wanamaker's giant store. *The Gross Clinic* was also on view at the Columbian Exhibition at Chicago in 1893 and at the Universal Exposition in Saint Louis in 1904. In these world's fairs of marvels and technological break-throughs, stunts and county-fair atmosphere, this Bon Marché of civilization that counted its crowds by the hundreds of thousands, *The Gross Clinic* offered the first great account in America of the idea of exhibition itself, of what might be exposed in public, and of how the energies of exposure might be accumulated and directed

Conspicuousness

One of the most striking phrases of the newly emergent American sociology, a discipline that implies a conception of social life as role and performance (as can easily be seen in the later work of Erving Goffman and the convergence of sociology and anthropology in recent years), was the phrase Thorstein Veblen coined in 1899, "conspicuous consumption." The first of these two words is the more important to us because it invites us to imagine all life directed toward an audience. In 1899 this word "conspicuous" arrived just in time to describe the ten-year domination of public life by Theodore Roosevelt, who has been described by John Chamberlain as "a careerist, a showman of his own personality." As Dixon Wecter put it, "Roosevelt created a character and lived up to it with winning consistency."[6] He did so, we might add, in public, brought into focus for the national and world audience by the daily newspapers, for whom his exploits and performances were the kind of godsend usually guaranteed only by the hurricane and baseball seasons. The newspapers require, oddly enough, predictable sensational events that arrive just as regularly as the paper itself does each day. Roosevelt's career, as John Milton Cooper, Jr., aptly noted, was "the first major career in American politics to be conducted wholly within the era and under the influence of modern journalistic media."[7]

Between the Civil War and the First World War, the mass circulation newspaper had become one of the dominant and novel sets of spaces within which public reality appeared. Today, television, with its very different pressure on and drive toward certain types of events and personalities, plays an equivalent role. Even a different type of face is required once the change from the newspaper to television has taken place, just as a different voice was required once radio had replaced the lecture platform. The newspaper circulation wars of the 1890s in New York were fought over readerships that could reach the millions. The new materials of personality and action suitable to be made conspicuous were only slowly discovered in the different realms of culture. We might describe the years between 1890 and 1910 as a series of experiments in the modeling of a highly visible structure of identity under the new circumstances of conspicuous performance.

These conditions of identity writ large would be appropriate for the "most famous man in the world," as Roosevelt had been called, but they would equally describe the very structure of character for the novel that gives the richest account of this new world of fame, Dreiser's *Sister Carrie*.[8] In Dreiser's novel the Broadway career of the youthful, energetic, but relatively talentless Carrie who rises to be, at last, a "somebody," is played off against the alternative descent of a man on his way to becoming that great American dread, a "nobody."

The very same conditions lay behind the fame of the writer whom we might call America's first coast-to-coast literary figure, Samuel Clemens, whose better-known name, Mark Twain, should be seen not so much as a pen name but as a trademark (as it always appears on the copyright page of his works), a brand name for the various enterprises of lecturing, door-to-door subscription sales of novels or travel books, printing investments, and public appearances, all headquartered in the gaudy Hartford mansion that would, like his name itself, come to be seen as part of his identity. Twain even turned his own features and clothes into elements of his performance.

William Dean Howells, in the reminiscences that he published in *My Mark Twain*, described his meeting with the man whose very hair and mustache seemed part of a costume. Twain was wearing a sealskin coat, fur side out. He had a "crest of dense red hair," and Howells noticed the "wide sweep of his flaming mustache." To Howells this conspicuous sealskin coat, however warm Twain found it, "sent the cold chills through me when I once accompanied it down Broadway, and shared the immense publicity it won him. He had always a relish for personal effect, which expressed itself in the white suit of complete serge which he wore in his last years, and in the Oxford gown which he put on for every possible occasion and said he would like to wear all the time."[9]

In the same period the laws of conspicuous and performed identity were even more fundamental for that abstract person, a corporation. The historian of technology David Nye has written an analysis of the more than one million photographs in the archives of the General Electric Company.[10] Nye has shown that between 1890 and 1940 the corporation represented itself to itself and to the public that it was shaping into its pool of customers by means of a segmented performance. The internal magazines for managers that pictured the teamwork and good times of the summer camp at Association Island differed from the newsletter for workers, the journal for scientists, and the news ads aimed at the general public. Yet the corporation was in the process of setting in place, inventing we might say, three realities: the product itself, projected through advertising, brand names, and corporate imagery; the company, seen as a hierarchical and yet interdependent family through newsletters and other internal publications; and the consuming public, national in scale, eager for the new electrical way of life, loyal to

General Electric products. Both the new public and the new corporation were geographically so extensive that to manufacture corporate patriotism, or what came to be called "consumer loyalty," among people numerous enough to form an army required a constant newspaper-like and newspaper-dependent diet of visual and narrative reminders that created the uniqueness and conspicuousness of the company. To create corporate identity, brand-product identity—such as the Mazda light bulb—and the identity of a purchasing public, the million photographs were required as tokens of a world that needed to make itself visible in order to remember that it existed. Just as in Eakins's paintings of performance, the three realities, that of performer, act or product, and public, all come into simultaneous existence by a process of mutual conferring of reality.

It was also by means of photography in the 1890s that Jacob Riis had made America aware of how the other half lived. The same camera that played so large a part in the creation of reality for the modern product and corporation also brought into focus suppressed and forgotten social facts. The machinery of fame and exposé were once again the same.

The phrases "larger than life" and "a giant among men" so often used to describe Teddy Roosevelt implied not so much the traditional rhetoric of the heroic as a more diffusely available, heightened reality. It was a version of this enhanced, speeded-up, intensified reality that newspaper headlines or advertisements and mass public events, whether the newly crowded baseball games or the sales days at stores like John Wanamaker's, made convincing. A certain transfer of reality takes place for someone lucky enough to be in the presence of Eakins's Dr. Gross, to be an actress like Dreiser's Carrie, or to be a ticket holder for one of the lectures of Mark Twain's world tour of 1895–96. The atmosphere of this surplus reality is captured in a description of the department store in a recent book on the Bon Marché, the Parisian equivalent of Wanamakers: "Dazzling and sensuous, the Bon Marché became a permanent fair, an institution, a fantasy world, a spectacle of extraordinary proportions, so that going to the store became an event and an adventure. One came now less to purchase a particular article than simply to visit, buying in the process because it was part of the excitement, part of an experience that added another dimension to life."[11]

The democratic right to enter such heightened spaces was just as available to the common man through his access to famous and talked-about things in the new brand-name products, which were, on one level, no more than a commonsense solution to the new national market, as Twain's lectures were. The Singer sewing machine, the Kodak camera that swept the nation in the 1890s, or Coca-Cola, a drink with a brand name so successful that it would come to stand for America itself—these were what we might call "famous" objects. As things they differed from ordinary goods just as a star does from a person, or a trip to Wanamakers from just going out to the store. The overall creation of this surplus reality for persons, things, or events defined by inversion the newly negative condition of being a "mere camera," a "mere doctor," or a "mere human being—not a Kodak, not Dr. Gross, not Teddy Roosevelt. Everyday reality comes to be "merely" so, once a higher dimension of conspicuous and performed reality has been added, like a new economy of being, on top of it. The star and what came to be called the "little man" or, as I am calling him here, "mere" man, are created at the same moment.

The public world that trained its eyes to see that the headline of the newspaper, since it was an eye-catching fact, stood at the top of the pyramid of news, being the "star" event of the day, was also a public world that had developed, in its explosive building technology, the skyscraper, the most deliberately theatrical and conspicuous building type since the medieval cathedral. Thanks to the Otis elevator and the high cost of inner-city land, the years between 1880 and 1920 saw the classic phase of the Chicago and New York skyscraper. The Woolworth Building, built in New York in 1913, has been called the first skyscraper as advertisement.[12] The skyscraper is the star on the stage of the city streets, the conspicuous sign of the prestige and importance of the company. Just like the mansions of the rich that were rising along Fifth Avenue or the eccentric and grandiose mansion of Twain, the skyscrapers naturally appealed to the newspapers housed in some of the most striking of the new buildings.

The refinement and sophistication of high visibility as well as the development of new techniques to dramatize and convert into events even the most static or abstract of facts were cultural accomplishments that came to a climax in the great national expositions, which were, after London's Crystal Palace Exposition of 1851, a periodic and prominent fact of the years up to the First World War. The Philadelphia, Chicago, and St. Louis fairs permitted the industrial world to convert its machinery into exhibitions that, by speeding progress up, made progress itself visible, invention and national power visible.

Alongside these many experiments that converged finally toward a national strategy of celebrity, product promotion, political fame, and high visibility of a kind available to persons, places, things, and ideas, the cultural period between 1880 and 1910 also produced an ongoing meditation, often anxious and angry, that struggled with the psychological and social consequences of the new power. The predictable autobiography for this period, *The Education of Henry Adams*, put on display, once the book was no longer privately circulated among friends, the hesitations of a public actor convinced that he had never found the right role and so must exhibit his awkwardness and failure as substitutes for the display of what Eakins had put on view: the pleasures of mastery. The costs and distortions built into this centralized, national space of appearance, for which the newspaper was one expression, and the national market as symbolized by the Sears catalogue another, were tallied and recomputed by writers as different as Henry James, Mark Twain himself, and Theodore Dreiser.

The counterweight to this novel, economically driven blend of identity and product that I am calling "conspicuousness" was a new and profound regrounding of privacy. The greatest works of domestic architecture in the years 1890–1910 were the houses built by Frank Lloyd Wright in the Chicago suburb of Oak Park. These houses create a new internal openness by breaking down the cell-like home of the Victorian middle class. At the same time Wright's houses present to the outer world a mysterious, low-slung privacy. The very feature of a house that announces in capital letters the wealth and importance of the family within, the entrance, often posed on its pedestal of unnecessary steps and flanked by pillars as pompous and grand as funds permitted, is absent in the new Wright homes. It is often difficult to see where to enter these homes, as though they did not wish to invite strangers at all. The façade, that upright, decorative statement facing the street, disappears in favor of a three dimensional form, equally rich and interesting on all sides. The houses hug the ground almost in disdain of the visibility that the vertical dimension commands. In an age of skyscrapers, Wright reclaimed the symbolically "low" territory for its advantages for privacy. His houses protect inner life and they renew it. The Robie House, to take only the most famous example, could be said, in traditional terms, to have not only no facade but not even a front. It refuses to address the street, to announce the family within, to be their social face or at least the outer face of their prestige and wealth. It is nearly impossible at first glance to see the approach to the house or the entrance to it, both normal and conspicuous features of the façade.

Like all of Wright's work, the outside of the Robie House makes a stranger, a viewer, feel excluded rather than involved in a performance. The observer is mainly aware of an inner life that is self-contained and has no need of observers, visitors, or admirers, an inner life that is rich, mysterious, and detailed. About this inner life, the Chicago houses, as would the later Kaufman House and the Guggenheim Museum, remain silent except to make us aware of its spirituality, nobility, and uniqueness. Within this space, Wright designed the materials for a new democratic intimacy and privacy, one of the fundamental cultural achievements of the last hundred years, an achievement dependent not only on artists like Wright, but equally on the developers of the suburb as a way of life and on the invention of first the radio and then the television as spaces of appearance that replaced the newspaper and the crowd-surrounded public stage as devices for the transfer of events and personalities.

The honesty of materials that Wright stressed was part of the obverse side of high visibility. Here Wright joins forces with the realists in literature who tested and revealed the dishonesty and idealism that lay concealed in many descriptions of reality. The requirement that we see and value the stone, wood, tile, and fabric of the house is like a pure food and drug act for architecture. Wright's insistence on honest, natural materials, never covered or disguised, is parallel to the insistence on rooting out adulteration and fraud in food and medicine, or corruption and deceit in government. Lincoln Steffens's *Shame of the Cities*, as well as the muckrakers and writers of naturalism, share Wright's goals of visibility and naturalness.

Signature and Memorability

Thorstein Veblen, whose *Theory of the Leisure Class* of 1899 remains one of the classics of the remote and estranging stare of late Victorian anthropology, described the conditions under which conspicuous consumption would overtake conspicuous leisure as a strategy. He wrote that the new techniques would work best in "those portions of the community where the human contact of the individual is widest and the mobility of the population greatest." He went on:

> The exigencies of the modern household system frequently place individuals and households in juxtaposition between whom there is little contact in any other sense than that of juxtaposition . . . In the modern community there is also a more frequent attendance at large gatherings of people to whom one's everyday life is unknown; in such places as churches, theaters, ballrooms, hotels, parks, shops and the like. In order to impress these transient observers, and to retain one's self complacency under their observation, the signature of one's pecuniary strength should be written in characters which he who runs may read.[13]

The signature that Veblen speaks of here is the brief token of an identity, the minimum of legible individuality. That it must be written on a scale that he who runs may read is a requirement not only for the display of wealth, but for the production of public reality no matter what the realm. The new chain stores, such as the Atlantic and Pacific Tea Company and the Woolworth's five-and-dime stores, used the colors and design of the façade of the store itself to package the store's identity as a signature. The red sign and the old- fashioned gold-painted wood letters of the Woolworth's sign are still in use from Two Forks, Iowa, to Berlin. To this day the advertisements for the John Wanamaker store carry the literal signature of the founder in bold type across the full page. The signature within this period takes on the scale of the headline. Consider for a moment the champion headline maker of all times, Teddy Roosevelt. William Allen White's description of the man himself illustrates the conversion of physiognomy into signature. White begins by saying, "Theodore Roosevelt was a giant, an overgrown personality."[14] The physical description that follows has the exaggerated quality of a blown-up photograph or what we would now call a superrealist painting. The features are distinct enough and of a size to be seen in a crowd of 50,000, half a mile from the platform. It is a personality projected onto the scale of skyscrapers.

> His walk was a shoulder-shaking, assertive, heel-clicking gait, rather consciously rapid as one who is habitually about his master's business. He shook hands vigorously with a powerful downward pull like a pumper, with a firm but never rough handclasp. His shoulders sloped a little off the square line, and his head often, perhaps generally, was thrust forward from the neck, a firm short pedestal for his face, which jammed his head forward without ever requiring a stoop of his shoulders. His countenance was dominated by a big, pugnacious nose, a mustache drooped to cover a sensitive mouth in which a heavy underlip sometimes protruded, indicating passion. Occasionally, he used the lip as a shutter, purposely to uncover a double row of glittering teeth that were his pride.[15]

The lip that rises like the curtain of a theater to show off the bright teeth uncovers the cartoon-like signature that came to be recognized as the visual summation of the man. Howells describes a similar theatrical unveiling of signature by Mark Twain. "Nothing could have been more dramatic than the gesture with which he flung off his loose overcoat, and stood forth in white from his feet to the crown of his silvery head. It was a magnificent coup."[16] Each of the features of White's description of Roosevelt is seen close up and in vigorous action. Each detail is immediate. We seem to be seeing the action of the lip or the teeth from less than three feet away. The vigor of the description of Roosevelt turns him into a character from a tall tale. He is close up the way the front of a train running toward us down the track would be.

To locate the tradition of White's picture, in which the appearance is made up of disconnected, oversized details, almost like the faces in nightmares, we would have to go back to Dickens and his lurid but comic style, in which faces and personalities are designed, like the odd Dickensian names, to make a character unforgettable even over a crowded novel of nine hundred pages and fifty competing personalities. Mark Twain's first description of Huck Finn's father as he appears to the frightened boy has exactly the same quality of White's Roosevelt. "He was mostly fifty and he looked it. His hair was long and tangled and greasy, and hung down, and you could see his eyes shining through like he was behind vines. It was all black, no gray; so was his long, mixed-up whiskers . . . He had one ankle resting on t'other knee; the boot on that foot was busted, and two of his toes stuck through, and he worked them now and then."[17]

The bold verbal sketch that invites the illustrator's pen or the cartoonist's few witty strokes had been the essence of Dickensian characterization. Whether in Twain's physical melodrama or the actual cartoon-like appearance of Teddy Roosevelt, an appropriate descriptive rhetoric had been invented to attract the attention of a public that had to be seen in terms of a crowd. Roosevelt's words themselves were sometimes prewritten cartoons—"Talk softly and carry a big stick!"—in which thousands of cartoons are already present in the words and bearing of the man. The most famous package ever invented—to use the language of advertising—was the Coca-Cola bottle of 1916, an ingenious container that provided the costume in which the liquid within performs in public, the bottle or the appearance being the signature of identity on a conspicuous scale.

Eakins's painting of Dr. Gross provides a final technique for the signature of conspicuous identity. By his spot-lit, isolated position, his erect, vertical bearing, his dignity, his domination of the scene, Dr. Gross is already highly visible. But by means of the bloody hand and knife he is made conspicuous and unforgettable. The bloody hand is what we might call Eakins's device, even his gimmick. He uses the poetics of intensification that we have come to identify with advertising. The bloody hand and knife or the cut breast of *The Agnew Clinic* seize upon deeper layers of feeling than mere respect or professional awe can command. As in advertising, where fear or sexual desire, competitive triumph or social anxiety, can be generated and then linked to the product or surface of belief that is the topic of the advertisement, the shock or fear confer unforgettability on both Gross and the painting itself, thus seizing a permanent hold on the memory. Eakins, by this device, has guaranteed that his painting will be talked about and notorious, eye-catching and controversial. Most important of all, once seen, it will be unforgettable. The taboos of sexuality, nakedness, violence, the excavation of irrelevant fear or shame that can then be harnessed to the object or idea in search of high visibility—these become underlying factors in the creation of signatures and conspicuous identities.

Disappearing in Public: Howells and James

The magnification of personality under the new conditions of appearance and performance, public life's morally corrosive relation to the simultaneous need to fashion and defend a private personality geared to the domestic and intimate realms of life, its treacherous dynamic of rise and fall, overnight sensation and overnight collapse, its displacement of the conversational and the personal—even in the erotic sphere—by the mass psychology of the platform and the crowded hall with their public seduction of voice and spirit: these features of a potent and expansive public life were subject to an unusually profound and hesitant analysis in three of the greatest novels of the 1880s—Henry James's *Bostonians*, Howells's *Rise of Silas Lapham*, and Twain's *Adventures of Huckleberry Finn*.

Howells's novel begins with its millionaire businessman going public, submitting to an interview with a newspaperman. The interview looks back over Lapham's early life with his rise to success, and then pictures for the public his anecdotal, down-home side, making him both famous and human at the same time. Lapham consents to be made into a type. Now profiled in the "Solid Men of Boston" series, not only is he a successful entrepreneur, but he *stands for* entrepreneurship, just as Edison stands for the inventor; Einstein, the scientist; or Twain, the new western literature.

The close relationship between what interests the newspaper public and the novel-reading public becomes obvious when we see that Howells himself, just like the reporter, is writing about Lapham in order to describe a new phenomenon of wide social meaning and, at the same time, to satisfy the curiosity of the public about new self-made millionaires. Where do they come from? How do they live? What are their ethics? The self-made man is a new social type, like the new American girl that writers from Henry James in *Daisy Miller* to Dreiser in *Sister Carrie* defined and exhibited as a type. In his opening chapter Howells defines himself and his project as parallel to the new publicity of the newspapers, yet deepened by the energies of self-consciousness about the machinery of making known, exposing, exhibiting, and locking into place a new type.

The close ties of the machinery of fame to representability and typicality, and its hidden affinities for exposure, collapse, and the shredding of public identity, are common central features of the rise and fall of Verena Tarrant in James's *Bostonians*, the fall and collapse of Silas Lapham that is, of course, in Howells's title, his rise, and, finally, those chapters of *Huck Finn*, nearly a third of the whole, in which Huck and Jim play servants and supporting actors to those two masters of the public space, the Duke and the Dauphin, whose many performances elude only by seconds and well-timed flight the exposure and disgrace that the unwanted costume of tar and feathers makes into a finale to their flimsy but lucrative self-exhibition.

The full intensity with which Mark Twain had laid siege to the new public world in his greatest novel can be seen when the fundamental premise of the novel is made clear: Huck and Jim are two heroes who cannot appear in public, the one because he is supposed to be dead, the other because he is a runaway slave. For Huck, who does not yet know that Pap is dead, and Jim, unaware that he has been legally freed, to appear in public without an alias, a story, a false identity, is to risk the loss of all freedom. Even the normal social space of homes, of streets, of conversation and recognition is for them a space of danger. Yet superimposed upon the violent but ordinary public world of lynchings and feuds is the additional set of claims of the magnified space of performance and crowd, actor and preacher, billboard announcement and rented hall.

To hide from even the routine of social recognitions implies that one is captured rather than presented in public. Once Silas Lapham begins his appearances—in the newspaper by means of the interview; in the social geography of the city by means of the striking house that he is building to represent his prestige; and in polite society by means of his family's bungled appearance and his own self-exposure, after he has drunk too much at the dinner party given by the aristocratic Coreys—he is risking the great public fall that will climax in his bankruptcy, the death blow to his "run" in the public eye.

James, too, in posing the career that Verena Tarrant might have had on stage as the alternative to the hidden, silent marriage in which her charm and smile would be redesigned for the domestic audience of one, her voice lowered, implies that this is also a choice to live or to die. The public self of the star, or of the type, crowds out and extinguishes a presocial or a prepublic self that finds itself unusually fragile once it accepts the seductions that drive it to appear and to perform.

Since both James and Twain are openly concerned with the literal performances of hired halls and hissing or applauding audiences, it might seem that Howells's more old-fashioned social novel is only obliquely aware of the new landscape of appearance. But what is the whole of *The Rise of Silas Lapham* but a series of moments of exhibition brought about by that moment in a man's life when, with two marriageable daughters who must be put "on show," his entire life must be exhibited—not only *their* accomplishments and beauty, but his total, earned social standing? The house that Lapham sets out to build and then accidentally burns is a stage on which to mount, for public view, his social worth at the key moment of his daughters' marriageability. Appropriately, Lapham's fortune has been made in paint, a surface that, as Frank Lloyd Wright would point out, conceals the nature of the substance that it covers.

Howells's novel itself, while being about exhibition and visibility, is one of the first major novels of American realism, a form devoted to placing in public view accurate accounts of social life without either idealization or the distortion of moralizing . The power of the realist privilege to let social life be seen and to let wider ranges of experience appear and be included within the line of vision of the novel can be felt when Howells puts on view, as Jacob Riis would do photographically, the sordid urban scene, letting it stand adjacent to the lives and settings of the Coreys and the Laphams. Howells's own exhibition of the two Lapham daughters, Penelope and Irene, becomes an investigation into the phenomenon of the new American woman.

It may seem distorting to speak of the novel as a series of acts of exhibition, but that it is just that becomes clear once the events outside the marriage plot are considered. In bringing together two families from distinct social worlds in a series of visits, dinners, and office meetings, the novel places them on view for one another. Their language, styles of decoration, and sense of manners create, by means of contrast, a covisibility. They make each other conspicuously what each is. Lapham exposes himself, once drunk, and reveals the bragging upstart that the Coreys had anticipated. His wife lives in fear that she will make mistakes that will expose her unfamiliarity with society. The small piece of paper that Mrs. Lapham finds that exhibits to her what she imagines is her husband's infidelity turns out to reveal only his nobility. Bankruptcy reveals or exhibits the true financial worth of an otherwise speculative set of facts—Lapham's wealth.

Howells's novel is concerned through and through with the dangerous paths of exhibition and with a world that exhibits itself, only to then be exposed, until, finally, the exposure itself is torn aside to reveal a further surface beneath. Lapham, first displayed in the newspapers as solid and rich, is progressively revealed as insubstantial, then as noble in refusing to transfer his losses to innocent investors, and finally as solid and vigorous as he dwindles into his final decline, reduced to a single line of paint and a small country life.

The society of cautious and incautious self-display that is Howells's Boston had not yet swept out into the melodramatic and political society of the lecture platform and crowded hall that characterized the Boston and New York of James's *Bostonians* with its intensified possibilities of celebrity and stardom as a way of life. Only Dreiser's *Sister Carrie*, published some fifteen years later, would produce an account equal in intelligence and scale to James's romance of fame.

James's plot is shaped around three performances: first, Verena's trancelike, naive, and fervent speech in the crowded, shabby room filled with the odd-lot society of Boston reformers and spiritualists; second, her more polished debut as a lecturer in the select New York Society of Mrs. Burrage's Wednesday Club; and, finally, in the extraordinary scene that ends the novel, the performance that does not take place, the empty stage of the sold-out music hall, crowded with the stamping and the whistling of the disappointed crowd. Her photographs and life story sold in penny versions, her name on all lips, her pictures in the windows of the stores, and her name on handbills plastering the theater, Verena is prepared for fame. Yet the final scene invites us to imagine a last-minute escape from a life of performance.

The climactic act that asserts the full possession of an individual self is the act of disappearing. Concealed in a cloak, Verena vanishes just when the sold-out house guarantees the cranking up of the machinery of high visibility. Earlier steps taken toward achieving this full private self were small acts of disappearance and invisibility—having secrets, for example, or withholding information, practicing reticence or leaving the house for long, intimate walks. These earlier steps made up a series of domestic acts of not speaking, not letting the facts appear, not being entirely visible to another person. By this strategy of negation a private self is born and sheltered in the novel.

The starting point for James's account is not the fashioning of a public form for ordinary personality, but rather the shaping of a private realm for instinctively public personalities. For these natural performers, the question is: How might a genuinely private self ever be fashioned out of personalities that seem to arrive written in headlines, faces born to adorn billboards? With the coming of photography we arrived at the very important concept of the photogenic. Some variant of this notion applies to every form of representation or appearance. The photogenic is that which seems born to be photographed, most real in pictured form, most present not in person but in images of itself. Verena Tarrant is "genic," in this sense, to the world of publicity, just as Mark Twain, Charlie Chaplin, or Thomas Edison were, or as the voice and manner of FDR were "genic" to the new radio culture of the 1930s.

The genius of James's novel is not to ask the question of how, out of normal human materials, blatant, performing personalities are made. Instead he begins with Verena's instinctively public self and asks how, out of this, an intimate and human-scale personality might be crafted. It is this reversal of terms that generates the progression of Howells's and Twain's novels as well. Lapham begins in the newspaper, but by the end of the novel he has crafted a small-scale dignified obscurity. He has miniaturized his fate, as Verena has. At the heart of *Huckleberry Finn* lies the winning back of small-scale intimacy—for which Jim's calling Huck "honey" is one of the tokens, and their nakedness on the raft another—from a world that conscripts them into performances and overcrowded, dramatic public realities. To put it paradoxically, all three novels turn on the complex victory brought about by disappearing in public.

Intimate Performance: James's *Bostonians*

James, like Twain, was concerned with the paths of power over another person. In America the relation of slavery set an outer limit to the more restrained or concealed models of domestic power, since in slavery the other is owned, his will suspended. But to be the manager of a rising celebrity whose every detail of appearance, every public statement, gesture, and idea must be planned might also be seen as an absolute form of power not different from the master-slave relation. The choice between the life of celebrity and that of marriage could be posed, as James saw, in terms of the inevitable, central intimate relationship of each way of life—husband and wife for marriage; manager and star, promoter and star, for the public realm. To mold another person in education, as Olive did Verena, is, in this context, a somewhat sinister power, as is the mesmerizing process by which Selah Tarrant starts his daughter's performances. He acts out the parental "gift" of life and talent to a child, but in so literal a way that the umbilical cord seems as yet uncut.

James has placed at the center of his feminist novel, with its natural question of what it would mean for a woman to be free, the purchase of Verena from her parents by Olive Chancellor. Olive pays the parents, almost seeming to rent their daughter on a year-to-year basis, or at least she pays for their own disappearance from the scene of Verena's life. She buys the right to become her framing influence. Educating, marrying, managing, owning, and inspiring are all relations of power that occur within intimacy. All are asymmetrical: they are not relations of mutual action and control, but rather examples of complementarity, like the parent-child relation. James's reactionary hero, Basil Ransom, speaks out for the traditional complementary relation of man and woman, but Olive and Verena, too, are a complementary and not an equal pair. Olive will provide the money, the social access, the education, the will, and the anger. Verena will speak, enter the public world, provide the youthful and sweet-tempered vehicle, the spirit and the beauty, through which Olive's ideas, resources, and energy will appear in public.

What does, finally, appear in public is an eroticized privacy that, like the naked body in each of Eakins's clinical paintings, charges the public space with its intimacy. The description of Verena's first lecture in *The Bostonians* is a careful and profound analysis of the public self. Verena is worked into a state or inspired as though by hypnosis. A nearly identical scene occurs in *Sister Carrie*, when Charles Drouet comes backstage to save Carrie's first dismal performance by breathing a confident self into her. The gap between Verena's self and her performance is that between a vehicle and a source.

> She began incoherently, almost inaudibly, as if she were talking in a dream . . . She proceeded slowly, cautiously, as if she were listening for the prompter, catching, one by one, certain phrases that were whispered to her a great distance off, behind the scenes of the world. Then memory, or inspiration, returned to her, and presently she was

145

in possession of her part. She played it with extraordinary simplicity and grace.[18]

The performed self is at so great a distance from the intimate self that hypnotism, dream, trance, the memorization of a role by an actress are all needed to make the distance and the moral peculiarity felt.

Ransom is aware that the effect of Verena's performance has nothing to do with the argument or the ideas. "It was simply an intensely personal exhibition" (p. 61). The trick lies in the offering of a nakedness and the use of it to authenticate ideas, as a person used to be offered as a sacrifice when a city was founded, the reality of death conferring reality on the abstract civic fact.[19] James describes a world of ideas given immediacy by a transposed intimacy and sexual energy. Later, in his stories of the 1890s, he would picture the modern literary world as one in which the artist is asked to make his works genuine by appearing in public and producing his own personality as a performance that gives "interest" to his works.

Verena, at the end of her speech, "turned away slowly towards her mother, smiling over her shoulder at the whole room, as if it had been a single person" (p. 63). A sexual vocabulary surrounds the talk, from the beginning, when Ransom feels that Verena's father's hands placed on her head to inspire her are a "dishonor to the passive maiden" to the conclusion, when Ransom laughs at "the sweet grotesqueness of this virginal creature's standing up before a company of middle-aged people to talk to them about 'love'" (p. 64).

If we ask what the intimate power of Verena consists in, it lies in the fact that she is herself both the speaker of the ideas and a personal allegory of them. She is the enactment of the yearning for freedom, including the paradoxes of freedom: that she is mesmerized into a performance about freedom for women by her father; that she is bought and sold, managed and produced for the public like a traveling Indian on show; that she is hidden away and then displayed before those who have bought tickets, passed from sponsor to sponsor. She is the iconography of her ideas as Theodore

Roosevelt was the strenuous life that he promoted and lived. The ideas take visual form in the materials of personality.

Just as ideas such as feminism or the vigorous life were given performance in publicly memorable dramas—the Rough Riders at San Juan Hill, for example—so, too, inventions and products were disseminated within the economy by performances of small dramas and tests. San Juan Hill is, so to speak, the publicity for the Roosevelt ideas. Daniel Boorstin has described a key moment in the publicizing of the sewing machine, the instrument that became the first of the household appliances that penetrated and reshaped domestic life.

> To persuade the public that his machine would really work, Howe took it to the Quincy Hall Clothing Manufactory in Boston, seated himself before it and offered to sew up any seam that anyone would bring. For two weeks he astonished all comers by doing 250 stitches a minute, about seven times the speed by hand. He then challenged five of the speediest seamstresses to race his machine. The experienced tailor whom he had called in as umpire announced Howe's victory and declared that "the work done on the machine was the neatest and strongest."[20]

The inventor dramatizes his machine in this heroic round of challenges and boasts, umpire and victory announcements. The public in the form of the spectators around the stage and then—through word of mouth, newspaper reports, or handbills that recount the event—the larger buying public that is the ultimate audience receives the machine by means of its ability to perform in public, to become a commercial. Verena's speech, too, is not an argument for feminism, but an endorsement of it, a commercial for it.

Alongside his display of the varieties of publicity and performance, James must describe the varieties of privacy from Basil Ransom's reserve to Olive Chancellor's abashed, tense, and sexualized shyness. One of James's greatest accomplishments in this novel is the delineation of the painfully physical shyness that is Olive's one performance. Her white-lipped anger, her sudden tears, her tense expectation, as well as her passion, are all transparent in her face and tense bearing. For her, although she dreads being in public, there is never any genuine privacy, because her aspect broadcasts her mood in spite of her will. Blushes, frowns, clipped-off words, breathlessness, blazing eyes—she has no hidden feelings at all. She is a martyr of involuntary publicity. Her moods are written all over her face.

Opposed to this high-strung, almost hysterical privacy are the silence and reserve of Ransom. The political realm as Ransom embodies it is not yet distinct from loyalty or from the passionate realm of feelings. James has injected Ransom into a new social and political world in which the political has become distinct and public. Even more, it has appropriated for its own uses those private energies that are intimate and sexual so as to display them as charisma. It is this step that James can study in the young girl whose beauty and rhapsodic feelings are placed on the platform to burn in public under the costume of politics the energies of fervor and passion.

The Masters of Performance: *Huckleberry Finn*

The full encounter between the public and the sexual that might seem at first to be one of the strongest and darkest elements of both James's and Howells's accounts of performance and exhibition turns out to set a sharp limit. Because both James and Howells require the marriage plot for an analysis of social fact, the notion of privacy has in advance a specific and privileged content. Throughout James's work the erotic always entails not only the private, but to some extent the secret.

What is usually taken to be one of the defects of Twain and particularly of *The Adventures of Huckleberry Finn*, that Twain avoids any account of sexual relations or even adult relations between men and women, turns out to be one of the novel's greatest strengths, permitting him to display in *Huckleberry Finn* the full energies of the new public world—one to which he, unlike Howells or James, was drawn in his self-imagination and of which his entire career is an instance as complex as any in his fiction. In the purely male world of the raft Twain can construct the actual texture of late-nineteenth-century public space, a space of power and deception whose final topic is not intimacy but survival.

In the Duke and the Dauphin Twain parades the range of performances and frauds, lies and scams that reveal the amateur lying of Huck as the defensive tactic that it is. The Duke is the master of the temperance meeting, the revival camp, the traveling Shakespearean performance, and the carnival sideshow. The professions of these two scoundrels—actor, revivalist, preacher, printer—cross the field of public appearance. They turn the raft itself into a practice hall, stock it with costumes that replace the nakedness of Huck and Jim, and break down the great division that Twain had so carefully wrought between the land as the world of deceptions and lies and the raft as conversational and intimate, naked and exempt. With the Duke and the Dauphin come the framing lies about their own identities—as royalty fallen on hard times—and the perfected staging in which Jim, tied up with ropes, plays just what he turns out to be, the already recaptured runaway slave.

With his two great symbols of the underbrush of culture that Twain as the American master of the one-night performance in a rented hall knew very well, he can imbed dizzying layers of role and performance. The old man who, in order to seize position on the raft, passes himself off as "the wanderin', exiled, trampled-on and sufferin', rightful King of France" (p. 124) must practice, on that raft, the role of Juliet. The playbills describe him as "the Illustrious Edmund Kean the Elder." In total he is the old man playing the Dauphin, pretending to be Edmund Kean, who is acting the role of Juliet.

The failure of this too richly layered offering leads to the second night's performance, in which the king comes out prancing on all fours, naked. Although the skit is too short for the audience's taste, they love it enough to have it repeated. As Huck says, "The people most killed themselves laughing" (p. 151). They turn up in droves, not to hear the high-cultural language and see the costumes of Shakespeare, but to see the naked human animal, prancing around the stage. Unable to perform, the actors expose. Unable to rise, they descend. The naked, capering old fool sells the ridiculousness of his own flesh, taking in $465 in three nights.

Just as the Duke had successfully revealed Jim as what he actually was by printing up a bill identifying Jim as a runaway slave, so too the old man in his performance makes public only his naked foolishness. What is performed by Jim or by the king is privacy itself. The secret is exposed. Twain, like Eakins in his clinical paintings, and James in his metaphoric exposure of the private self in Verena's performances, has tied the space of performance to self-exposure—the surgically opened breast, the capering old man, the rapture of the virginal girl.

Free of the Duke and the Dauphin, Huck and Jim alone on the raft are engaged in the tender and risky experiments in feeling that, taking place between a boy considered dead and a vanished slave, occur in spite of and at the mercy of a public world for which they must lie and perform. Twain's novel, like James's, gives off the electricity of experimental intimacy within a private world only occasionally free from invasion or conscription. The uncomfortable moral improvisations of Huck in his feelings for Jim are stuttered through with a necessity that, in James's novel, can be felt in the high-strung affections and fears of Olive Chancellor as she concocts euphemisms to account for her feelings for Verena. In James's case even the romance between Basil and Verena, for which neither northern nor southern societies provide a code of courtship, asks us to picture lovers improvising their way across an unmarked social terrain of intimacy where "mates" are captured almost in a primitive recreation of male and female sexuality. That each of these novels revolves around the strategies of escape, mystification, outwitting of the public world's styles and performing claims, and disappearances engineered by characters who are spontaneous masters of lying and performance, as both Huck and Verena are, invites us to imagine that the primary victims of this world are not its failures but its apparently triumphant artists of performance. Only with Dreiser's *Sister Carrie* would this world receive at last its heroic tribute.

PART THREE

Regionalism

chapter five

Membership and Identity

Regionalism and individualism in its strongest form constitute the primary antagonists within American culture to the uniform and abstract minimal affiliation that I have earlier described as a democratic social space. It has been my argument from the beginning of this book that a paradoxically rich abstraction governs cultural life in America, winning out again and again over the apparently dense claims of either radical singularity, which we commonly call personality, character, or personal identity, on the one side, or the thick nuance of traditional cultural ideals of community, region, or other forms of substantial collective identity, on the other. It is now time to look closely at the competing claims of regionalism and individualism as alternative paths to a democratic social space and a linked aesthetic or system of representation.

In this chapter I will once again be claiming that it is in the guiding signals of the American economy of mass-produced, ever-changing goods, along with the ever-changing frames within which those goods appear and are distributed, that the leading and defining edge of national life is to be found. Accompanying invention and enterprise, and equally important, is the ever-changing census of people guaranteed by immigration. Immigration changes more than the relative value of claims of worth based on "old family" versus new settler. The ever-changing mix of countries of origin and patterns of later intermarriage mark out the changing frame of the culture itself. Enterprise, invention, immigration, and intermarriage are richly interconnected facts in a culture of abstraction. In fact, the combination of these four features subsidizes what we call, on the aesthetic plane, abstraction.

Each has at its center the act of erasing the past. Inventing a new tool or dance displaces and makes obsolete skills, habits, and social relations that had, until then, given satisfaction. Immigration and intermarriage leave behind and abandon a culture that can, in the future, only be revisited in nostalgia and even then, only for a time. The future exists at the expense of the past in intimate, psychological ways in intermarriage and immigration, but in social or economic ways because of invention and enterprise. These four national energies commit the United States and most individuals within it to the costs and giddy benefits of creative destruction.

Simply put, abstraction as a cultural fact that we can find exemplified in Whitman's or Wallace Stevens's poetry, in the philosophy of Emerson, in the language of Henry James, or in the paintings that led to American domination of the postwar art world of the 1950s and 1960s derives from economic features of American life that set patterns for domains far beyond the economy itself. The business of America is business. Or, to speak metaphorically, the business of America is immigration, not only of persons but also of the things and of the systems that willed change makes possible.

The culture of America occurs in a form that has taken its profound signals and patterns not from religious life or a religious view of life, not from history and the accumulated victories and defeats of a national spirit, but from the business of immigration, the business of settlement, and the business of the mobility of people and of the frame within which they move.

Recent accounts of America's culturally decisive economic life have laid stress on capitalism, consumption, and the consumer society, on advertising and on the sheer number of goods made available. The department store teeming with thousands of products arranged in seductive displays for the theater of shopping has been used as the best image for this new plenitude that might be said to define a new kind of culture, a culture of consumption.

My own emphasis is different. If we imagine that it is not the number of goods that is decisive, but the rapidity with which needs are invented or met in new ways, then the emphasis shifts from quantity of goods or the process of acquisition to the speeding up of invention and to the accompanying instability of the activities and objects of social life. An increasing percentage of goods and ways of doing things, including what we call ways of life, passes into quaintness or obsolescence, while new ways and objects establish themselves and yet newer versions are thought of as possible, just over the horizon. Only a few of those possibilities will actually become real, but the very category of the possible and the next-on will necessarily gain weight within the larger system of the past, the present, and the future look of the world.

To pass from steel-nib pens with their accompanying inkwells to fountain pens with their internal barrel of ink to ballpoint pens to typewriters to computers as the ordinary system of writing, all within one lifetime, is a simple example of the mobility of the frame within a culture of invention. An eighty-five-year-old woman who as a child went to school at the start of the century and sat at a desk with a round hole for the inkwell can sit down near the end of her life at her grandchild's Macintosh computer. The same woman would have found the cultural world around her change its system for the delivery of everyday stories from theaters to films and radio to television and videotapes viewed at home. The multiplication of similar instances creates within lived experience a willingness to consider any possible next-on system seriously. That horses and carriages gave way to automobiles, trains, and airplanes within a hundred years for personal long-distance travel transfers the emphasis from goods or systems to the calculus of rates of change over time for any or every good or way of doing things or way of life, whether that of the jazz musician, the Mississippi riverboat pilot, or the creator of computer software.

The true pessimism of the Turner hypothesis in the United States would not be realized merely by the disappearance of free land and the closing of the frontier. Rather, it would lie in the contemplation of the possibility that the rate of change over the past two hundred years might be an exceptional, brief burst of transformation within a system that will at some later point revert to relative stability and satisfaction. Will better systems of transportation supersede airplanes, as the air system and the private automobile had earlier superseded the horse or the wind-driven sailing ship, which in various forms had dominated for millennia? Will some as yet unimagined technology soon replace the television-like pictures broadcast into the home, as those broadcasts had replaced theaters that had lasted thousands of years or movie houses and radios that had lasted in a dominant form for only one generation?

The most damaging Turner hypothesis would be to speak of the closing of the frontier of invention. If we pictured a day in which companies could no longer boast that 30 percent of their profits for the year came from products that did not exist the year before, then we would encounter the darkest possible Turner hypothesis: that the episode of inventiveness that followed the discovery of controlled electricity, magnetism, and the internal combustion engine was just an episode like the great burst of creativity in the visual arts in Renaissance Italy. Might the past two centuries have been no more than a short-lived interruption of an overall conservative cultural relation to novelty?

If we were collectively to affirm the literal meaning of the term "conservative" and hold onto whatever already exists while forcing the new to pass strenuous tests of worth before being permitted to compete with and to destroy present ways of life, then the system of creative destruction within which American culture has lived enthusiastically for the past hundred and fifty years would disappear.

Each new system is, in fact, unable to compete initially. It is not mere competition that leads to creative destruction. Decades of subsidy built up the airlines and airports of the world, while the railroads protested that only these subsidies prevented them from winning out and strangling the new and as-yet unprofitable system before it could mature and compete for passengers and freight. It would be relatively easy for society to withdraw its willingness to favor the next-on system against whatever system now exists. The interstate highway system, the suburb, the paving of roads, and the provision of parking are all required before the automobile can seem to be the best form of transportation. At that point it can destroy the railroads, which had in their turn benefited from free land that subsidized their start-up decades and permitted them to destroy the canals with their even earlier subsidies.

Conservative cultures can always point to the fact that it is only if we decide to favor the next-on world and then shower it with subsidies that the instability of capitalism and technological invention can be realized. The Turner hypothesis, understood as the closing of the frontier of invention, could be realized in all its pessimism and not just because in the long run it became clear that this two-hundred-year period of invention was a mere episode. The closing of the frontier of invention could also occur as a result of social anxiety that led to the choice to end subsidies to ever newer possibilities, and even to begin granting defensive subsidies to any endangered object, system, or way of life. Such subsidies are common in Europe and America to preserve the way of life of the farmer and the family farm.

If this revolution in subsidies occurred, we would face, along with the disappearance of creative destruction, the loss of the future's priority over the present and, especially, over the past. Aesthetically, we would face the disappearance of what I have called American abstraction, the "loose inkling of types" that made up Whitman's idea of commonness. We can see such a loose-fitting, minimal identity as a strategy of readiness for a next-on world certain to be different in detail and in structure from the present one. The democratic aesthetics of abstraction should be seen as one by-product of a system whose real goal is our alignment with the as-yet unknown future opportunities that would follow from change, rather than the provision of democratic equality within representation. Nonetheless, commonness, in the great and celebratory project of Whitman and Emerson, happens to provide a remarkable version of a democratic aesthetics in the long-lasting project of abstraction as an unintended but welcome consequence of adaptation to quickly changing frames of life.

In this chapter and in the chapters that follow I will examine two alternatives to abstraction: regionalism and realism. Each has its own path to an alternative democratic representativeness. Both are, in American experience, secondary to the larger project of abstraction. In America, regionalism and realism take their specific form from the fact that they are alternatives and not the central aesthetic strategy.

Realism, as we have known since at least Eric Auerbach's *Mimesis*, assigns weight and worth to individual differences, the very target erased from so many directions in Whitman's idea of a national poem and poetic project. Realism reaches democratic representation within a society by a strategy that we might call turn-taking. One at a time, each person or thing deserves one moment of representation by means of its unique differences, the very differences shed in Whitman's search for commonness. In Whitman's poems the individual differences of personality and life history have been brushed aside by the uniformity of sleep and silence as well as by the uniforms of work. Paradoxically, as I have shown, those differences are also eradicated by the poet's imaginary act of replacing each of his fellow citizens, even the bridegroom in the bridal bed. In Whitman's poetic portrait of his fellow citizens, those very differences that would constitute their claim from the side of realism, with its specific detail and attention to uniqueness, vanish.

Equally, the broad umbrella of what I will be calling regionalism collapses or fades under the seductions and opportunities of the loose and mobile forms of identity that rapidly changing economic life encourages and rewards. One telling way to state this claim would be to say that given the choice between possibilities and substance, possibilities win out every time even when linked, as the preference for possibilities must be, to that thin version of substance required if we are to be prepared to adapt to the next-on possibilities. What, then, becomes of substance in either character or community under rapidly changing circumstances like those guaranteed by the acceleration of invention and technology?

A particularly important version of substance in American life is posed in the lives of recent immigrants. Some would view the struggle over assimilation as a loss of the thick communal and family substance of the prior culture. Assimilation is usually pictured in these descriptions as a one-way street. The Polish or Mexican or Chinese immigrant assimilates to something taken to be a stable American culture. In fact, that culture itself, from its side, is different in every generation. One reason for the tone and direction of those differences is precisely the blend of immigrants who, having arrived, now make up one large part of what everyone assimilates to as a common culture. Assimilation is a double process in a rapidly changing cultural frame, and it is precisely the economic mobility of the frame, as I will show in this chapter and the chapter that follows, that guarantees the double project of assimilation. At the same time, it guarantees, that the best description of each generation in America is that every single person must be and think like an immigrant, a newly arrived citizen of an only partially familiar world. Technology and creative destruction level the field between old-timers and newcomers in favor of a world in which all are newcomers.

In the final two chapters of this book, I will deepen the account of the kind of intense singularity that I have claimed was the first alternative to what Whitman celebrated as commonness. I will do that by arguing that in realism singularity of detail and voice are the traces of a belief in picturesque singularity, uniqueness of event or life story, uniqueness of personality or character. Realism, in spite of its use of types and the typical, lives off our confidence in its representation of just this or just that moment or event, person or place. In the analysis of realism in Chapters 7 and 8, I will account for the tactics of the literary and visual pursuit of uniqueness and individuation.

I have already treated Whitman's tracking of the common (of what is as true of you as of me, as true of the present as of the future), calling his goal American abstraction. Realistic detail and the singularity of voice and that life story told by just one voice, the subject of Chapters 7 and 8, represent one familiar alternative to the model of abstraction. Implicitly, realism, understood in this way, embraces the strongest form of individualism.

In this chapter and the chapter that follows it will be the second alternative to abstraction, that of groups or communities stable over time, which I will describe by means of the encompassing term "regionalism" and the literature linked to the worth or to the fate of regional identities. Abstraction, realism and regionalism seem to me, in a unique way, to provide a map of the alternatives within American culture, or, in fact, within any society accepting creative destruction. Any society that has abandoned, as the United States has, what anthropologists have taught us to think of as culture—a set of practices and beliefs that are stable over time and passed on from generation to generation—finds itself with these three new alternatives, abstraction, realism, regionalism. They make up the self-representation for societies without culture, when we use that word in its familiar sense of tradition-driven, relatively closed communities. The implication of the word "closed" can be taken as a reminder that it is immigration and technologically inventive capitalism, in combination, that force us to think of alternatives to the idea of culture for human groups that expect the future to be radically different from the present, and expect that their own membership will be, because of immigration and intermarriage, radically different from their present blend of citizens. As a result, any such society is forced to lessen its reliance on the past for a code that might give shape to either the present or the future.

The Wider Meaning of Regionalism

I want to begin by proposing that we lift out the term "regionalism" and give it a wider use in our cultural history of the last two hundred years in America. By using regionalism in this novel, but I hope not irritating, way, I will try to give a sketch that will bring to the surface aspects of the politics of cultural identity under American conditions. To do this I will confront the purely intellectual debate over regionalism and identity with some of the unique, practical conditions within American cultural life that have from the start made regionalism paradoxical, unstable, and, finally, episodic within our national life since the time of the Civil War. Naturally we need to see the Civil War itself as the one attempt to make permanent and political a fundamental regional and cultural difference by means of secession and the founding of a distinct culture and nation based on slavery.

One important phase of my argument in this chapter will be to change perspective and look not only at regionalism's opposition to some unified idea of the nation or society as a whole, but at its political pressure on the individual to shed his or her many-sided, overlapping, but fresh and strangely mixed, poly-identity. We might better eliminate the word identity and call such a poly-identity a person's *memberships*, since one can be a member of a church, of a chess club, of a political party, of a profession, of a region, of a race, of a family, of a gender, and can regard these as memberships rather than as identities. The *identities* of Doctor, or Gay, or Southerner, or Socialist, or Chess-master, or Woman, or Roman Catholic can make up a list that describes the many-sided life of just one person.

Memberships involve affiliations. Identity often, but not always, involves descent, or it depends, as Clifford Geertz has pointed out, on a biological idiom. Affiliation and descent are the deep terms underlying the surface terms "memberships" and "identity."

The requirement to choose one of a wealth of overlapping *memberships* and regard it as an *identity* is a feature of the politics of what we could call "priority identity" or "preemptive identity" so that in the political sphere of action and interests each person can be seen and regarded as Hispanic or Jewish or Gay or Female and can be, as we say, "counted," and counted on to support an agenda. Simply put, one difference between memberships and identity rests on whether you feel obliged or not to decide about yourself whether your priority identity—the identity by which you are "counted in" and represented politically—is Southern, or Roman Catholic, or Female, or Novelist, or Black, or Bohemian, or Lesbian, or Disabled, or Senior Citizen if in fact you are, as a person, all of these at once.

Who insists on your priority identity? Who has the right to claim you as "one of us" and to denounce you if you refuse to go along with the public solidarity required? Or, on the other hand, can you choose to present yourself as "bohemian" or as neutral or as a "background" Jew or Southerner who no longer speaks with an accent or as a Gay who does not wish sexuality to be the primary, conspicuous fact about your life? Do groups, on their side, have the right to claim a property in your identity? Does your birth preempt your identity once and for all because you were born female, black, southern, disabled, gay?

What account can we give of those far more decisive group cultures—memberships—that are time-specific in modern America, such as childhood, adolescence, Yuppiedom or senior-citizenship? These are full cultural programs, not inferior in complexity to being gay or being Jewish. That there is a full culture of adolescence cannot be denied. In recent decades, perhaps for the first time, a culture of senior citizens has come into being with its own way of life, recognizable clothing, retirement communities, perhaps even its own states (Florida and Arizona), its own types of entertainment, political representation, and so on. The American Association of Retired Persons (AARP) is now a more profound membership in America than the Irish-American Club, the Sons of Italy, or the Croatian Catholic Church.

Adolescence and senior-citizenship are short-lived, shared cultures and ways of acting that involve systems of taste, language, and attitude. Each of us passes through these cultures, but they actually spell out more detailed rituals and ways of life than any other, more enduring traditional regionalisms within modern culture.

What do we do with these *regions of time* within our poly-identity that have, often, no distinct hierarchy, no single political representation? Increasingly in the twentieth century there are also socioeconomic regions that cut across all geographies: one can be a suburbanite or a rural dweller or a young urban professional in each and every climate, state, and traditional region of the country, and these "regional identities" (suburbanite, yuppie, rural dweller) define profoundly similar ways of life in pockets scattered across the geographical map.

I mention these regions of time (adolescence and senior-citizenship) and those regions that are ways of life (being a suburbanite, rural dweller, yuppie) because in both cases we are speaking of *phases of life* rather than traditional *ways of life*, in the sense understood by anthropologists and sociologists. Such new regions involve both biological and economic facts in impermanent and partly voluntary ways.

An increasingly important cultural question centers on temporary or what we could call "fading Identities." We enter into and later exit from an account of ourselves that, while we find ourselves in the middle, seems to be what we would traditionally call a "culture" or a way of life. Adolescence is such an American cultural account of oneself that the very young anticipate when ten or eleven years old, then enter into and live fully within for a few years, and finally exit from in their twenties. The identity of Adolescent is like a spell that descends and then lifts as another way of life takes over to act, in its turn, as a culture used to act.

The word "yuppies," we need to remember, depends on the first letter "y": young urban professionals. There are no muppies or middle-aged urban professionals, nor have we heard about suppies, senior urban professionals. The way of life fades into another life-form sometime in one's thirties.

Gay urban culture, as it exists in San Francisco, New York, or Boston is also a culture (however biological the sexual preference for one sex or another might be), a culture that one enters, affiliates with explicitly, joins as a member, usually in a person's twenties. It is more clearly a membership than what Clifford Geertz would call a primordial loyalty. Like all memberships it tends to fade into inactive membership over time.

My quick sketch of overlapping memberships raises two political questions about affiliation and membership. First, what autonomy and exceptions can any one region of identity claim so as to opt out of any larger national uniformity? Second, what kind of uniformity can a local identity insist on in relation to the poly-identities of its members, all of whom are also members of many other regional-isms? Regional identity is a middle terrain that has limited rights in both directions—outward in relation to national society and inward in relation to each individual member who would not accept being assigned exclusively to this or that regional category. It is important to note that it is only in relation to catastrophic politics and apocalyptic conditions that a collapse occurs in which poly-identities disappear into what we might call a single hunted identity, as happened to European Jews 1930 to 1945. In this extreme condition, poly-identity and the nuances within membership both vanish. We would make a grave mistake to apply these apocalyptic conditions of regional identity to ordinary social life.

By the notion of nuances within membership I mean whether one is an "active" or inactive member, a practicing or lapsed member, a member "above all else" or in an occasional and casual way. As a nuance within membership we might remember that only those depending on us as a reliable constituency for their power will insist that we are *above all else* senior citizens or Jewish or southern or gay and that we must broadcast that affiliation, or be, as the word insists, "out," meaning *challengingly present in the civic space* as gay or southern or Jewish or senior citizens in a reliable and steady way, standing up to be counted.

Often representatives, in order to pressure their followers, insist that the only alternative to this challenging presence in the civic space as X or Y or Z is the admission that one is "hiding" the identity, ashamed of having it, in the closet, trying to pass for something else, and so on. In reality there are dozens of nuances not described by this choice between being bravely "out" and being ashamed, or "passing" for something else (as the dictators of Identity have come to call it) or closeted or in hiding. Pride and shame are not the only ways of expressing membership. Indifference, subordination of one membership to another seen as more important, background membership, lapsed membership, inactive status, occasional interest mixed with more common indifference, once-a-year Irishman, part-time lesbian, self-designated roles, hatred of all memberships whatsoever: these are just a small number of alternatives to the false choice in every membership situation between being bravely out and being closeted, ashamed, and hoping to pass for something else. Shame and masquerading are weak possibilities in the crowded terrain of affiliation and membership.

To sum up the argument to this point: The notion of membership is not only inherently plural—we all are members of many different civic groupings. It is also nuanced; all possible relations to membership are valid and common. Only a mix and ever-changing mix of categories, along with the chance to break out of or deny the force of any and every one of these categories can accurately account for the relative, but still real, power of chosen but not fated cultural identity within societies like American society, where the force of anything inherited or transmitted is weak, and where the past is relatively weak in comparison to the future.

One final important fact about memberships: From the point of view of the individual, multiplied memberships are the best protection against the demands of any one membership. In fact, multiple memberships weaken the very place of membership itself in life and thinking, because of contradictions among the imperatives and received truths coming down from each group. The end result is to force anyone with multiplied memberships to listen and believe selectively, to exercise choice, to become practiced in refusal and resistance to automatic solidarity, and to become through these processes a reflective, independent, democratic, and tolerant actor within society. In other words, multiple memberships guard both membership and independence as ideals to be treasured, and train us in choice, in resistance, in knowledge of incompatible but legitimate alternatives, on which tolerance is, in part, based, and in the full exercise of discrimination, on which democratic cultures depend.

The civic presence, which is the public side of membership, exists in rich and overlapping forms. It can be seen both in acts of joining and in acts of refusing to join while continuing to support, as well as in acts of opposing. It is found in contributing money, in voting, in meeting together, in acting as a lobby or pressure group. Civic presence also occurs in visibly sharing cultural rituals and languages, in phrasing or understanding a variety of things in the same way, in referring to the same key historical events, core situations, and assumed facts. Any, all, or some of these and other details of civic presence are typical of membership and especially of the rich, braided public life of overlapping memberships.

Plural Memberships in Economic Culture

In the United States the larger topic of membership and identity offers a revealing angle of vision on the question of multiculturalism, a question affecting many cultures or even most advanced cultures today. From my point of view it is useful to stress that it is because of economic success or economic promise that the issue of multiculturalism arises in its twentieth-century form in America. It is not religious immigration, as in the earlier cases of the New England Puritans, the Amish, or the Huguenots, and it is not political persecution, but vast opportunity-driven economic migration that underlies modern, and above all, modern American immigration and internal migration. Why should I stress this point at the outset? One reason is that by submitting to the logic of the initial economic promise, we can less easily resist the larger, often unexpected details of the economic logic once they come into play. If those implications should weaken or destroy or limit other values, we would find that our power to deny or resist this weakening or destruction would be surrendered in advance by the very motive—economic opportunity—that initiated the process in the first place.

It is important to ask if features of that very economic formula that invites immigration and creates—at least initially—multiculturalism would not inevitably at a second, third, and fourth stage either diminish or transcend distinct cultures and traditions. In this the pull of economic opportunity might work precisely opposite to that other force—military conquest, invasion and occupation—that has in the past so often created hostile, embittered multiculturalism of a near permanent and refractory kind. Unlike opportunity-driven immigration, military conquest and occupation are likely to support, deepen, and sharpen cultural differences, freezing the conquered into a sullen and aggressively unchanging version of their culture as it existed just before the defeat.

In a parallel to military conquest, we might imagine that if American multicultural society had been created for the most part by religious immigration and not by economic, opportunity-driven individual and family migration, we could then ask if the resulting society would sustain, strengthen, or weaken the differences among the many distinct faiths that had, each for their own reasons, sought sanctuary or tolerance by immigrating.

The economic magnet that produces national diversity in a country like the United States also operates in cities, which have traditionally drawn those seeking opportunities from the countryside, from villages, towns, and provinces, and from diverse local cultures and ways of life. Large cities accomplished within nations what immigrant cultures like the United States have achieved between nations. Both cities and immigrant nations draw, by means of an economic magnet, diverse opportunity-seeking strangers who are often young, energetic risk-takers. Even within the United States the most common pattern of mobility amounts to a generation-after-generation reaffirmation of immigration by later descendants who move on, seek a fresh start, and find themselves once again joining new mixed communities distinct from those within which they were born.

The city, as opposed to its countryside, and the immigrant nation, as opposed to its countryside, the world, share these features because they are economically driven systems of chosen diversity. Economic motives differ profoundly from more communitarian motives of immigration. Religious immigration by groups of persecuted believers might be taken as the best example of communitarian immigration. Such groups imagine the creation of an enclave culture in control of every detail of a way of life. They ask only that the wider society "leave us alone." The Puritans in New England in the seventeenth century, the Amish in Lancaster County, Pennsylvania, the Hassidic Jews in New York City, and the Mormons in Utah are classic instances of communitarian immigration.

Communitarian, exceptional cultures—such as the Amish or the Hassidim, along with the uniquely stressed culture of first- and second-generation immigrant families and, most commonly of all, African-American culture because of the uniquely damaged history of slavery—have played too central a part in the analysis of identity and membership in American society. Important and rich as these examples are, they offer a misleading picture of the later and common stages of the economically driven culture of assimilation and erasure that American culture has always been. By starting out with individualistic or family-level economic motives, Americans often discovered that the later defense of communitarian features of ethnic or religious life was weakened in advance wherever those features conflicted with the logic of the economic starting point.

We sometimes speak as if multiculturalism implies the side-by-side existence of sharply different cultures, each of which, like the Amish or the Mormons or the Hassidim, are internally coherent and continuous over time. The pattern of ethnic neighborhoods of first- and second-generation hyphenated Americans in the city would be one misleading image for American culture over time. The geographical model of regionalism gives to the side-by-side, enduring-over-time account a physical reality. The map on which there seems to be, even today, a "South," a "West," a "New England," and a "Midwest" pictures for us this side-by-side, distinct, and enduring model of cultures. But the plural and parallel model of culture has never won serious ground in the United States. We are not regional in the radical way that such examples as the Amish or Hassidic Jews would make typical. These two groups are rare in having mastered the problems of binding the generations to one another, transmitting a temporally frozen culture, and controlling the marriage partners of the young, along with their access to the wider educational system.

When we consider these relatively small-scale examples of successful cultural regionalism, we see at once that their combination of features describes precisely what is seldom the case in the larger culture: strong parental control over the next generation; relative decoupling from the larger culture in ways of dress, speech, dietary patterns; resistance to or rejection of public education; insulation from the media and popular culture; and, finally and most important of all, effective barriers to marriage outside the group. It is precisely these features that are rare elsewhere in the culture and account for the fact that the Amish, for example, are not even remotely typical of the experience of immigrant groups in America.

In recent years the models that we use for cultural difference and identity (but not for membership) have common features precisely with the Amish or Hassidim and other refractory, traditional cultures of separation that are well-defended and distinct groups that, I claim, are atypical of the larger picture of American geographical regionalism of the nineteenth century and the ethnic or hyphenated regionalism that developed in the aftermath of the great wave of European immigration that ended in 1914. We might imagine a similar, short-lived ethnic or hyphenated regionalism will follow on the second great wave of far more diverse immigration that began twenty years ago and continues to the present.

In his important essay "'Ethnic Conflict': Three Alternative Terms," Clifford Geertz has drawn out the use and sometimes complex force of the terms "Primordial Loyalties" and "Standing Entities."[1] The idea of primordial loyalties deliberately contradicts the liberal idea of a purely abstract, free-standing individual, the citizen per se, the citizen of John Rawls's *Theory of Justice*. This free-standing individual has often been challenged by the communitarians, who have disowned as a fiction what Michael Sandel has termed the "unencumbered self," a self without imposed loyalties, that is, natal loyalties. The richness of this debate is alluded to in Geertz's term "Primordial Loyalties." Among such loyalties Geertz lists the tie of those who speak a certain language or dialect, practice a certain religion, stem from a certain family, have undergone together a certain history, or live in a certain place or locale where they practice a certain way of life. Each of these is a natal fact. Geertz points out that in contemporary American thinking about identity there is what he calls a "radical biologization" of identity questions and of ethnicity because, in America, the central place in all arguments must be given to black-white divisions rooted in the history of slavery and discrimination. If black-white relations do model or give a paradigm for all other relations (those between the sexes, between ethnic or religious groups, between neighborhoods), then radical dichotomy, blood thinking, and a "diffuse and totalizing biological idiom" appear more readily in the formulation of identity questions than in a culture without this particular central model or paradigm.

For contemporary American cultural debates Geertz's choice of the word "loyalties" has unfortunate consequences that play into the hands of those on one side of the argument. The use of this term implies that any later choice to decline to hold or assert a given identity, to no longer practice the religion or publicly count oneself as this or that, amounts to "disloyalty" or even "denial of what one really is," even to the point of "betrayal" of the others to whom one seemed to *owe* by definition primordial loyalty. Loyalty is a troubling concept that involves a false commitment to one side of the debate.

To add an important contrast, one that Geertz does not introduce in his argument, we could say that identity questions in America are locked in place between the fatal model of black-white relations and the quite different model and idiom that follow from that other central historical topic to which all questions also return—immigration. With immigration new and non-biological, nondichotomizing idioms arise, idioms of personal choice. To have two models is better than to have only one, because the inconsistency of their requirements frees both thought and action.

chapter six

Episodes of Regionalism

A History of Regionalisms in the United States

Regionalism, as the very word suggests, dissolves or modifies the premise of an abstract common ground of citizenship or democratic personality. Regionalism rejects the premises of a democratic social space. Instead it proposes some plurality of side-by-side, but less encompassing identities as the genuine cultural units where wholeness and intelligibility occur.

We usually set regionalism over against nation, against some presumed unitary national identity. Sometimes this is called hegemonic identity. But in America regionalism's real alternative is mobility, change over time, both changes that we make and changes that occur around us in the economic frame within which we conduct our lives. Mobility includes the right to go somewhere else and to be someone else, the right to start over, the option that the young above all have to make what is called "a fresh start." It also includes the right of children on their way to adulthood to select from, discard, forget, and create their own emphasis within the many things inherited from parents as "their natal identity," or what Geertz calls their primordial loyalties.

For children this also includes the right to invent new categories of identity unheard of in the past generation—beatniks, hippies, yuppies, slackers, nerds. Mobility is spatial and temporal. It governs difference of place as well as the right to renew, discard, and invent categories of life and experience. The right to start over and move on includes the right to no longer be known as a southerner, a Texan, an Irish-American, an adolescent, a nerd, or a Roman Catholic.

The strongest statement possible about obdurate regionalism is that it becomes a way of restating mobility as disloyalty, a way of insisting that people are the property of their categories and that any mobility involves the "denial of who you really are." The claims of loyalty have unique force and are, for that reason, often invoked in matters of identity. It has a far weaker relevance to notions of membership because these are necessarily plural. Within overlapping memberships, loyalty might be so weak as to be meaningless.

To our normal ideas of personal mobility must be welded the particular modern fact of short-lived ways of life. Not only do individuals change their lives, but the economic and social forms of life among which we might picture ourselves choosing are themselves rich in mobility, even turbulence. Ways of life, sets of skills, and moral codes are all subject to obsolescence, mutation, and invention. When we read Mark Twain's *Old Times on the Mississippi* we need to keep in mind how many skills, technologies, and economic patterns were needed for there to be steamboats on the Mississippi for the young boy to dream about. But we also need to remember how quickly, in Twain's lifetime, this way of work and life became obsolete. Similarly, the life of the cowboy, the great cattle drives, rose and fell in one lifetime in the years after the Civil War. In modern economies the forms of life move and the claims of regional or stable identity weaken in the face of the obvious survival value of change and mobility.

At the moral level regionalism involves the right of other members of the group to claim you statistically as one of this or that category, and in the numbers in each category lie the importance and power of leaders who claim to represent the interests of regions and sectors of interests. From the leader's point of view the mobility and the right to mobility claimed by individuals can only be regarded as disloyalty, defection, and denial.

Regionalism seems at first to be a form of democratic representation: let each state have two senators. And if states are not the only kinds of regions then let each ethnic group have two senators, each religion have two senators, let each gender have a proportional number of senators, each class within economic life have the proportional number of senators and representatives. Or so it would be if such categories were accurate maps over time.

How long in America is anyone an "ethnic"? Since everyone descends from people who came from elsewhere why are not German-Americans today called "ethnics," or the Scotch-Irish, who arrived two hundred years ago? The answer is that we use the word "ethnic" to refer to the first few generations of transition. After three generations the mobility of place and the intermarriage rates lead to children who no longer think of themselves as half French, half Polish, or part German, a little English, some Italian, and some Lithuanian, especially once they move and marry away from the institutions that enhanced ethnic identity: clubs, churches, sports teams, and so on.

If a man wishes to refer to himself as an Italian-American or his wife as Jewish-American, their children are not at all likely to call themselves Italian-Jewish-American, and their grandchildren are not (after marriage to a Portuguese-Greek-American) likely to be called Italian-Jewish-Portuguese-Greek-American. Hyphenation is a one-generation mirage in a culture of intermarriage, and those who insist on it do so because they intend to attempt to police and control the marriage patterns of their children. Americans are not hyphenated, unless we restrict the claim to say that after the second hyphenation, the hyphens themselves fall away. All that we mean by the word American is an identity too many hyphens long to matter any longer.

Historically, the policing of the marriage patterns of the young has failed, and a hundred years after immigration (and now it is a hundred years after the great immigration wave of 1880 to 1914) these hyphenated terms that were so strongly felt from 1925 to 1940 (one generation after arrival) have melted away in mobility and intermarriage. The same should be anticipated a hundred years from now for the great 1980s wave of immigrants from China,

Mexico, Vietnam, Central America, Portugal, Lebanon, and Russia. Living in one place and doing the same work generation after generation, marrying in each generation "one of our people," is the least representative American story.

Short-lived Regionalisms and Bubble Economies

Cultural life in America swings like a pendulum between a diversity of sectional voices and an ever new project of unity, between the representation of the nation as made up of weakly joined districts and the representation of a central national order. A hundred and fifty years ago our then strongly sectional culture was split along geographical lines: The New England Mind, The Southern way of Life, The West of the Pioneers with their energy and violence. Each section had its own voices and themes, its own philosophies and religions, its unique spirit and humor. A new common identity was rebuilt out of these regionalisms only by the Civil War, by the mythic figure of Lincoln, by the railroads and telegraph that reconquered a geography grown too large for the earlier federal unity of Washington and Jefferson, and by the elaboration of an American way of life made up of Singer Sewing Machines, Coca-Cola, Winchester rifles, and Ford Model T's—a common way of life created around democratically available mass-produced goods rather than by the right to vote or own property.

It is only to this geographical form of regionalism that we usually apply the cultural or literary term. As a literary genre of the late nineteenth century we think of regionalism as an element within the larger descriptive, sociological, and even scientific practices of realism. As a literary-cultural movement we identify it with a resistance to modernity in the name of older, even if not traditional, ways of life, with a hostility to the growing importance of urban culture, and with a defiance of or resistance to the homogenized economy—the market as it is sometimes called, an economy that distributed the same goods and way of life everywhere, just as salesmen sold Singer sewing machines or Mark Twain's latest book door to door in every corner of America.

Cultural regionalism was given literary form by the novels of Sir

Walter Scott, in which a defeated people, in the aftermath of their eclipse as a distinct nation, were given cultural permanence by means of a literature in which their ways of speech, dress, food, habits of thought, and moral style were set down by the novelist in his new role as historian and cultural anthropologist.

The long connection of literary regionalism to defeated or dying ways of life was already fully present in Scott's works. The longest-running literary topics in American regionalism—the South and the West of the so-called western novel—were both, like the Scotland of Scott's novels, literary constructs in the aftermath of a defeated or superseded way of life. I want to stress that these celebrated ways of local existence within regionalism were not at all necessarily *traditional*, consisting of many-generations-long habits and practices. The American West of cowboys, cattle ranches, Indian wars, and cattle drives was a very brief phenomenon that appeared and disappeared in one lifetime. Yet in regionalism, this post–Civil War West, this Texas, seems to be a way of life like that of the Breton fishing communities in France or the shepherds of rural Spain—a way of life based on ways of being and working that have endured for many hundreds of years, ten or twenty generations.

The device of speaking "as if" cowboys and cattle drives or the railroad economy or the canal and Mississippi River steamboat economy, or the New England whaling economy, or the cotton culture of Mississippi between Eli Whitney's invention of the cotton gin and the Civil War were not *bubble economies*—quickly built and rapidly expansive, prominent, quickly transformed, destroyed by trains or by the discovery of oil in Pennsylvania or by the end of slavery—is one key falsehood at the heart of all talk about community and culture in America. We must always insist on the short lives of culture in America. Jazz culture, for example, lasted forty years, the period of the radio, of hotel ballrooms, the aftermath of Prohibition. The cowboy culture lasted just about as long. New York City Jewish culture lasted one generation, as did Pittsburgh's heavy industry and immigration culture, its steel mills, coal mines, and the river-transportation system that served them and linked the city to the nation at large. Seen from the point of view of traditional economies and cultures that last for centuries and are handed down from generation to generation as a way of life, many economic and cultural effects in America are little different from the short-lived way of life of the miners in California after the gold rush of the late 1840s. The sharp difference between an economy of "creative destruction" with its rapid wearing out of ways of life on the one side, and on the other side the implications of regionalism that every culture is made up of permanent ways of life whose loss is always tragic, is one of the deep contradictions at the heart of American regionalism and a unique modern American paradox.

The cultures celebrated by the novels of nineteenth-century geographic regionalism depended for their integrity and distinctiveness and endurance on isolation, often geographical, but sometimes merely structural. They depended on economic viability and endogenous marriage patterns and on the power of each parental generation to replicate their culture in the lives of the young. Isolation, economic viability, intragroup marriages, and the power to transmit ways of life from parents to children are the four foundations of regional culture.

When we approach the literary movement of regionalism from the other side, a paradox emerges. At the concrete level, various regionalisms are invented and abolished (or at least set under siege and turned defensive) by the same technological facts that sponsored representation only to wipe out the very thing being represented. In the late nineteenth century that technology was the system of easy transportation, the railroad system, especially its small trunk and branch lines that linked so many remote regions to the centers of population. The trains moved observers through regions, bringing the visitor, the summer people, the reporter with a notebook. It is out of this access that regions as such became of interest to the national culture. These same trains provided escape routes from small-town life and regional culture for the restless and the young on their way to Chicago or New York. The small-town train station invented yearning and restlessness itself as a precondition for future mobility.

Paradoxically, the very connectedness that makes regions visible on the plane of representation spells their doom on the plane of the real. The geographical regionalism that leaps into expression in the aftermath of the transportation system, finds the trunk-line railroad depot an open door through which its self-contained cultural stability exits forever. To be recorded and erased occurs in the same movement of the pen and the observing eye.

This paradox within regionalism is repeated in the later literary regionalism of ethnic groups, where in so many novels we notice, at the edge of the family portrait that is being drawn, the sensitive child who is, we can guess, the future author of this very book. His or her escape from this world and nostalgic reconstruction of it in print are two sides of the same coin. The author, a former member of this culture, writes for and within the wider culture to which he or she, as a writer, has already become loyal while serving it as a translator of the culture from which he or she had earlier departed. Such novels as *The Joy Luck Club*, *Studs Lonigan*, *Call It Sleep*, *Invisible Man*, and *The Mambo Kings Play Songs of Love* embody this structure.

We should be intrigued by the late-nineteenth-century coincidence of a literature that celebrates or informs us about self-contained "time-less" traditional communities, their ways of life and rooted speech, customs, and the completion of a railroad system whose trunk lines let outsiders reach with new ease into every pocket of the cultural landscape. Richard Brodhead has written about the striking connection between what he calls "vacation culture" and "second homes"—the summer life of the urban middle class in the late nineteenth century—and the "preservation by invasion" of quaint, once remote "old-fashioned" villages, coastal regions, and settings, now easily reached from the city and nostalgically beloved for their way of life by city dwellers who invaded and created a carefully "restored" prolongation of now vanished ways of life.[1] This is, let us note, the world of their second homes, their vacation homes. It is a fascinating fact about vacation homes that they frequently involve regression to an earlier way of life. The many hunting and fishing lodges built in the Adirondacks out of logs are only the most obvious example. Thoreau's cabin at Walden Pond is the model of a second home or a vacation home, similar to a Russian *Dacha* or a Swedish cabin in the woods.

It was the money of summer people—city money—that preserved and employed the remaining inhabitants of Sarah Orne

Jewett's isolated coastal Maine, which became a magnet for summer people in just this period. Jewett's stories are a key example of the connection between "self-contained," isolated traditional communities and the wider system that made any such isolation illusory once the train station linked every small town to the national grid, and once urban leisure and the search for contrast created the summer home, the lengthy vacation, and the modern "antiquing" of the past by writers, painters, and decorators.

The presence of transportation, especially the train station, in every regional novel is one clue. In Sherwood Anderson's *Winesburg, Ohio* the station, along with the hotel for transients, is one of the key locations. In such diverse regional books as Faulkner's *Light in August*, Jewett's *Country of the Pointed Firs*, Owen Wister's *The Virginian*, and Willa Cather's *A Lost Lady*, it is the train station that is the church of modern small-town life. The ever present station reminds us of the fact of choice, the arrival of the visiting intellectual and the departure of talented youth in search of a wider world. The station makes the place of outsiders and observers, including the writer, and over her shoulder, the reader, the central fact.

In Edith Wharton's novella *Summer* the outsider who arrives to sketch authentic old houses and who researches in the town library is our surrogate and it is through his eyes that we view the small-town world. The climactic chapters of the book, already a study of a remote and regional community, take us on a day visit to the mountain or hill people, who have moved the remote and isolated culture one step back from the quaint, mildly remote culture of the village. It is this play of regions that gives region itself meaning. The scholarly outsider drawing authentic houses for a New York publisher to print for his urban audience's nostalgia, the town itself, and the mountain people outside town make up in combination the three cultures that give us the regional novel as a form.

Regions become known as such by those who move from one to another and are able, as a result, to see contrasting ways of life. Owen Wister's novel *The Virginian* is not about Virginia, but about the meeting, courtship, and marriage in Wyoming of a Virginian and a New Englander. In its first chapter we arrive at the train station that already links the Wild West to the East, North, South, and Midwest. That act of moving from one world to another finds its professionals in the reporter, the artist, and the intelligent visitor. But it exerts a deeper attraction on an ever larger number of middle-class figures who establish a second home, a summer place, to keep open a double cultural membership for themselves, one foot in urban modernity, one foot in the more and more fictive world of antique, traditional values that, paradoxically, only the money of urban outsiders now can keep alive as if it were still a going concern economically. Once again it is the trunk-line rail system that made this possible, and the automobile that kept it possible. It was the national magazines and the book culture of Boston and New York that promoted the regional.

Early-Twentieth-Century Regionalism

Each swing to regionalism splits the country along different fault lines and each rewon unity involves not a return to a lost identity, but a new plane of association. In early-twentieth-century America a new regionalism that was not geographic but ethnic appeared as a result of massive immigration. The local color was not that of climates and regions, but of hyphenated Americans: Jewish-Americans, Italian-Americans, Irish-Americans, WASPs, Chinese-Americans, Polish-Americans, Swedish-Americans, and Russian-Americans. This was a regionalism of languages, folk customs, humor, music, and beliefs set against the pull of what came to be called Americanization.

And yet even to call these groups distinct "cultures" is to accept the regionalist myth about their experience. Cultures are what is transmitted, what exists across generations; cultures involve duration. What strikes us now about the many books and cultural formulas of early-twentieth-century hyphenated American regionalism is that these works are all functions of a transitional generation between cultures; they are one and all immigrant, hinge-generation novels, and are in no way about the struggle between cultures over time, that is, over generations. Their presumption is generational break rather than a continuity of generations, and about this break they are typically more sad and nostalgic than angry. They constitute not a provincial literature, but a port-of-arrival literature. Even the term "ghetto" is for the most part inaccurate, since a short-lived housing pattern cannot be legitimately called by the same term, "ghetto," as the permanent many-generations-old housing and legal structures of central Europe. In Philadelphia the district called Germantown has long ago ceased to be German. In Cambridge, Massachusetts, the districts that thirty years ago were largely Italian are now Portuguese, what was Greek is now Haitian, what was Irish is now Central American or Asian, because these are the new arrivals at the port of immigration. What stays constant is the percent of those born in another land and the percent of children in the schools whose home language is not English.

The rings of suburbs to which the children of the earlier immigrants have now moved can hardly ever be defined by any ethnic markings whatsoever. Even to use the European meaning of ghetto is to misunderstand the fact of ghettos within a society of intermarriage and mobility, a society in which the next generation will not live in some other ethnic district of the inner city, but will instead abandon the city altogether for the newly created suburbs, where quite different districts and subdivisions will arise. They will, in other words, reimmigrate and dissolve rather than choose among what seemed to be the fixed terms of choice. The culture overrides rather than settles. Emerson's circles reappear on the twentieth-century American map as ethnic urban enclaves, later giving way to patches of suburbs, encircled in their turn by nearly rural ways of life served by shopping malls and highways. The suburban development of the automobile culture overrode and canceled the battle lines drawn within the ethnic districts of the city, even where the latter remained as vestigial areas of lesser and lesser overall importance, as is the case in Boston, where the early-twentieth-century map of Irish and Italian districts still corresponds to reality.

The common examples of the ethnic-regional novel' such as *Call it Sleep, Studs Lonigan, Christ in Concrete, My Ántonia, Invisible Man, The Joy Luck Club, The Mambo Kings Play Songs of Love,* are not works of stable provincial literatures, truly regional literatures, as was Austrian or Swiss literature of the nineteenth century; they are instead, one and all, immigrant, mobile, transitional novels where the key dramatic fact lies in the relations between generations and, in Sir Walter

Scott's sense, in the elegiac relation to a disappearing way of life—that of the parents and grandparents. Decisively, these novels state the key American theme: No longer will cultural transmission define the relation of parents to children. Children will gain the needed cultural information outside the home, on the street, from songs, in school, from the media and from the experience of the workplace.

In the case of the regionalism of hyphenated Americans it was not the railroads and the everyday objects of a thriving economy that created the dissolving and blending force. To this ethnic regionalism that followed the mass immigrations of 1880 to 1914 was opposed the core culture of the system of public education coupled to the culture of public entertainment and the pull of economic advancement, always purchased at the price of a surrendered culture, most obviously by the requirement within the schools and business world of the use of the English language.

Another unifying force was mobility itself. Only by remaining within a ghetto, the port of arrival, could members of an ethnic group maintain and preserve the coherence of language, ways of life, religion, and, most important, marriage within their ethnic group. To move even once was to enter the general American condition. For New York Jews the move from the Lower East Side or from Brooklyn to the Long Island suburbs was their entry into the general American condition.

The weak power of parents over children in twentieth-century America, even within those ethnic communities where parental power had been, in the old country, most absolute, dissolved the bond on which all other sanctions guiding cultural transmission depend. The relatively small value of all things known and thought valuable by parents for the lives of their children declines once an economy is based less and less on traditional occupational paths—carpenter, baker, barber, housewife—because those traditional paths involve knowledge that the previous generation has and the younger generation needs.

When the young try to locate themselves in a landscape of work that their parents never faced at all and know nothing about, the lore of the parents becomes a hindrance because it is more often wrong than right. Parents send their children into whaling or into steel mills just when those occupations themselves have collapsed. It is the creative destruction of the economy—its new structure from generation to generation and the new paths that the new structure opens up as it closes down the only paths known to the older generation—that weakens the grip of the older generations, with their "old ways," and makes, we could say, immigrant families the central model for all families, because they experience in a dramatic way (since their language cannot be the language of their children) the more general collapse and danger of transmission between generations of knowledge and ways of life, and the opening up in the wider culture of means distinct from the family for inculcating each generation's way of life, sense of opportunity, outlook, and values.

The weak power of the adult generation to pass on a culture to the young follows from circumstances in which parents cannot guide their children or give them economically decisive tools for their adult lives. In cultures where the family owns land, or a family business, or has the skills and equipment, along with an established reputation, for fishing, baking, or medicine that will confidently carry the next generation through their lives, the power of the adults over the young of the next generation is directly proportional to the fact that the young owe this economic or skill debt to their parents.

Because the older generations in America begin by failing the young in economic wisdom—since the frame changes so rapidly—they cannot instruct them in cultural, behavioral, or ethical matters without meeting skepticism or defiance. If they can't give them and guarantee them a path to making a living over the next fifty years, they can't impose on them a way of life either. Because the young have to find out for themselves, under the shifting conditions of their generation, their own way, they naturally reserve for themselves the right to invent their own wisdom about sexual mores, family life, food, clothing, where and how to live, what to think about politics, and so on.

My central point here is that a rapidly changing economy and work structure destroy the value of intergenerational wisdom and increase the value of wisdom unique to each peer group. In a society of creative destruction the landscape of work and the means for making a living will change dramatically, and the secondary components of any way of life will follow tamely along in imitation. Therefore, the case that we normally think of as exceptional—the immigrant's rapid transformation in the first, second, and third generations that drives a wall of silence and misunderstanding between the generations—is in fact not an exceptional case at all, but a vivid model for the general American condition. With constant economic restructuring, every generation must emigrate from and immigrate into a new way of life, of thinking, of training, and of earning a living.

Thus the second form of regionalism (the ethnic form of hyphenated Americans of the first third of the twentieth century) reveals not a patchwork quilt or multicultural array of stable ways of life, but instead intergenerational strife that gives us a model for the culture as a whole. *Call It Sleep* and *Studs Lonigan*, *My Ántonia* and *The Mambo Kings Play Songs of Love*, set before us not the model of cultures, but the techniques and representational look and feel of the requirement to shift with each new generation from an obsolete but beloved parental way of life to a still inchoate but uniquely functional new culture that will serve the tribe of children, only to become—once they are mature enough to want to pass it on—obsolete forty years later.

What I have insisted that we place in the center of our thinking about regionalism is the economic commitment to a rapidly changing culture of invention, with its dizzy cycles of creation, loss, and transfer of wealth and power. Such an economic commitment turned out to be far more decisive than the purely individual right to escape or to move on. Individual mobility was historically profound because it was the means of renewing the act of immigration—leaving behind and moving on—that was each individual's first drop of American identity, whether one or twenty-one generations ago. We can see a ceremonial repetition of immigration in each generation. In particular, the move from the rural countryside to the large cities involved as much trauma as the original immigration from overseas. A new culture had to be learned, and each new city resident turned away from the way of life left behind with the rural or small-town family. Dreiser's *Sister Carrie* is the great American description of this second immigration.

A generation later the immigration from cities to the new suburbs that dominated American life after 1950 entailed the abandoning of supports for identity that neighborhoods had supplied in favor of the economic sorting out that richer and more modest suburbs imposed. Once again the stress of abandoning and entering culture repeated itself.

A substantial fraction of American young people immigrate at eighteen by going away to college and leaving behind their friends and family life so as to enter and learn the culture of a far more diverse but very temporary new world, entered at eighteen, left behind half a decade later.

Late-Twentieth-Century Regionalism

In recent years there has begun a new form of regionalism that is neither geographical nor ethnic. The regionalism of our own times is a regionalism of gender, race, sexual orientation, and later ethnicities imagined on a racial model—Chicano identity, Asian-American identity.

The civil rights movement after 1954 had as a cultural corollary the debate over black identity in America. The women's movement that followed drew from it, just as the nineteenth-century suffrage movement had followed and drawn its vocabulary from the abolitionist movement against slavery. Later gay and lesbian identity movements, along with ethnic identities now conceived not on the model of the earlier hyphenated identities, but on the more radical model of black or female identity, reopened the full spectrum of regionalized culture. Native-American, Chicano, Gay, Black, Asian-American, Lesbian, Female: these were the new regional cultures in the United States, displacing the Southern, Western, and New England regional cultures that had divided the map a hundred years earlier. Now a third episode of regionalism had set out its claims—in this case, against a central technological culture made up of the new media, television and film, and also against the older forces of education and mass representation. The model set in place for regionalism by black or female identity was refractory in a way that earlier episodes had not been. These new regional forms of identity were the first within American experience that neither mobility nor intermarriage nor the passage of generations would alter. Earlier geographic or ethnic regional identities had usually been temporary and subject to reaffirmation or neglect by every new generation that might move or intermarry or simply forget to honor and proclaim southernness or Italian-Americanness. The very mechanisms of the culture would erase them over time.

In Owen Wister's *The Virginian* the central hero—the "Virginian"—moves west and marries there a schoolteacher born in New England. William Dean Howells's *Hazard of New Fortunes* represents the southerner, the midwestern businessman, the German-American immigrant, and the New Englander. They are all found together in the same novel because, one and all, as if to honor the only real American tradition—mobility—they have relocated to New York City. Relocation enables business ventures, a common social life, friendships, and possible marriages among all those who have similarly resettled. Owen Wister's novel, often called the first important western, is also one of the most important novels of immigration because in the United States the port of arrival is only the first stopping point in a process that will be repeated in generation after generation that resettles in a new place, abandons a settled life to, in effect, reimmigrate. Immigration as an ongoing, repeated project is the under-story of Wister's novel. Although that novel seems to set out a new region—the Wyoming West—it does so by means of the very characters and mechanisms that guarantee the temporary nature of the rugged West as a distinct region. The train, the school system, the resettled characters from a variety of earlier regions, and intermarriage will guarantee the children a freedom from any of the traces of the now abandoned earlier regions that nurtured their parents: the South and New England. In Wister and Howells the representation of region involves the simultaneous representation of the ways through which region will be abolished, above all the triad of mobility, intermarriage, and the fresh start of each next-on generation facing its new conditions.

When we use the word "regionalism" for African-American or female identity, a new and irreparable situation exists. To be an African-American or a woman is an unnegotiable identity. Insofar as other groups, including ethnic groups and gays, took over the African-American model, they chose to see their own regional identity as final. If to be African-American or female were to be taken as a model case by means of which all other regional identities were to be described, then we would for the first time have a natal fact, or what Clifford Geertz calls a biological identity, set in the life of each child as an already given fact of birth. The meaning and implications of this fact could only sink in over time when each child discovers his or her place in a larger cultural, symbolic matrix.

For any such natal or fated identity, the two key personal acts of choice, mobility and marriage, were no longer the mechanism by which one might reaffirm regional identity by choosing to remain in the same community or the same geography in which one had been born and to marry within the group and therefore determine that the starting point of one's own children would be, insofar as possible, the same as one's own. Moreover, the alternative of moving away and/or marrying outside the boundary of regional identity—the act that for earlier regionalisms guaranteed a new starting point for one's children distinct from one's own—was also not available.

Even more important, the rapidly changing economic frame that I have called the mobility of mobility itself was irrelevant to these identities in a crucial way. These are natal facts, as in traditional cultures all identity features were, including social status and economic sector. Whether one was a farmer, a baker, a laborer, or a merchant had been fixed at birth. Our contemporary use of race identity and gender identity as models serves to smuggle back in a fated, traditionalist idea that affects all wider cultural identities as though they too were given at birth as race and gender are.

Mobility and intermarriage vanished as significant mechanisms once the model of regional identity was African-American identity or female identity. The role of adult choice was replaced by the project of finding out, and after finding out, affirming or denying who or what you already were and had been since birth. The politics of this kind of choiceless identity creates the current literary interest in what is now called the literature of passing. Passing or allowing oneself to be taken for white or Protestant or heterosexual is the new ethical dilemma of this form of regionalism. The word "passing" has become one of the strongest remaining ethical rebukes, as inauthenticity had been in the peak years of Existentialism.

The use of African-American identity as the model case over the last thirty years must raise the question of whether American slavery with its unique history and consequences does not disqualify any use of African-American experience for the general case. Is African-American identity, for historical reasons, more like Amish or Hassidic identity within the earlier systems of regionalism, where both were exceptions that were contrary to the norms rather than even potentially normative? It may seem a grotesque suggestion to link such small peripheral groups as the Amish and the Hassidim to the fundamental experience of slavery and African-American experience. I do so only to point out the consequences of imagining Chicano identity or gay identity or Asian-American or female identity as intractable regions within American culture. This third, recent episode of regionalism sets a fundamental challenge to the mechanisms that had earlier swung the pendulum between region and commonness.

The true mobility of American culture is not simply the mobility of persons, whether from place to place, up and down on the scale of wealth and social prestige, between success and failure, or between wealth and poverty, but rather the mobility of the frame itself, the overall horizon, a mobility that makes the word "culture" and the ideal of the transmission of culture or a way of life weak and misleading.

In a country where children do not typically inherit their parents' farm or live their lives in the county where they were born, the idea of "settled" communities, and neighborhoods, and of ways of life and thought that might be passed on, flies in the face of the fact that 20 percent of the population moves in any one year.

Only carefully fenced communities severed from the larger economy, as the Amish are in Pennsylvania or as groups governed by such prohibitions as religious dietary laws—like those of orthodox Judaism or practicing Muslims—create enforced separation from this system. The uniqueness of this example shows that the plural and parallel model of culture has never won serious ground in the United States. We are not regional in the radical way that the Amish or Hassidic Jews are, two groups that have mastered over time the problems of binding the generations to one another, transmitting a temporally frozen culture, and controlling the marriage partners of the young, along with their access to the wider educational system.

Without a grasp of these features we use the very word "Culture" in ways that smuggle in the false premises of a traditional or anthropological tribal meaning of enduring ways of life, successfully transmitted by parental generations to their children with only slight modifications, and in which the key details of economic life, location, inheritance, and marriage patterns are under the control of the adults. Should we even use the word "culture" for modern economic conditions under which these features have less and less hold? The paradoxes within the two different forms of regional literature that I have considered in this chapter suggest that the anthropologist's term "culture" is oblique and deceptive when used to describe American experience.

PART FOUR

Realism

chapter seven

Realisms of Detail, State, and Voice

The novel usually provides the essential literary evidence offered for an account of culture. What kind of evidence is it that the modern realistic novel has to offer? The abstraction described in earlier chapters of this book, with its natural fit to a culture of immigration and economic mobility of persons and things, would naturally seem to draw its best instances from philosophy or poetry, from Emerson or Walt Whitman.

The novel has an almost fated relation to realism, to concrete detail, to ordinary and specific experience located in just this moment of history and this specific spot. For that reason the alternative that realism poses to regionalism and to abstraction as a democratic poetics of the concrete and specific relies on what we believe that realism does in its one-at-a-time focus on a person, experience, place, or moment of specific presence.

In this chapter and the next I will attempt to define the changing technology of literary and, in places, visual realism. The genuine alternative that realistic detail offered to abstraction is fundamental to the modern history of American culture. That realism is not one formula or kind of evidence at all is what I hope to show in this part of my argument. Climactic works of realism, such as Faulkner's *Sound and the Fury*, represent the rich alternative to the masterpieces of abstraction, above all Whitman's *Leaves of Grass*.

The accumulation of the evidence for what counts as real in realism leads in this chapter to a claim that the realism of voice is fundamental in American literature from Stowe's *Uncle Tom's Cabin* to at least the time of Faulkner's *Sound and the Fury* and West's *Miss Lonelyhearts*. After my earlier stress on silence and the silent representation of people in Whitman, where silence is, so to speak, the Latin of an immigrant culture of many demotic languages, this concluding linkage between American realism and the individuated voice is intended to offer the same Emersonian surprise as the new technology of radio with its unseen voices occasioned in the second quarter of the twentieth century after the earlier domination of photographs and silent films, where human presence, as in Whitman, occurs at the sacrificial cost of silence. The interplay between realism and the technologies of popular representation in the late nineteenth and early twentieth centuries is one of the important themes of this final pair of chapters. The match and challenge between literary representation and the rival newspapers, films, radios, and television will dominate Chapter 8. Because a number of defining steps within late-nineteenth-century realism occur within the European novel in the aftermath of Gustave Flaubert's *Madame Bovary*, the argument of this chapter will set the American literary experience within the examples and terms of the wider European experience of progressively unfolding realism.

Evidence for Reality in Realism

"Looking for a handkerchief to wipe her tears she smiled; we were silent for some time, then I put my arms round her and kissed her, scratching my cheek till it bled with her hatpin as I did it."[1]

In this scene from Anton Chekhov's novella *My Life* describing a kiss that will lead to marriage, we find the key features of what I will call pictorial realism. We *see*, as though standing very close to the two characters, a step-by-step, real-time scene. The sentences make up what we call a description, and they tell us only what could be seen by a camera or by a reporter: the act of looking for a handkerchief, a smile, the silence, the arms put round her, the kiss, the scratched cheek bleeding from the hatpin. No inner life or speculation occurs, no response is recorded. Neither metaphors nor memories nor analysis occurs. In particular, there is no mention of the pain caused by the hatpin or the surprise when it was first felt. The scene is physical and it is fully visible, even though it is an intimate scene where no one but the lovers would be present.

The reality of the scene is confirmed in an odd way. The hatpin, scratching his cheek till it bled, is the evidence for the reality, for the believability, for the realism of the scene. This hyper-real, visualized, and felt detail, the jab of pain within the kiss, makes us feel that this one kiss is just what happened, and that it is unlike any other kiss.

All critical writing on realism has noticed such odd striking details. Usually there is only one detail that stamps the scene as real, breaking this one kiss off from every other one that the character has ever experienced in his life as well as from every other literary kiss that readers, who might have read hundreds of scenes just like this, have ever encountered. By means of the hatpin the kiss is made memorable, scratched into the reader's memory, just like the scar that the lover's cheek might display on his face for the rest of his life.

What we call detail in pictorial realism is always close up. We find ourselves, by means of small, noticed things—often, like the hatpin, things not seen until this moment—right in the center of the scene, face to face with these people. We find ourselves in real time in which just this scratching (progressive present tense) is taking place, and just for the two seconds that it would take to happen in the middle of the kiss. Actions that begin and end in a few seconds, like a smile or searching for a handkerchief, also mark out the granulation of time here—ten seconds, five seconds, two seconds.

"Description levels, Narration orders."[2] This statement by Georg Lukács embodies the crux of one charge against description and descriptive realism. The hatpin has become equal in importance to the kiss. The handkerchief has been mentioned at the same level of attention as the smile or the embrace. The small and the large, the central and the odd, but vivid, secondary fact share the stage in the same bright light. The mundane things of life—handkerchiefs and hatpins—share attention with smiles and those first kisses that seal betrothal and mark a once-and-forever turning point in a life.

For a writer like Flaubert, one motive for such details was to reduce large states and conditions to the prison of the concrete and the everyday. At her dinner table Emma Bovary and her husband endure life together. "Charles was a slow eater. She used to nibble a few nuts, or lean her elbow on the table and beguile the time by tracing little lines on the oil-cloth with the tip of her knife."[3] The horrible ultimate detail of amusing herself by making marks on the tablecloth with her knife, the act of a naughty child for whom even this pointless scraping is better than nothing and so counts for amusement—this is the detail that counts as evidence for the realism of Flaubert's account.

But in Chekhov's story a very different motive drives the story to the leveling of detail. Smile and handkerchief, kiss and hatpin: each has its moment of isolated concentration as the description moves past it. In Tolstoy the horse pulling ahead to win the race and the blue fly on the horse's flank each have their full, frontal moment of attention. Detail levels. And as Paul Valéry pointed out, since in description the details can appear in any order whatsoever, the intellectual component of art is diminished.[4] Here again, to narrate is to order temporally into before and after, cause and consequence, but to describe is to order arbitrarily, sometimes smile before handkerchief, other times, handkerchief before smile.

The scale of description is also arbitrary, as Valéry noticed. A military battle can be described in five lines, and a man's hat in two pages. Scale, order, foreground and background, important and trivial are all put at risk, because, we could say, in description there is only foreground, only central actors. In one sentence or moment of attention it can be the smile, or the handkerchief, or the silence, or the kiss, or the hatpin scratching the cheek that is front and center, alone on the stage. Naturally, in such a rotation of attention, the most unexpected sensation becomes the most memorable. In this case most important is the hatpin and the scratched cheek. Roland Barthes, in an essay that taps into the long tradition of argument about detail and realism, speaks of such details as creating the effect of the real.[5]

These several objections to "real detail" that Lukács, Valéry, and Barthes—along with many others, including Eric Auerbach in his dismissal of modernist realism in his landmark book, *Mimesis*—can be brought into sharp focus in a passage of descriptive characterization from Chekhov's *My Life*. In this passage we have almost a parody of how the ordinary comes to feel unique and real by means of odd, pointless, unordered detail.

> In the evenings he drank too much in the village or at the station, and before going to bed stared in the looking glass and said: "Hullo, Ivan Tcheprakov."
>
> When he was drunk he was very pale, and kept rubbing his hands and laughing with a sound like a neigh: "hee-hee-hee!" By way of bravado he used to strip and run about the country naked. He used to eat flies and say they were rather sour.[6]

The details have a false specificity. Why do we learn about his eating flies and why do we learn of his comment that they tasted sour? Aren't these nothing more than specific, pointless details? Will this character ever really run naked in this story? Will fly eating turn up later at a crucial moment? The answer is: no.

What explains the sequence of these pointless details? Arbitrary, merely odd; close up, but merely individualistic or individualized: How many queer and singular traits does it take to make up a character? We feel almost in a competition to top the previous "individualizing fact"—the man who neighs like a horse; the man who runs naked around the countryside for fun; the man who eats flies and says they taste sour. Small, exact, unique facts, arranged without order, in this number just because it seemed enough. Uniqueness and the feel of the reality of the passage seem purchased at too high a price, as sometimes seems the case with Charles Dickens. At other times in pictorial realism odd details create an almost mystical feeling of the here and now. Flaubert's description of Emma Bovary's parasol achieves this.

> She turned back at the door and went to fetch her parasol. She opened it out; it was of shot silk, and the sun shining through it cast

flickering lights over the white skin of her face. She smiled in the moist warmth beneath it, and they heard the drops of water dripping on to the taut silk one by one.[7]

Such precious notation of a just-here, just-now moment of perfection is also rendered in the unique, real-time detail of pictorial realism, the raindrops, one by one, hitting the sunlit silk parasol. Writing about photography even before the Civil War photographs of Mathew Brady, Oliver Wendell Holmes noticed the new medium's automatic production of just such evidentiary details: "The very things which an artist would leave out, or render imperfectly, the photograph takes infinite care with, and so makes its illusions perfect. What is the picture of a drum without the marks on its head where the beating of the sticks has darkened the parchment?"[8]

Detail and Allegory: Realism and Action

We need to notice that any hyper-real, memorable detail like the hatpin kiss, in its accidental quality—that's just what happened—opens the real scene to allegory and allegorical reading. The very accidental or arbitrary presence and focus on such a detail as the hatpin, the scratched cheek, the kiss that draws blood, makes it seem to augur a bad marriage, or to allegorize the nature of love as pleasure and unexpected pain, or even to allegorize the nature of pleasure, blinding us to the hatpin as we approach with eyes closed for the kiss. Exactly because this is a senseless detail, accidentally present, we freight it with meaning. We race to supply the most radical kind of sense: allegory and all-embracing application. The odd connection between "just-as-it-really-is" realism and allegory—that key technique of the "just-as-it-isn't" imaginary—is one of the strangest interpretive facts about detail-driven descriptive realism. Why are we asked to look at this trivial fact if it isn't really either representative (the normal justification in realism for detail) or, in its uniqueness, metaphoric and in the end capable of allegorical reading? The close attention implies meaningfulness, even while the concreteness seems to claim: this is mentioned because it just happened that way. Why does the allegorical temptation hover

over all realistic work, over the most empirical and factual form ever invented?

If we gave a twist to Lukács's phrase we could say: detail democratizes, whereas narration, like syntax in a sentence, creates subordination and hierarchy within attention. Even the false specific moment within a passage guarantees that everything, no matter how humble or accidental, is worth the attention of narrative, just as every person, every life-moment or experience, is worthy of equal notice, of equal descriptive and narrative focus.

If we say that description democratizes and that visibility, once guaranteed by detail, can never again fall back into the denied or overlooked, then what was the moral use of this evidence of reality? The ideas surrounding realism in literature and art had profound and intricate connections to democratic thought. Realism brought into the light and into visibility the unmentioned, undercounted members of society as well as sectors of life such as work that played little part in the polite, the poetic, and the idealizing with which art and literature have sometimes been identified. In Thomas Eakins's two great hospital paintings—*The Gross Clinic* and *The Agnew Clinic*—the usually invisible worlds of surgery are pictured, brought into the light, represented in the public account of reality alongside the commonly visible and therefore overrepresented world of a political speech, a sporting event, a fire in the city. The underreported poor join the census of the visible in the photographs of Jacob Riis, Alfred Stieglitz, or Walker Evans, each of whom set out to document, to represent with just the particular attention it is possible to give those who occupy the proud center of any photograph's space. Within literature, after Dickens and Scott, the representation of the excluded, the unmentioned and the unmentionable in society or in private, and intimate individual experience pushed back the lines of sight in culture until at least the time of James Joyce's *Ulysses*, with its full and detailed account of Leopold Bloom's successful visit to the outhouse. It is both experiences (sectors of experience) and persons that realism adds to the census of the visible.

In the 1850s Harriet Beecher Stowe conferred realism's visibility on the lives of slaves, Ivan Turgenev wrote the stories of rural and serf life collected as *A Sportsman's Notebook*, Leo Tolstoy wrote his great story "A Landlord's Morning" and *Sevastopol Sketches*, the first realistic account of ordinary men in war, and Gustave Flaubert wrote his story of provincial life, *Madame Bovary*. It is in these same years that Gustave Courbet painted the defining works of realism, such as his grand *Burial at Ornans*. Tolstoy, Turgenev, and Stowe put onto the map of representation what had until then been overlooked or unmentioned worlds and people. That this picturing came about first of all through a new literature of description and then through a new literature of witnesses or voices is the subject of this chapter.

One goal of this new visibility was social change. Representation itself was assumed to produce a revolt on the part of middle-class audiences, who had been protected from seeing or knowing the conditions of their own social existence. Reform relied on this revolt against intolerable conditions of life, a revolt that might lead to action, to legislation, to the abolition of serfdom or slavery, to changes in working conditions, to slum clearance, to pure food and drug laws and workers' compensation for injury. In some ways an equally important goal was the simple claim of worth for what had often been called "humble" people or "humble" things. One great accomplishment of realism was to replace the word "humble" with the word "ordinary" in our vocabulary. By realism's magic, "humble" people became from then on "ordinary people."

At the same time realistic representation was part of an ethic of honesty and completeness about experience that was independent of any change in social conditions. Under the influence of this ethic the most extreme face-to-face encounters were staged within pictorial realism. The competition to reach the outer limits of shock and surprise and by that means undo the ideal and the tritely beautiful was won early on in the history of realism by Baudelaire's description of a decaying carcass seen on "a beautiful summer morning so gentle." We see what must be a putrid horse, its legs in the air, as we read the poem. First a shocking moment of sight, at a turn in the road, then the horrid smell, followed by moralizing and brutal comparisons to a flower, and to a prostitute with her legs in the air: these ironic stages only prepare the way for what in realism is always the moment of truth. Suddenly we seem to have been brought close up, inches away from the repellent mass, close enough to see:

> Les mouches bourdonnaient sur ce ventre putride,
> D'où sortaient de noirs bataillons
> De larves, qui coulaient comme un épais liquide
> Le long de ces vivants haillons.[9]

In English a rough translation would read:

> The flies were buzzing on its putrid belly,
> From which crawled black battalions
> Of maggots that flowed like a thick liquid,
> Along those living rags of flesh.

The small size of the details recorded tells us how close we are, while the length of the stanza measures out how long our look and the poet's look will be held to this seething mass. The flies and maggots are locked in view with a glance that lingers and measures out its own fascination and disgust by waiting long enough to take their full measure.

Realism surprises us into unwanted moments or necessary moments of confronted sight. We face this carrion, and by means of the object, face what lies behind it, decay and death, the fate of the body in its relation to beauty. We are face to face with nature in a larger, more inclusive sense than is offered by the poem's opening line invoking a "beautiful summer morning so gentle."

The evidence of the real is supplied in the moment of detail that makes the poem not about thinking over or moralizing on a sight, but actually, insofar as description can do this, about seeing the sight for ourselves. The force of detail needs a frame within which it counts, and that frame is "real-time narration," the poem's mimesis of time in the moment of first sight, the flight to metaphors, the return for what we call a real look: a close inspection in which we measure out the full seconds of time we have to spend seeing this and hearing the exact words describing the flies and maggots. Real time weighs on us in an oppressive way to the extent that we are resisting and want to get away and think of something else. Detail measures visual space while real-time narration measures the temporal. In combination this pair grounds the conviction of reality within pictorial realism.

Aversion and fascination, cruelty and beauty, the poetic used against the grain of idealizing or merely pleasing notions of sight—these features in combination mark out the new territory in which a middle-class reader is set face to face with and, equally important, close up to, the real in one of its unmistakable, but often invisible forms. In this case, we find ourselves confronted with decay and death, the very facts usually made invisible by the earth that covers a human body or the carcass of a horse in its proper place, a grave, preventing us from seeing the slow transformation of the weeks after death in which, to use Yeats's words in a way not meant by Yeats himself, "a terrible beauty is born."

We could speak of burial as a system for deleting from the real the fact of decay, because it is, as we say, "removed from sight." Deletion and ellipse can then in turn be filled in by a moment of sight. All that occurs only in private, behind closed doors, across town or within the factory before we see the carefully prepared packages of ground meat in the supermarket, all that in novels happens after the three dots or once the chapter ends as the characters enter a hotel room together, all that is never mentioned in polite society or is, in a wider sense, "unmentionable" or covered by euphemism or silence can and has been since the 1850s returned to visibility or brought into the visible by means of the techniques of Baudelaire's poem. After realism no one ever forgets that the surface of the real, as we know it on a day-to-day basis, is rich in its deletions, unremembered, unmentioned, and that a cycle of return to awareness is one of the basic moves in art, at least as important as the turn of awareness to new or genuinely unknown things.

From Pictures to States

A less extreme and therefore more typical instance than Baudelaire's poem can be seen in Winslow Homer's drawing *Station-House Lodgers*. When Homer opens the door of the station-house in his illustration for *Harper's Weekly* in the 1870s his middle-class readers see for the

Winslow Homer, *Station-House Lodgers*, 1874. Wood engraving (23 cm. by 34 cm.). (Courtesy of the Fogg Art Museum, Harvard University Art Museums. Gift of W. G. Russell Allen.)

first time the chaos of bodies on the floor inside a night shelter. After a moment of social dismay, we also notice a kind of beauty the pleasing entanglement of limbs, the friendly and almost amorous group asleep crowded together on the floor. As we look in the door at one side of the room, we notice the man wearing a uniform at the open door across from us. He looks in at the very moment that we do, and his professional concern gives a name and tone to our own inspection. We also notice one waking or dazed figure, sitting at the left within the mass of bodies. This man individualizes the state, the consciousness of being here in this room as someone would experience it at the moment of waking up. He too has just entered the room, mentally, by waking up. In this figure we meet for the first time state-based realism as opposed to the pictorial realism of the inspector who looks in from outside. We as viewers are offered two alternatives of consciousness here. Naturally, we too are only looking in from without. We too are "inspectors"—that is, representatives of the world of order here to check up, to make sure everything is under control. But we also enter into the less pictorial relation of the posture and consciousness of the one waking man in a world of fellow sleepers, or of his waking up itself, confused and half aware, just as we are metaphorically waking up to this complex scene and to the social world it stands for. Our first confused seconds struggling to understand the dark mass of bodies map themselves within the work by means of the striking state and expression of this man. State-based realism rests on the convergence of two states: that of the reader or viewer and the state that we find somatically present within the work in a figure represented there. As we see in the station-house, whenever a door is opened onto a dark room, a path of outside light falls into the formerly closed world. Seeing within realism lets in light, turns on the lights.

To make clear the distinction that I want to stress between pictorial and state-based evidence of the reality of the scene I will have to give a deeper account of both alternatives and look at examples from both descriptive writing and illustration. To do this I will look first in detail at a small pictorial scene in Jane Addams's *Twenty Years at Hull-House,* of 1893, a representative book in the reform tradition, and then turn to two Civil War illustrations by Winslow Homer.

Pictorial Allegory: Jane Addams in the West

On a certain page of Jane Addams's memoir we open a door within deletion very much like Winslow Homer's station-house door. Jane Addams's small scene is so perfect an embodiment of the features of pictorial or descriptive realism that I will examine it in detail. It takes place when Addams is a young woman still in search of her mission.

> In one of the intervening summers between these European journeys I visited a western state where I had formerly invested a sum of money in mortgages. I was much horrified by the wretched conditions among the farmers, which had resulted from a long period of drought, and one forlorn picture was fairly burned into my mind. A number of starved hogs—collateral for a promissory note—were huddled into an open pen. Their backs were humped in a curious,

camel-like fashion, and they were devouring one of their own number, the latest victim of absolute starvation or possibly merely the one least able to defend himself against their voracious hunger. The farmer's wife looked on indifferently, a picture of despair as she stood in the door of the bare, crude house, and the two children behind her, whom she vainly tried to keep out of sight, continually thrust forward their faces almost covered by masses of coarse, sunburned hair, and their little bare feet so black, so hard, the great cracks so filled with dust that they looked like flattened hoofs.[10]

Investments are one of the key details of life we never look into carefully. They stand for the remote, invisible, relation of the middle class to many things from which they profit and on which they live. The moment of seeing for herself and then making us see is given in a few seconds of time, probably in a sight from the road. What we see here has the feel of a painting or a photograph with the farmer's wife in the center, the pigs between us and her, and the children half hidden behind her in the door of the grim farmhouse. The scene is purely visual; there are no details of sound or smell. No one speaks and no action takes place. The scene is fixed, as memories are. Addams speaks of a picture "burned into my mind" and by retelling it she burns it into ours. The point of view is not that of mere seeing. She is an interested party, a mortgage holder, as, indirectly, we all are. After seeing this scene she quickly orders the mortgages sold, even though the result of that act does not benefit the farmers at all. She takes the money and buys a "farm near my native village and also a flock of innocent-looking sheep," creating a pastoral world that will prevent her from ever again thinking of this woman as "my farmer."

As with many pictures burnt into the mind by realistic narrative, the outcome of looking at these intolerable social conditions is meant to be a subsequent moment or even a lifetime of action. It might lead to work to reform the banking laws or to individual charity that rushes in and puts money in the farmer's hand, or, as in this case, to a sale of the investment that thrusts the whole situation back into deletion. Because we learn that drought conditions and not cruel bankers have caused this horrible scene, we know that even out of sympathy we cannot alter nature. We might even feel that what we see here is the stupidity and greed of farmers who tried to farm in those parts of the West where annual rainfall was too low to support agriculture, and who created the Dust Bowl and other ecological disasters because of their ignorance and greed.

The scene Addams presents is what I call self-allegorizing realism. The pigs eating their own kind are juxtaposed to the woman protecting her young. Relations of the weak and strong are forced into consciousness: humanity protects the weak; animality preys on and then devours even its own brood. The pigs are sharply focused in the single odd detail of their humped backs. Like many details in realism, this one is more effective just because it is not relevant to what follows.

The children are also seen in detail: coarse masses of hair and bare feet so black, so hard, with great cracks so filled with dust that they looked like flattened hoofs. The detail brings us close enough to see the cracks in their blackened feet. The detail also merges them down into the animal world, as does their hair. They are halfway fallen into animality, but held back by the protective mother. Only she stands between them and the pigs, but their feet have already half-turned to hoofs. So the allegory suggests.

As Addams looks and as we look, the scene sorts out the moral problems of looking, just as Homer's inspector and his just-wakened sleeper had in the station-house. The mother looks on with indifference, unlike Addams, who will rush off to sell her mortgages. The children behind her are eager to see just as we are, standing opposite them, looking over Jane Addams's shoulders. But the mother tries to delete the scene; she wants them not to see. Addams uses an odd phrase for the mother's action: "she vainly tried to keep them out of sight." Does this mean keeping the children out of Addams's sight, out of our sight? Or out of the pigs' sight? Keeping them "out of sight" really means, oddly enough, the reverse: keeping this scene out of their sight. But it is around this rich phrase, this spinning, multipurpose phrase, "out of sight," or trying and failing to keep them and it and everything "out of sight" that the passage turns. The humanity of the farmer's wife is expressed in her hopeless wish to censor what her children will know by sight, what they will have to face at so young an age.

For realism, in the very act of forcing us to see, to locate human-ity in preventing someone from seeing is a rich act in a world where there is only the visual. One thing defined is the difference between children and adults, a refinement in the earlier human-animal split. To be adult is to see and know. The farm wife does not go back inside and shut the door. Jane Addams does not turn aside, nor does she let her reader.

I have drawn out the allegory of the scene, an allegory of looking and not looking, alongside an allegory of the human relation of strong with weak contrasted to the animal relation, because one of the most troubling or manipulative features of brief realistic mo-ments like these is that they are so often allegorized or used with the effect of allegory. Pictorial realism relies on quick, brief images. Few examples would be longer than half a page. The scene brings us face to face with strangers. We know nothing of how good or bad, industrious or shiftless, these people are. The complete infor-mation is locked in the surface. We will never see them again. The visit, the sight by the road, the investigative report all tell us self-contained realistic narratives of this kind.

Case-based Realism

When the pictorial is used in this way we have what I call case-based realism. We regard the facts here as both typical and inno-cent. A pure apparition occurs as we travel down the road and turn the bend. No background information is known by either reader or observer. All is just as it appears. There is no time in the anecdote, no structured past of which this is a result, no tomorrow in which later events happen. Discovered and uncovered by the traveler, as by the reader traveling along the pages of this chapter, the scene is just like a door suddenly thrown open onto a room, then quickly reshut.

Travel always confronts us with pure images of this kind. We see just what Addams refers to as "conditions." We see a child in rags leading a goat across a hill or we see a man fixing a wheel beside the road. We do not know their names, their stories, whether they are good or bad, whether they enjoy the act they are doing or are enslaved to it. Causality and ethical reality are absent in such pictures. The real story behind the scene is unknown, and the life that occurs in these conditions can only be imagined. This is the deep meaning of saying: the fundamental theme of all documentary realism is the life of strangers insofar as it might be self-explanatory and complete in one and only one image, one glimpse or one memory.

This lack of knowledge is combined with a strong pictorial presence. We are "struck by" what we see; it scratches our cheek like the hatpin in Chekhov, or is "burned in," in Jane Addams's phrase. The scene itself makes us stop and frame it for memory or for thought. Such lack of knowledge where there is unforgettable visual presence creates a situation that invites us to project meaning into the scene. Quickly, we supply the ethical and social account out of our own preexisting narrative stock. We could say that we stop to notice the scene just because we already have the allegory or the account for which we see at once that this is a perfect illustration, a perfect case. This means that we are drawn to allegorize the sharp, individual case exactly because we know so little about it, while at the same time we have a ready-to-hand strong conviction that it effortlessly illustrates. We are unfamiliar with these people and how they came to this state.

Jane Addams, clearly uneasy about living off her investments, resolves at once that "I will no longer profit from this misery." The scene allegorizes her own already latent convictions about nature, about the strong and the weak, about mothers and children, humans and animals.

We need to notice the deeply significant silence of all the figures in the scene. Naturally this is part of its painting-like completeness, but it also defines the distance we stand from the scene. We are far enough back to see it all at once, but close enough to be implicated in it. The distance at which Addams can see this scene without having to greet the woman, or without the woman glancing at her and responding to her presence, is one key fact about pictorial realism. We are far enough back in space not to have to encounter, to speak with, to greet those we see. We are far enough back so as to be unnoticed by the actors. This silence is fundamental within pictorial realism, in which evidence is made up only of what has been seen. Photographs, paintings, and descriptive texts, like this one, bring the visual and the narrative arts closer to each other than at any other time. Each artistic formula brought the middle-class audience face to face with, and close up to, the visual form of conditions. Typical conditions, persons seen as types, and types within a determining environment: such are the narrative components of Jane Addams's scene and of pictorial realism. I will return, in a later section, to the profound fact of silence within pictorial realism. One way of specifying that silence is to think of it as voiceless realism, or realism in which the central figures are deprived of voice and of the right to tell their own story in their own words.

Winslow Homer in the Civil War: From Pictorial to State-Based Realism

I will now use two sketches by Winslow Homer made on the battlefields of the Civil War to make the transition from pictorial to state-based realism. Homer's *Sharpshooter* and his *Soldier Loading a Rifle*, two of his thousands of sketches from the war, might each seem at first to supply evidence to those back home of the look and feel of the battlefield in roughly the same way. In fact, these images mark out two distinct paths of evidence of the reality of what is depicted, and two alternative routes for the back-home viewer's contact with the great unseen reality of the war.

Homer's black chalk drawing of 1863, *Soldier Loading a Rifle*, pictures for us the most common single act of war. In this act the soldier is seen at work. He is a careful craftsman engaged with his tools. We see him full-length, from cap to shoes, dressed in his uniform, in a concentrated and active stance. We stand close to him; his toe is near the frontal plane of the picture. He is a stranger to us, and as in most realistic work, he is a type, defined by his actions, his garb, his posture, and his location. We see him at the scene of his labor, a battlefield, much as we might see a surgeon in an operating theater or a professor in a classroom. Because we know nothing specific about him, or about this battle, or this particular day, he generalizes easily, as happens in realism, into every soldier,

Winslow Homer, *Soldier Loading a Rifle*, 1863–1864.
Black chalk, white chalk corrections, on green wove
paper (426 by 326 mm.; 16 3/4 by 12 13/16 in.);
pieced. (Cooper-Hewitt, National Design Museum, Smith-
sonian Institution/Art Resource, NY. Gift of Charles Savage
Homer, Jr., 1912-12-99.)

every battle, every day, and it is by means of one of his typical acts,
one of his habitual and repeated central acts, that he is seen. In scale
he has been treated with the dignity and with the isolation that
convey importance and completeness. He does not have to share
this pictorial space and our attention with any other person. He
elicits the serious attention and respect that Eric Auerbach saw as
the heart of realism in *Mimesis*. The soldier is, as we might say, worth
a picture, worth the care of that other craftsman, Winslow Homer,
who sees him as a fellow worker, a fellow practitioner of expertise.

We are face to face with this man, his complex body arrayed around the long diagonal of the rifle, which while being loaded stretches almost from corner to corner.

Winslow Homer's Soldier is one of thousands of ordinary men and women given dignity and centrality by means of the realistic account of their work. Homer's wood engraving of a young woman in a factory, *The Clanking Shuttle*, confers this same serious attention, respect, dignity, and generality on the woman at work with her machine in the factory setting. She too is full length, erect, and fully concentrated on her repetitive task. This is the ordinary and the everyday, not the dark satanic mills, and not the rustic clowns seen only in comedy. She is the heroine of her world as the soldier is of his, for this moment. These images are among tens of thousands of drawings, engravings, and photographs that place us in a world we have never seen, and set us face to face with the human center of that world, a typical factory girl or a soldier doing the typical act that defines full participation in that world day after day, year after year. What is defined by the pictorial image is what came to be called "conditions." These include the circumstances of a life, the environment that shaped the life pictured within it, just as tools shape the arm that uses them. Conditions are always "typical conditions" or average conditions. Those shaped by them often wear a uniform, as soldiers or butchers do, as baseball players or factory girls do. Conditions are themselves uniform.

What Homer sees and records in his thousands of sketches is also what Whitman sees and lists in his *Song of Myself*.

> The spinning-girl retreats and advances to the hum of the big wheel[11]

or

> The jour printer with gray head and gaunt jaws works at his case,
> He turns his quid of tobacco while his eyes blurr with the manu-
> script.
>
> sec. 15

Each worker is isolated for a moment of attention, pictured with her or his tools, active in the moment of labor. Even in a list like

Winslow Homer, *The Clanking Shuttle*, 1870. Wood engraving (4 1/4 by 3 7/8 in.). (From William Cullen Bryant, *The Song of the Sower*, New York: Appleton and Co., 1871.)

Whitman's each person merits a moment of attention and stands alone before our eyes in the isolation of a poetic line or two that is his alone, hers alone. We face them and come to know them one by one. Such figures I think of as *everyday strangers*. As we see them we understand the picture, because we are familiar with the work of spinning, weaving, loading a rifle, and we allow the individual to be absorbed in the function, in the performance of the well-known movements of the trade. There is no inner world and, more important, there is no story that these scenes hint at. No history or phase of an unfolding or secret drama darkens the transparency of these motions, postures, costumes and attentive moods. Here we have the essence of Whitman's voracious words "I see. . ." I see the soldier loading his rifle; I see the spinning-girl; I see the printer; I see the girl at Homer's clanking shuttle.

Here an important paradox appears. To call these figures everyday strangers might seem to imply a relation of estrangement or lack of felt connection. This is far from the case. It might be better to call these figures "fellow citizens," or people known to be within our world of concern and interest. The very lack of personal stories, of inwardness and of unique traits, might be, in fact, the very best premise for the representation of the fact of belonging to the same society and the same sphere of care. We do not know their names or stories. To know either would place them within our familiar or intimate worlds or the odd world of fame or notoriety that makes certain others known to us as well as our familiars and intimates.

The very essence of democratic society, when we contrast it with earlier tribal and clan-based groups, is to give reality to those outside our familiar or intimate sphere in ways that convince us of, or remind us of, their call on us for concern and interest. If this is true, then we might say that the visual and the photographic, along with the narrative use of its equivalent, pictorial realism by means of description, is uniquely important as a form of democratic representation precisely because it sets before us these *everyday strangers*. In fact, no narrative story can arouse our interest in everyday others without individualizing each person because of the unique events in time and space that are being told about that person. The pictorial with its silence, its absence of "the story behind" the visual facts, preserves intact the mere fact of "fellow citizens" those who are also members of what we call "our world." This is also a way of saying that pictorial narrative is uniquely able to convey humanity per se, that is, humanity without the individualization of each person's unique life history, personality, way of thinking and inner feelings. It is this humanity without individualization that we find in Homer's spinning girl or his soldier loading a rifle.

State-Based Realism: Winslow Homer's *Sharpshooter*

Homer's *Army of the Potomac—A Sharpshooter on Picket Duty*, which was printed in *Harper's Weekly* on November 15, 1862, seems at first to confront us with the same kind of visual and descriptive detail. But here we go down a different, more intimate path to enter the action, a path of somatic identification, the same path of somatic identification that I introduced in the figure of the just-awakened figure in Homer's station-house.

We feel kinesthetically the remarkable balance of the soldier, his body draped around the branch of the tree, one leg along the branch, the other free in space, his back and buttocks over the branch, his upper body leaning this side of the slender branch to create a perfect balance. His hand rests on a yet smaller branch to steady his arm. The rifle rests on the branch, perfectly still. He aims with absolute concentration and his trigger finger rests almost casually on the trigger in the moment before firing. The hand is almost ghostly white. To describe the scene we need somatic details of balance and posture. We empathically enter the complex posture, the front shoe turned sideways, the knee high.

The most important detail of the drawing is the invisible face. In any image in which a face is present we establish our first contact with the inner world of the subject through the face and its details of expression. Denied this path, we take the position of the body as a whole, its action and condition, as our entry point. By using just that moment of action when the sharpshooter's face has vanished into his concentrated act, Homer requires of us a somatic empathy that lets us enter his whole body. This stunning corporeal situation requires us to imagine it somatically, to enter the state of being, both body and mind, of the concentration of this act of see-ing—sighting. Since we too are engaged in an act of looking at this moment—at Homer's engraving—the sharpshooter's professional, keen-sighted, balanced attention to a detail far away defines our own look at Homer's engraving—not a glance, not a gaze, not a voyeur's or spy's quick and furtive glimpse, but a marksman's stillness and complete attention, a killer's look at the victim unaware of his attention and of the bullet about to be fired.

In state-based realism we cross into the physical space of the action, take the point of view and point of feeling of the figure before us and give ourselves up to consciousness of the full being of the situation, one that strangely draws us into mimetic awareness of

Winslow Homer, *Army of the Potomac—A Sharpshooter on Picket Duty*, 1862. Wood engraving (23 cm. by 34.8 cm.). (Courtesy of the Fogg Art Museum, Harvard University Art Museums. Gift of W. G. Russell Allen.)

our own state. Homer too, if we imagine him in the act of drawing this scene, concentrates, peers, uses his tools and feels out the precarious balance of this body at rest in the tree. We the viewers, the artist, and the artist's subject, the sharpshooter, superimpose ourselves on one another in this example of state-based realism.

Whitman marks his change from pictorial to state-based realism in *Song of Myself* by abandoning the words "I see. . ." in favor of the stronger words "I am. . .," as in the line "I am the hounded slave, I wince at the bite of the dogs" (sec. 33). The words "I am" are sometimes indirect: not "I see the beggar," but "I project my hat, sit shame-faced, and beg" (sec. 37). The strongly felt posture of shame with its prop, the no longer worn, but outstretched hat, takes us into the somatic feel of begging. The strong "I am" is also richly present in a scene where seeing itself is impossible within the rubble of a fire.

> I am the mash'd fireman with breast-bone broken,
> Tumbling walls buried me in their debris,

Heat and smoke I inspired, I heard the yelling shouts of my com-
rades,
I heard the distant click of their picks and shovels,
They have clear'd the beams away, they tenderly lift me forth.

I lie in the night air in my red shirt, the pervading hush is for my
sake,
Painless after all I lie exhausted but not so unhappy,
White and beautiful are the faces around me, the heads are bared
of their fire-caps,
The kneeling crowd fades with the light of the torches.

sec. 33

Like the image of Winslow Homer's sharpshooter this scene in
Whitman is an actual moment, a posture never exactly to be repeated, unique to the crushing building, or in Homer's case, to the
tree. An exact life-or-death, breathless, moment within time has
been seized of which the scene in its visual details is only a small
part. To say, as Whitman does, "I am the mash'd fireman" is to enter
more exactly a situated world of smoke, heat, distant clicks, and
tender lifting.

Nor is this a unique moment in Whitman's *Song of Myself.* When
he accounts for his own poetry he reaches across by means of the
most unprecedented intimacy. In a remarkable play on the use of
his breath in poetry to lift up his fellow countrymen, Whitman
makes the state of despair and the inspiration of poetry the state-
based model for his art.

I seize the descending man and raise him with resistless will,
O despairer, here is my neck,
By God, you shall not go down! hang your whole weight upon me.

I dilate you with tremendous breath, I buoy you up,
Every room of the house do I fill with an arm'd force,
Lovers of me, bafflers of graves.

Sleep—I and they keep guard all night,
Not doubt, not decease shall dare to lay finger upon you,
I have embraced you, and henceforth possess you to myself,
And when you rise in the morning you will find what I tell you is so.

sec. 40

In this remarkable passage Whitman, both poet and nurse to his countrymen, blows new breath into their lungs. Each word of the passage is both the literal circumstance of rescue and the poetic relation of bringing irresistible new spirit into the lives of his readers. "Here is my neck," he writes, naming the poem as his body, "hang your whole weight upon me." "I have embraced you" in the writing of this poem. "I seize . . . and raise": these two words define his full poetic practice. "I dilate you with tremendous breath." To read or speak his poem is to undergo this full dilation by his breath. Or as he writes in the forty-seventh section:

> (It is you talking just as much as myself, I act as the tongue of you,
> tied in your mouth, in mine it begins to be loosen'd)

No poet had ever before grasped the magic and literal fact that whenever we speak his words, even in silent reading, we find him already inside us, a tongue in our mouth, breath in our lungs, superimposed on us in carrying out his project to speak for us all and have us, then, recognize him by speaking back in our moment of pronouncing him, the very spirit that has no path of resistance. Here is state-based realism in its ultimate democratic form.

The somatic state of the sharpshooter in Homer's image, and our entry into it, depends on a remarkable fact: this man fills out the entire frame of the image. Just as his body is draped carefully around the branches of the tree, so too the four edges of the print are draped around his boot, his cap, his back, and his rifle barrel. We seem to be closer to him in space than we could possibly be on the battlefield, because in battle he works alone, secretly hidden in the tree. If the frame were pulled back and he were just a small aspect of the visual scene, we could not attend somatically to him. State-based realism is necessarily a close-up, nearby, body-to-body experience. It is an intimate realism.

If we remember for a moment that sharpshooters were the most feared, because unseen, highly accurate killers in the Civil War, we can imagine at once the rest of the scene that Homer does not show us, a larger scene that would make somatic identification with the state and state of mind of the sharpshooter impossible. Imagine that the picture includes his target, a soldier quietly reading a letter from home, or drinking from a canteen, or walking unsuspectingly along a road that will, a second later, be the scene of his death. To see the victim would force us empathically into his state, or rather into pity for his ignorance. We would feel dramatic irony about what we can see and he cannot. Homer's complete somatic, or state-based, image is only part of a larger pictorial image, and to see that we would have to back up far enough so as to have both sharpshooter and victim in the same line of sight. Once back that far we would have to divide consciousness between at least two figures and we would be too far from both to see the exact physical details that make somatic, or state-based, perception possible. Because what Homer shows us is—for this picture—the "whole scene," we know his subject to be a state rather than an action. The larger frame would confront us with a moral action, a world of killer and about-to-be-slain. As it is, in Homer's picture we are near enough to see the neatly balanced canteen tied in a precise loop around a small branch. The finesse and artistry of the sharpshooter is evidenced by the delicate loop he has tied the canteen with before assuming his own balanced state of rest in preparation for taking his shot.

By denying us the entire action, Homer defines a new aesthetic whole, the state of the man perched in just this posture at this moment of time. We enter that state without protesting in the name of the unseen victim or feeling the complex anxiety that the idea of hidden, expert killers cast over the war. The moral or ethical neutrality of state-based realism was one of its major innovations, and this neutrality included the possibility, as here, of entering the state of the slayer as easily as the state of the man about to be slain.

State-Based Realism and the Early Novel

With state-based realism we reach the most radical of literary facts, the creation in the reader or the spectator of strong, pervasive states linked to and often parallel to, or mimetic of, the state of being of figures within the work of art. The pity and terror of Aristotle's definition of tragedy are states induced in the audience watching *Oedipus Rex* and they are states of characters within the tragedy.

State-based realism was fundamental to the rise of the novel and to the craze for reading that swept Europe in the eighteenth century. Solitary and silent reading, often done in private rooms, often done at night, often done in bed, made possible a more radical induction of certain key states, whereas our presence in a crowded theater or amphitheater for a spectacle makes possible the strongest possible version of quite different states that profit from the feeling of multiplication—feelings of total loss, of patriotism or of deep religious belief, to name only a few.

From Samuel Richardson's *Pamela* in 1740, through Rousseau's *La nouvelle Héloïse*, to Goethe's *Die Leiden des Jungen Werthers* in 1774, the novel became the rage of Europe because of the mimetic attention to the solitude of its central figures, which matches the solitude of the reader, and through its exploitation of the strong, impassioned states of fear, love, and melancholy that set out a basic grammar of extreme states. Goethe's *Werther* offers the most direct evidence of state-based realism because of the number of suicides committed by readers imitating the suicide of the character whose melancholy and sense of loss had become their melancholy and their loss. The emotional curve of Goethe's novel, from the elation of a fresh beginning in a new land to the ecstatic promise of happiness, and then the plunge into loss, emptiness, and a sense of nothing left to live for, mimics the very curve of a reader's hope and delight at encountering the first pages that begin a great work, and his or her later depression and world-emptiness as the end approaches.

We could call these mimetic states or speak medically of contagious states. Melancholy and a feeling of emptiness might be endemic to the lives of many novel readers who pick up a novel to fill time and fill up their lives, and who are, necessarily, alone, if not lonely, and solitary, if not abandoned, even before beginning to read this particular novel about the most radical forms of these already existing feelings. State-based realism relies on powerful, likely, preexisting states, especially those natural to the moods and conditions of solitary reading itself.

The European novel produced early on two minor forms of great popularity that make explicit what we might call reading in order to undergo intense states of being. Those two minor forms are the gothic novel and pornography, which like the later romance and detective story people read compulsively so as to enjoy and experience predictable states. In the gothic novel it is fear that is the fundamental state of the reader, who is often alone and often reading at night about a central character also alone at night in a mysterious house or landscape. The reader in bed never knows what surprise or shock will appear on the next page. These white pages that hide the unknown until we turn them mimic exactly those doors that, within the novel, the heroine must overcome her fear to open, those drawers and caskets, boxes and packages, those graves and attics which again and again she must approach and face and explore. Gothic realism is dependent on this parallel fear.

In pornography the state sought by every reader and provided by every work is sexual arousal. The reader who reads alone the story of *Fanny Hill* witnesses and participates in the many scenes of the arousal of the characters, their adventures and climaxes, in parallel to his or her own arousal and climax.

The states on which such realism is based must be intense states of consciousness and body such as melancholy, fear, sexual arousal, laughter, and delight. We should not claim that all merely cognitive similarities between reader and character are states of this kind. Lambert Strether in Henry James's *Ambassadors* is curious about Mme. de Vionnet and we as readers are curious too. Detectives are often confused or mistaken or suspicious, and we are too. Strether accidentally spies on Chad and Mme. de Vionnet, and we too are guilty witnesses of the boating scene. Being surprised, which always happens both to characters and to the readers reading about those characters, is not the foundation for a state-based realism. In painting, many acts of intense looking that we see within the work are mimetic of the viewer's act of looking at the work, often in ways that precisely instruct the viewer that she or he is like a person looking at a naked woman or like a jeweler inspecting a gem up close, or like a general surveying a scene of battle, and so on. At times this is rich enough, deep enough, to create a somatic and state-based realism. I believe that it is in Winslow Homer's *Sharpshooter* but not in his *Station-House*.

We need to preserve carefully the strong states of fear, sorrow, mourning, laughter, sexual arousal, melancholy, elation, and delight—the soul-filling states. We need to keep them distinct from mere cognitive states, moods of all kinds, and from all other interesting feelings if we aim to understand the conviction and evidentiary force of state-based realism. In literature and art we find ourselves with just the genres that we do—tragedy, elegy, pornography, comedy—because of the fact that only certain extreme states are fundamental in aesthetic experience. Both reader and character can burst into laughter, and laughter is, historically, the most widely found shared state in art. Tears of pity, sorrow, and mourning are the second most widely found and used state. Fear is the third.

From Pictures to States: Walt Whitman's Western Wedding

Although pictorial and state-based realism are distinct paths of evidence and conviction, there are important moments in art where we begin in one form and magically change over to the other. The step from pictorial to state-based scenes occurs only rarely in *Song of Myself*. When we find it happening within a painting-like scene a technical act of magic takes place as we move from seeing to being, from Whitman's "I see . . ." to his "I am . . ."

> I saw the marriage of the trapper in the open air in the far west, the bride was a red girl,
> Her father and his friends sat near cross-legged and dumbly smoking, they had moccasins to their feet and large thick blankets hanging from their shoulders,
> On a bank lounged the trapper, he was drest mostly in skins, his luxuriant beard and curls protected his neck, he held his bride by the hand,
> She had long eyelashes, her head was bare, her coarse straight locks descended upon her voluptuous limbs and reach'd to her feet.
>
> sec. 10

This full-scale painting of the western frontier, with its array of actors and its central figure of the bride, is seen, at first, at a respectable distance. We are aware of a scene large enough for one glance to take in the cross-legged group of smoking Indians, the trapper and, at last, his bride. Initially, Whitman defines each person only by his or her clothing or garments: first, the Indians with their moccasins and blankets; then the trapper dressed mostly in skins, but also dressed in his luxuriant curls and beard. After these heavy and masculine blankets, skins, moccasins, and beard, we reach the bride, who seems, in Whitman's description, to have only the covering of her hair; no garments are named after we have been led to expect that his portrait will list what each member of the wedding party wears. Of her he says: "She had long eyelashes," a detail that implies a zoomlike close-up that suddenly makes us intimate with her. It implies that we are standing close enough to see this fact that would be invisible from thirty feet away. Now we seem to be as close to her as the groom himself is. To use the word "bare" in the phrase "her head was bare" lets our attention pass from her eyelashes to the hair of her head, but now indirectly and in a way that sets in play the more encompassing meaning of "bare," the idea of being unclothed.

After the eyelashes we see that her "coarse hair descended upon her voluptuous limbs and reach'd to her feet." Whitman omits to say that her coarse straight locks descended upon the dress or the Indian robe or blanket that covered her voluptuous limbs. By speaking only of the hair and the limbs, the eyelashes and the texture of the hair (coarse), he puts us as close to her as the bridegroom holding her hand, and he invites us to see her or imagine her sexually, as only the bridegroom here has the right to do. Since Whitman has inventoried her by means of her hair and her eyelashes, he leaves a blank space for the final, undescribed triangle of sexual hair.

The pictorial representation with which this painting-like scene begins gives way to a more intimate, and in this case more empathic, state-based narrative—that of the husband. After the thick heavy blankets of the father and his friends, the trapper, too, is seen as hair and skins, but his bride is voluptuous limbs, long eyelashes, and descending full-length locks. Here the pictorial, face-to-face, static image—as though arranged for a daguerreotype—a fully visualized world of surface details such as clothing, finds itself nuanced and transformed into a state-based narrative of the new husband's erotic nearness to these long eyelashes and voluptuous limbs. For this second stage of the pictorial, the central fact is the disparity between the visual evidence of a painting, where there can be no ambiguity about the garment of the bride, and the quite different evidence of poetry or narrative, in which not to name or list the garment after listing the clothes of all the other actors in the scene creates the possibility of nakedness in the aftermath of the word "bare" or the suggestion of the presence of her voluptuous limbs, which, by naming them instead of her clothes, the poet makes us see. The eros with which the bride is enumerated simulates or enters the state of the groom filled with desire for the body of his new bride. What began as a pictorial, framed wedding portrait, seen from a distance, glides into a world only known by invasive participation: co-possession of the bride. Whitman, the trapper, and the reader share what is legitimately only the trapper's state.

Beyond the Pictorial

From any single image, like the one burned into the memory of Jane Addams or like the image of Whitman's wedding party, we can go in three directions.

First, outward to the allegory and subsequent action that follow. Allegorized realism follows a deep cultural form, that of the sermon. Because sermons commonly begin from a fragment of biblical narrative or even an everyday event, any culture with a history of sermon-making carries over those instincts into secular and political occasions. Expounding the images of pictorial realism became one of the staples of secular sermonizing and ethical life and one of the standard practices of literary criticism, which has often been in effect a kind of secular sermon.

The second direction is toward narration. We commonly ask: what is the story behind that image? To tell the story is to set the pictorial into narrative with its attendant causation, its explicit ethical and other structures that no longer accept the image or the visible as self-explanatory. It no longer "speaks for itself." To insist on the real story behind an image such as this is to betray a caution about or even a suspicion of pictorial narrative, because we know that the whole story or the real story might make all of these just-as-they-appear details turn to irony or moral ambiguity. Even to propose narrative is to insist that this image is a singular case, not necessarily typical or innocently representative of conditions. Narration would deny the universalization of the image that just seems natural when taken as a detached picture.

The third direction would be to move laterally to other pictures, each one also self-contained. Eventually, wider representation might build up by sheer numbers. With picture after picture a more reliable whole is set in place. Here too, a skepticism about single images plays a part. Only if other images confirm this, or only if a transparently tendentious genre of pictures does not reveal itself, will we accept the picture. In this third direction we move out toward taking a census of the visible.

The features of pictorial and state-based realism that I have defined so far are characteristic only of the experience of looking long and carefully at one image. In dwelling on an image we enter it as though it were, for a moment, the whole world, the real. Our time spent attending to it, simply as time, honors or respects the conditions and persons within the image. If we think of the phrase "I don't have time enough for *that*" or "Do you expect me to waste my time on *that*?" we can see just what level of honor, respect, or love is implied simply in the demand for time and the viewer's willingness to give time.

In Whitman's *Song of Myself* we stop to notice, to honor, and to include within the space of representation, person after person, occupation after occupation. We find ourselves with a fast-moving, short-term attention, required and then replaced, line after line, moment by moment. One part of the task that Whitman set himself has much in common with the new idea in the nineteenth century that political society must, every ten years, take a census. Not only must citizens be counted, but the conditions of their lives must be known if society and politics are to function. The facts of national life must be brought to light. Everyone must be counted; all states and ways of life must be included. Whitman sets himself to picture the states and conditions of his fellow citizens and he does so by means of occupations, by means of well-known types, and by means of quick pictorial notations that have the structure of photographs. The "Song of Myself" is most often a song of myself by means of others, each allowed a line or a few lines of attention, each brought into the light of poetic attention.

> The opium-eater reclines with rigid head and just-open'd lips

or

> As the fare-collector goes through the train he gives notice by the
>   jingling of loose change

or

> The western turkey-shooting draws old and young, some lean on
>   their rifles, some sit on logs,
> Out from the crowd steps the marksman, takes his position, levels
>   his piece
>
> sec. 15

Such quick, sharply registered scenes, presented a dozen at a time in "Song of Myself," carry the central features of visibility and shared attention that make realism of this kind essentially a democratic project of representation. As Whitman put it, "Each who passes is consider'd, each who stops is consider'd, not a single one can it fail" (sec. 43).

Each figure is seen frontally, at a distance, engaged in his or her life. This is the ordinary and the everyday and because, contrary to our stake in the heroic or the moral, we all have equal shares in the ordinary and the everyday, we all expect the small flashlight of attention to turn to us. Each scene is given only a brief line or two, so that more and more can have, in their turn, some moments of undivided attention. In each scene, there is only one central actor, opium-eater, fare-collector, or marksman at the turkey shoot, and a magic circle excludes accidental nearby figures so that the focus can be complete. We know them by their work or actions and each is the type of all other blacksmiths, turkey-shoot competitors, opium-eaters, or spinning-girls.

Free of drama or of individualizing words or moments, they are, as people are in paintings, without past or future, just as they are now, in this glance, forever. The actions must be repeated ones, like the moment of chopping a log, one blow of the ax that stands for ten thousand such blows over a lifetime. Representation samples: this turn of the wheel out of a million, this rifle-aim out of the thousands of national turkey shoots, this moment of intoxication out of thousands of others. People are sampled as well as actions. Just this girl, here and now, with all other spinning-girls implied behind her; these blacksmiths with all other shops and fires and anvils behind them. The practice of representation, in the political sense, that sends one congressman from every five hundred thousand citizens can also be applied to literature by means of types, sampling, anonymity, and representation.

Whitman's brief pictures attend for a moment to unnamed people. Without unique traits they carry out generic, everyday actions. As with figures in a painting, we don't know them, except as appearances. It is this way that we, in everyday life, know "passers-by" in the streets—the driver of a car, the policeman directing traffic, the young woman on her way to work. This pictorial relation is the one that we stand in to a familiar world, familiar because we recognize and grasp who these people are, what they are doing, why someone might be—in Whitman's day—around an anvil, with a fire, striking with heavy hammers. Yet it is not a small-town world where we would know the name of the blacksmith, his story or the reason why he still works late into the night, and so on. These people in Whitman's images are comprehensible strangers, seen once and once only, passers-by in the city streets. They are freed from their stories, as all people seen only once are.

The pictorial has a frontal and complete structure. There are no shadows that hide from us the rest of the action. There is no policeman lurking around the corner who will soon arrest one of the blacksmiths—actually an escaped felon pretending for a moment to be only a blacksmith. Such an ironized or expectant story does not exist in the pictorial. We are not about-to-be-surprised, a condition that is fundamental to listening to stories as opposed to seeing pictures.

The pictorial within realism allows a distance, like that at which we see the working life of the young woman at her spinning wheel without getting any closer to involvement with her. She does not speak and she has no story. That silence is part of the dignity of the actors, but it is also a protective fact, because by seeing without speaking we remain in a comfortable and distinct space apart: she in her world unaware of us, we in our world seeing her through a pane of glass.

Whitman's contemporary Winslow Homer produced hundreds of illustrations and prints that carry out in the realm of drawing and printmaking the representation of the dignity of each of the ways of work of his countrymen.

Silence and the Witness

What we acknowledge in pictorial realism is the power to "burn unforgettable images" into the memory forever and by that means to create unforgettable visual states of affairs. Jane Addams records a small set of these brief and shocking images and offers them as an explanation of her life at Hull House. All visual images in narrative are rendered as descriptions, and it is brief paragraph-long or page-long descriptions that preserve the near-instantaneousness that is a crucial feature of the power of sudden, unexpected images. All such examples are photograph-like in placing us face to face with people and conditions whose past and future are unknown to us. The pure present time of a picture releases the actors from causation and responsibility, from fear or hope. They have presence at the price of having pure presence. Where they come from, what happens next, whether they are good or evil, the victims or the agents of these conditions that we see in front of us, cannot be shown, because in the image they are precisely not part of a story with its links of past, present, and future, its assignment of responsibility and credit. The world we see pictorially is the whole world: no rescue awaits just off stage; no bank in town is there to be visited with the hope for a loan. Just this is all there is.

Finally, in pictorial narrative the actors are silent. They are seen, and because seeing implies being far enough away to see the entire scene—not too close, not too far—we know that a subtle protective distance is built into a scene like Jane Addams's image of the farm. We see this from the road as we pass. We know it as we know things about strangers. Travel often confronts us with the purely visual (in part because we do not know the language, but also in part because we do not have the right to inquire of the people that we see). We are not acquainted, and because, in travel, we move in a world of strangers they are known to us pictorially as what we call "sights." The boy leading a reluctant goat across the road, a woman in tattered clothes asleep by a hedge, two men fighting and rolling in the dirt outside a store, a group of well-dressed picnickers under a tree: these sights of travel are always pictures of strangers whose stories are unknown to us. When we say "his story is unknown to me" we state the important way in which the pictorial, the merely seen, stands outside narrative, outside stories altogether. Its essence is a presumed but unknown story. About this story the people seen in a photograph or in Thomas Eakins's *The Agnew Clinic* are silent. Silence is a crucial fact about the visual, because it would only be by means of speech that this present moment might take its place in antecedent causes, in surrounding conditions, in hopes or fears for tomorrow, and in the assignment of credit or blame. When we say, in looking at a photograph, "What's the story here?" we are after the knowledge that would fill in both social and moral facts about the true state of affairs behind what appears here as brute fact.

The visual is one of the prime examples of what we mean by brute fact, and by what we know to be the defect of brute fact, which in its strong, unforgettable presence is likely to mislead us about the real story of which this pictured state is a sample in space and time. It has been, as we say of photographs, "cropped." If we want to see more in space or hear more of the time before and the time after, the pictorial will yield nothing beyond its strong claim that what we see in front of our eyes clearly exists. The picture is evidence for the existence of just what we see but with the added important implied truth that we see it *as though what we see were all that exists.*

That what we see is "the whole story" and is representative of what we cannot see, and that its details, as we say, "speak for themselves" are key assumptions of the pictorial. The pictorial could be called a "self-allegorizing" form, because the instance in front of us invites us to leap to the largest social and moral conclusions without any other evidence than the one scene by means of which those ideas might be illustrated. Scenes can only be self-allegorizing where the audience shares ideas, values, and ways of reading single, detached pieces of evidence. The self-allegorizing works because it lines up with what we already know or feel, and with how we already think. It is in pictorial realism that the strange paradox of the close tie between the empiricism of realism and the seemingly opposite claims of allegory must be noticed.

In this summary of "missing features" in the pictorial or visual form of realism, I have stressed the brevity in written pictorial narrative of the description—usually only a few sentences; the absence of past and future; the exemption from narrative and story (or even the hostility to story); the important silence of the figures seen in pictures who cannot or do not explain themselves or tell us about themselves, or rather allow the scene to speak for them and tell us all we need to know about them. I have stressed as well the physical distance implied in the visual; the category of the stranger; the link to travel or other forms of one-time encounter such as the investigation or the fact-finding trip; and finally the consequence, once all these features are put together, of a self-allegorizing relation between the brute fact of the image and social or moral generalities. Pictorial realism works on our feelings, as Jane Addams's example makes clear, by means of sudden impact. It depends on strong feelings like horror, pity, or guilt that this unforgettable image ignites in the viewer as the prelude to taking action. That action is what we call reform, whether accomplished by new laws, individual charity, or a change in the mind of the viewer and reform of his or her investment strategy.

Voice and Testimony: From *Uncle Tom's Cabin* to *Miss Lonelyhearts*

If we think of the pictorial as evidence of the real as undeniable fact, then the nature of that evidence as a single instance has to be remembered. What is present in a picture is one person, one situation, one case, as we might call it. Pictorial realism should also be called case-based realism. Our trust that this "really happened" just as it seems to be is buttressed by the neutrality of the description.

The facts of the scene are in front of us—pigs, a woman, her children. Here is one case, one example we can refer to, one memory we can recall. Statistical realism would tell us how many farmers were starving, how many mortgages were foreclosed this year compared to last, how prudent the farmers were in putting aside savings from good years, what percentage of them were shiftless or hard working, how good or bad the soil was for the type of work they did. Statistical realism—the ultimate modern basis for action—moves beyond the case, which might or not be representative, even if it is true in the sense of accurately reflecting what we call "the whole story." There is, as we say, the truth, the whole truth, and nothing but the truth. Statistical realism is impossible in either the pictorial or the narrative mode. Both the story-telling form of evidence and the pictorial form of evidence are case-based. One and only one condition or state of affairs is given presence.

Narration strips itself of most of its resources in its moments of description. Within nineteenth-century realism an important second form of evidence for the real was possible because a witness, a person speaking in his or her own words to tell the story of a life, was possible for the first time. The witness appeared along with dialect, the tolerance for ordinary lives, the new use of real-time scenes in fiction, and above all the willingness of authors to surrender page after page of their text to other speakers, their exact words recorded within quotation marks that tell us: the author did not write these words; he took them down as best he could. He effaced himself, suspended his style and vocabulary and habits of thought for these pages so that another could speak in her own words.

We do not often think how odd it is that a writer fills pages of his or her text with conversation or with the scenes that are defined by conversation. Certainly one remarkable fact about the realistic novel is that alongside the radically increasing percentage of description in the novel after Sir Walter Scott, there are also, in the aftermath of Scott and Jane Austen, ever larger scenes, exchanges, monologues, and other occasions where the author's voice and style are absent from the text, replaced by the often less sophisticated words of the characters. Whether we think of Stowe's *Uncle Tom's Cabin* or Crane's *Maggie* or Tolstoy's *War and*

Peace or such later works as the first part of Faulkner's *Sound and the Fury* or Henry Roth's *Call It Sleep*, the gesture in which the author steps aside to allow, in real time, a complete directly stated conversation or interchange to take place, with each word locked within the cell of quotation marks, should amaze us. It is an unprecedented fact in literature. In a number of famous works—*War and Peace, Buddenbrooks, To the Lighthouse*, the author disappears before even appearing. The first words of the text are quotation-marked conversation. Another self is present before the author appears. The attempt at authenticity or the appearance of authenticity within the quotation marks increased dramatically. Dashes, elided words, slang, dialect, broken-off thoughts, recognizable ethnic speech distinct from the author's, class and regional clues were all multiplied after Scott. In fact Scott guaranteed that he would be the greatest unread author in the history of the novel by creating unreadably authentic texts, pages across which the reader stumbles, conversations that must be puzzled out like a foreign page inserted in a newspaper.

The costs paid by literature between Scott and American ethnic writers of the 1930s were willingly paid out of a democratic impulse, on the one hand, and a notion of testimony and witnessing, on the other, that required that each person, in his or her own words, retain the right to tell his own story, her own story. No summary by the author, no retelling. Each person, as in a courtroom, speaks of what he knows, has seen, remembers, and will swear has happened.

Of course, much of what we remember from such voiced realism serves to define the casual daily-ness of exchange—the street talk of immigrants or city children in Roth's *Call It Sleep* or James Farrell's *Studs Lonigan*, where dialect and talk are part of what we could call mere authenticity. In Stephen Crane's *Maggie: A Girl of the Streets* we hear the conversation of Maggie's mother and brother after her seduction in this way:

> "She had a bad heart, dat girl did, Jimmie. She was wicked teh deh heart an' we never knowed it."
> Jimmie nodded, admitting the fact.

"We lived in deh same house wid her an' I brought her up an' we never knowed how bad she was."

Jimmie nodded again.

"Wid a home like dis an' a mudder like me, she went teh deh bad," cried the mother, raising her eyes.[12]

Crane's rather cheap irony here, using the mother's complaint to indict her own self-pitying drunken responsibility for all that has happened to Maggie, reflects the sophisticated puppeteer behind the naive dialect passage. But this almost traditionally comic and condescending double vision defines best the traditional use of "rustic" talk, even as we would find it in Shakespeare, and not at all the new voice-centered realism. In Crane we use the mother's actual words and feelings to ironize, that is, to disidentify from her perspective on the death of Maggie.

In Twain's *Adventures of Huckleberry Finn* we hear a story in which the author's voice has, in advance, given way to the racy idiom of the boy Huck Finn. This in turn prepares the way for his voice to give way to the many other moments in which someone is recorded in real time, speaking for himself. Jim's account to Huck of why he did not sleep is a perfect instance of a witness speaking in his own voice to tell a story that is his and his alone.

"What makes me feel so bad dis time, 'uz bekase I hear sumpn over yonder on de bank like a whack, er a slam, while ago, en it mine me er de time I treat my little 'Lizabeth so ornery. She warn't on'y 'bout fo' year ole, en she tuck de sk'yarlet-fever, en had a powful rough spell; but she got well, en one day she was a-stannin' aroun', en I says to her, I says:

"'Shet de do'.'

"She never done it; jis' stood dah, kiner smilin' up at me. It make me mad; en I says agin, mighty loud, I says:

"'Doan' you hear me?—shet de do'!'

"'She jis' stood de same way, kiner smilin' up. I was a-bilin'! I says:

"'I lay I *make* you mine!'

"En wid dat I fetch' her a slap side de head dat sont her a-sprawlin'. Den I went into de yuther room, en 'uz gone 'bout ten minutes; en when I come back, dah was dat do' a-stannin' open *yit*, en dat chile stannin' mos' right in it, a-lookin' down and mournin', en de tears

runnin' down. My, but I *wuz* mad, I was agwyne for de chile, but jis'
den—it was a do' dat open innerds—jis' den, 'long come de wind en
slam it to, behine de chile, ker-*blam!*—en my lan', de chile never
move'! My breff mos' hop outer me; en I feel so—so—I doan' know
how I feel. I crope out, all a-tremblin', en crope aroun' en open de do'
easy en slow, en poke my head in behine de chile, sof' en still, en all
uv a sudden, I says *pow!* jis' as loud as I could yell. *She never budge!* Oh,
Huck, I bust out a-cryin' en grab her up in my arms, en say, 'Oh, de
po' little thing! de Lord God Almighty fogive po' ole Jim, kaze he
never gwyne to fogive hisself as long's he live!' Oh, she was plumb
deef en dumb, Huck, plumb deef en dumb—en I'd ben a-treat'n her
so!"[13]

What Jim tells is not a secret, but it is so painful a domestic and
intimate fact, something known to him alone, that his choice to tell
it now confers intimacy and trust on whoever hears it. It is what is
on his mind, what "makes him feel so bad." The telling of this
private story opens up a realm of intimate experience that he has
chosen to share with Huck, unlike the visual, which is there for
everyone to see. To know what someone is thinking about, what is
troubling him, what he thinks of as the worst thing he has ever
done, what he castigates himself about, how stupidly or with what
cruelty he acted at a certain moment—to know this is to be already
admitted to the most personal of relations. Voice-based realism is
intimate to just the extent that pictorial realism is framed at a
suitable, silent distance, and voice-based realism is chosen rather
than distributed at large to whoever happens to see the publicly
visible. Paradoxically, the very goal of realism—to show in public—meant that it was for the public, for citizens at large, for
anyone, that the scenes of pictorial realism came to exist, and it was
just around this point that voice-based realism with its chosen
intimacy could go one step farther.

In Twain's novel this remarkable moment, told in Jim's own
words, transporting us back to the real time of the scene that he
recalls, word by word and gesture by gesture, captures the essence
of voice-based realism. The page of the novel encloses the entire
scene within quotation marks, but Twain requires a whole bag of
typographic tricks to create the scene; italics for individual words

or phrases, exclamation points for voicing, dashes, single quotes within quotes, apostrophes to mark dropped letters, freshly spelled words, repeated or doubled phrases, false starts and self-correction, spoken conventions that hyphenate pairs of words into such terms as "a-bilin," and sound terms like *pow* or ker-*blam*. The printed page is tortured to carry this scene; the typographical resources of English are pushed as far as any great author has ever pushed them.

Why has Twain done this? Note first of all that the scene itself is no longer a visual one. Huck listens to Jim and over Huck's shoulder we do too. The story has as its deep subject matters of sound and deafness, noises and responses to noise, questions or commands and the silent response to those spoken and sometimes angry words. The scene before our minds (Huck and Jim in camp) does not exist in the narrative at this moment. The story has devisualized itself so that Jim's words can be heard and so that the scene called up within those words, a scene given in second-by-second, real-time narration, can be heard and known as he tells it. Jim is a witness, testifying against himself, but ultimately for himself because his pain is the evidence of his goodness.

To read this scene at all I have to act it out. My voice has to try to become Jim's voice with his vocabulary, his excitement, his emphatic or italicized words, his pronunciation of words that I myself would pronounce differently. To grasp or read his story I have to align myself with him fundamentally, seeing with his eyes, hearing with his ears, feeling his anger followed by his remorse. On the page, the strange letters and marks that I decipher mark out for me his difference from myself. When he hesitates or can't say exactly, I do the same. His language and my language are as distinct as our two educations, cultures, internal thought patterns. The surface difference of recorded speech stand for the difference of status, race, age, historical period, and condition.

But the essence of testimony, of voiced evidence, lies in the fact that the difference gives way to a common humanity because Jim feels or acts just the same as we do beneath this strangely distinct language and vocabulary or strangely distinct skin color and condition. This obvious goal of realism to embody the world views in distinct spellings—so to speak—only as a preliminary to erasing them in the name of a common humanity is central to the nineteenth-century humanism of differences, in which understanding and common purpose are presumed to be within reach of Huck and Jim, or Jim and the reader, whenever fundamental human facts are at stake—family life and feelings, and in particular the parental relation to a child.

To state the obvious: Narrative that uses the resources of mimetic, spoken, real-time testimony has in its hands the key resort denied the visual or pictured scene. The audible realism of the witness whose story is his own, whose moral life and inner life appear in the basic facts of what is remembered and why, as well as in all details of vocabulary, emphasis, analysis, or characterization of the scene, retains for itself a whole realm of evidence that is fundamental, especially within the reading act. To hear Jim say these words is one thing. To read from the page and supply his voice from within ourselves as readers is another, more intimate participation in his story. In other words, one powerful element within voiced realism is precisely the fact that it is not directly voiced—as in a play on the stage—but must be voiced in my own inner voice imagining Jim's voice as I read. I have to become him for the page of the story. The capacity of the novel, after Scott, to insist that its readers become other voices, other inner lives, frequently those from worlds far from their own, is essential to its use of intimate demands for the novel's own purposes.

In the eighteenth chapter of Stowe's *Uncle Tom's Cabin* the drunken and dissolute servant Prue tells Uncle Tom her story. The entire chapter prior to this story is made up of quoted conversation in the kitchen. Many voices have for a moment taken over the page before the reader encounters these sentences. Tom asks Prue,

"Where was you raised?" . . .

"Up in Kentuck. A man kept me to breed chil'en for market, and sold 'em as fast as they got big enough; last of all, he sold me to a speculator, and my Mas'r got me o' him."

"What set you into this bad way of drinkin'?"

"To get shet o' my misery. I had one child after I come here; and I thought then I'd have one to raise, 'cause Mas'r was n't a speculator. It was de peartest little thing! and Missis she seemed to think a heap on't, at first; it never cried—it was likely and fat. But Missis tuck sick, and I tended her; and I tuck the fever, and my milk all left me, and the child it pined to skin and bone, and Missis would n't buy milk for it. She would n't hear to me, when I telled her I had n't milk. She said she knowed I could feed it on what other folks eat; and the child kinder pined, and cried, and cried, and cried, day and night, and got all gone to skin and bones, and Missis got sot agin it, and she said 't wan't nothin' but crossness. She wished it was dead, she said; and she would n't let me have it o' nights, 'cause, she said, it kept me awake, and made me good for nothing. She made me sleep in her room; and I had to put it away off in a little kind o' garret, and thar it cried itself to death, one night. It did; and I tuck to drinkin', to keep its crying out of my ears!"[14]

Prue's explanation is not only given in her voice and heard by Tom and through Tom, by us, but it is, like Jim's story in *Huck Finn*, deeply about sounds—the crying child at night, the mistress's words that pass it all off as "crossness." The sounds of child, mistress, slave, and hearer are all focused on a scene of Prue caring for—nursing—the sick mistress while being unable to care for or nurse the child. At the end we focus on the scene of death, which gains its real-time location from the exact narration of the one teller who can never forget the story, because it is her own story, and because it is the one story that has deformed her forever, changed her into a careless and death-seeking rebel.

Not only is Prue's story told in her own voice, it is about the spatiality of the voice. She must sleep near the mistress so as to be called at any hour of the night. Her child is put out of sight, but not out of the voice range where her cries reach back to the mother forced to abandon her. Tom has taken her aside so as to walk with her close enough to ask questions and hear her story. The space of understood sound is more intimate—necessarily intimate, intimate before any word is spoken—because of how close we must stand to another person to be able, as we say, to hear every word she said.

I would like to make the following claim: With its mimetic attempt to let the story be told not just "in his own words" but in his own voice or her own voice, in the "dialect," as we so weakly refer to it, realistic narrative created the first successful form of intimacy and inwardness since the letter, which in the hands of Richardson and Rousseau had propelled the novel into its central place in middle-class Europe. Like the intimate letter, the spoken story that Jim or Prue relates is a direct account of the most personal feelings and events. Such events are "shared" rather than told. They are like secrets because to be told such things implies that anyone who hears is trusted (as Tom is by Prue, or Huck by Jim) and included in the teller's innermost world. Like the letter, the spoken word is also a real-time event. And like the letter, the quoted words imply that the author is for the moment not speaking. The letter is made up only and completely of the unedited, unaltered, unsummarized, and most important of all, uncommented on (by the author in his distinct voice) inner statement of a distinct person.

It was the novel of letters that brought subjectivity and inwardness into literature in a new way, and it was the novel of voice-based realism that a hundred years later recaptured, by new means, the novel's capacity to render in an unprecedented way intimacy, inwardness, the realm of private thought and feeling, and the strongly felt reality of another distinct person, his or her moral and emotional world, his or her own sense of fate and life, uncontaminated by the embedding of all that is uniquely his or her own experience in the larger world of the author's purposes and world view. The typographical signs of a letter—the date, greeting, (Dear . . .), and close (Yours . . .)—worked exactly as quotation marks did in the later novel, protecting this personalized world from invasion or preemption by the author's thoughts, feelings, reactions, or words. In both the letter and the quoted passages, one decisive fact is that all material is given complete; no editing by the author has taken place, no three dots of deletion or ellipse. The words are just as written or spoken, every word present, just as the person chose to utter or write them. By means of either letters or voice-based realism, the very absence of the author certifies that a radical place has been opened up in the text for the full existence of another person.

In *Miss Lonelyhearts* Nathanael West merged letters and the voice of the victim to create, in the letters from "Broad Shoulders," "Desperate," and "Sick-of-it-all," a classic and ultimate superimposition of these two most powerful, intimate forms of realism. In the letter from "Broad Shoulders" we enter the moral world of a monstrous marriage.

> Things were a little out of order beds not dressed and things out of place and a little sweeping had to be done as I was washing all morning and I didn't have a chance to do it so I thought to do it then while my mother was in the house with her to help me so that I could finish quickly. Hurrying at break neck speed to get finished I swept through the rooms to make sure everything was spick and span so when my husband came home he couldn't have anything to say. We had three beds and I was on the last which was a double bed when stooping to put the broom under the bed to get at the lint and the dust when lo and behold I saw a face like the mask of a devil with only the whites of the eyes showing and hands clenched to choke anyone and then I saw it move and I was so frighted that almost till night I was hystirical and I was paralised from my waist down. I thought I would never be able to walk again. A doctor was called for me by my mother and he said the man ought to be put in an asylum to do a thing like that. It was my husband lieing under the bed from seven in the morning until almost half past one o'clock lieing in his own dirt instead of going to the bath room when he had to be dirtied himself waiting to fright me.[15]

Note here that by calling attention to the woman's misspellings, which readers recognize only because neither they nor West make such mistakes, the author separates us from her, differentiates us and leads us to feel sorry for her in a very different way—"poor uneducated woman." In Huck Finn every representational or orthographic fact brought us closer to Jim's mind and feelings. Here a cold, distancing irony that makes us see the wife as a child, because it is children who misspell most, divorces our sensibility right at every key moment in order to distract us by means of the attention to her spelling. Because this is a letter, not a spoken moment, orthography does not at all give the presence of her voice.

The audible realm of the conversation and the pictorial realm of the first glimpse are deeply alternative systems of representation in realism. The pictorial and descriptive become convincing by means of the odd, seemingly arbitrary detail, and this detail in its turn depends on the moment, in looking, when we focus or stand close to the object of our attention. In the spoken scene, it is the real-time play of distinct voices, and behind those voices, of distinct minds, perspectives, and mentalities, that guarantees the genuineness of the reality.

One thing being forced on our attention in both of these methods of realism is the feeling of physical remoteness that operates in society. Realism, in its descriptive detail—exact, carefully inspected—and in its recorded speech, brings us close up, face to face as we stand in speaking or hearing. When we hear "every word that is said" we are close enough to hear those words. They are not across the street or across the room—those distances at which people are purely visual facts. To hear speech we must be within the circle of conversation in which both speakers and hearers stand three or four feet from the people in the story. Similarly, to see just this detail of the long eyelashes of Whitman's trapper's bride we must be no more than four or five feet from her, "close up" as we call it in films or photographs, close up and certain of this evidence of the real. And it is by means of this evidence that one after another each member of the democratic population is brought voice by voice and voice after voice into representation and, therefore, into that part of the real where each person counts.

Inventing New Frames for Realism

Details within realism, whether visual, state-based, or voice-driven, are small-scale features of the larger work. Those larger works themselves exist on an equally dynamic and ever-changing scale of forms. We might think of the history of these changing forms almost as the history of a technology. For realism the analogy is more than a metaphor. Story-telling on the printed page has coexisted for more than a century with rival, forms: the photograph, the page of a newspaper, the radio with its voices, and the film with its odd coupling of the visual and a world of sound that includes not only voices and sound effects, but background music that acts like a manipulative set of emotional directions delivered alongside the work itself.

How the novel coexisted with, profited from, and sometimes lost out to these popular storytelling forms that also delivered a form of realistic representation is the topic of this final chapter. I hope to show that a form of creative destruction exists within literary forms no less than within transportation systems or systems for the transfer of messages at a long distance. The history of the realistic rival to abstraction is given here as an Emersonian history in which ever new circles have been imposed from unexpected and challenging directions on the techniques for giving form to the evidence of

what counts as real. Emerson demanded that all histories be the
history of surprises.

Realism and the City

In what follows I want to look at the transition from a system of
representation in the American city novel centered in literary realism and naturalism to a new system of representation that was no
longer political but modernist in its central emphasis on the artist,
on the accumulation of experiences, on the sexual, and on the
disconnection of moments of experience from one another. The
categories that I use to define this period from roughly 1890 to 1940
will, with modification, point beyond this period to the next generation's work in the novel. In particular, I will discuss the passage
from one model of social life and the social novel that reflects that
life—the model of conversation around a dining room table—to
models inspired by such media as the photograph, the newspaper,
the film, and the voices heard over the radio. These rival media will
define, I hope, a large tract of experiment and reconstruction within
the technique of the novel in the first half of this century.

The history that I want to trace is a paradoxical one. In brief it is
the change—at the level of content and ethos—within the city
novel from the type of victim narratives that are typical of literary
naturalism to narratives of bohemian freedom; from accounts of
suffering to catalogues of pleasure; from a picture of the city as a
single-minded machine of indifference and destruction to a picture
of the city as a small-scale field of daily opportunities for adventure,
for experience, for excitement. The city as we see it reflected in the
novel became, by 1920, a world rich in novelties of personality and
fate. If we consider the use of the narrative "accident," we can
quickly grasp this change. In a typical naturalist novel of 1890 to
1910 the classic example of an accident is a catastrophe, a house on
fire, an automobile wreck, the killing of a man in the street by a
stray bullet. By the time of Dreiser's *Gallery of Women* (1929) a typical
"accident" is likely to be the unexpected meeting in a Greenwich
Village studio with someone who will become part of an adventure,
a love affair, a whirl of activity and life-changing pleasure.

What is paradoxical about this history is that in many cases the same materials of urban experience continued to be used, but with new meanings assigned. The outsider continues to be the central figure, but by 1920 is no longer beaten down and destroyed, but free-spirited, improvisational, even joyfully marginal in the style of bohemian life. The novel holds on to an implicit norm of a middle-class way of life that is offstage and unavailable, but by the 1920s that way of life is no longer desired, or remembered nostalgically. It is even held in contempt. The milieu of poverty defines both the naturalist and the bohemian novel of the city, but the meaning of material want had changed from that of desperation to that of freedom from material interest. The central characters of both naturalist and bohemian urban novels are defined by the stance of dreaming, but by 1920 the point of view of the author toward the dream, or toward idealism and hope, is no longer one of irony, but one of participation in the dream of art and experience.

The location of the novel in a social world where the family is no longer a working center for continuity in experience, the representation of temporary rather than enduring experiences, and the turbulence of social life—its unreliability and insecurity along with its variety—are all given conditions of such works as Stephen Crane's *Maggie* (1893) or Theodore Dreiser's *Sister Carrie* (1900), as much as of such later bohemian works as Henry Miller's *Tropic of Capricorn* (1933) or Dreiser's great work of 1929, *A Gallery of Women*. How can the identical materials suddenly appear with entirely new meanings? How does the sexual disorder of the 1890s become the sexual bohemianism of John Dos Passos's *Manhattan Transfer* (1925) or Dreiser's *Gallery of Women*? How, for example, does the simple motif of drinking change its meaning between the late nineteenth century, when it stands for the despair and hopeless violence, the dead end of experience (as it does in Crane's *Maggie*), and the 1920s and 1930s, when it represents the glamorous world of experimentation with consciousness, the freedom from bourgeois values that alcohol and drugs represent as part of the urban milieu of Dreiser's *Gallery of Women*, not to mention the world of the urban cafe, the speakeasy, and the night club of Dos Passos, Fitzgerald, Hemingway, and Henry Miller? How does the city itself pass from killing machine to playground?

Photographs and Exposés: The Implicit Media of Naturalism

In the years between 1890 and 1900 Howells's *Hazard of New Fortunes* or Crane's *Maggie,* along with Dreiser's climactic *Sister Carrie* of 1900, defined the norm for a socially conscious account of the city. This social consciousness can be seen in Henry James's travel book, *The American Scene* of 1904, as well as in the photographs of Jacob Riis after 1890, and, most important of all, within the crusading journalism of the period. The city is seen as an array of problems that require and invite action. Even an aesthete like James thinks of the city as the "problem" of the alien (the rising number of immigrants), the "problem" of the language, the "problem" of the new relations between men and women. Each of Jacob Riis's photographs pinpoints a "problem" for the middle-class viewer's attention: overcrowding in the slums, child labor, the street lives of children, the dirt or darkness of city slum life, the harsh working conditions of urban labor. Each "problem" can be solved; conditions can be "improved" if only the viewer will "do something to help." The photograph, along with the newspaper exposé, should be seen as the key new media defining the kind of incontestable truth that naturalism and realism sought, in a metaphor appropriate to photography, to "bring to light." Darkness, shadow, obscurity, invisibility were all dispersed by the spotlight of the press, the flashbulb of the photographer, and the descriptive practice of the novelist, who "reported" back to his middle-class audience on what he had seen and witnessed.

The naturalist novel, it must be said, dealt with a level of experience darker than that captured by the photographs of Jacob Riis. Lives crushed by circumstance, by the system, by poverty; a world of inequality; the corruption of political life—these are typical of the material of such novels. The real center of concern is the problem of the conscience of the liberal middle class (particularly in a writer like Howells). But the question of indifference to, or action in the face of, suffering, corruption, and inequality that is

241

posed inside the Howells novel is naturally the central rhetorical question between every book and its typical middle-class comfortable reader. The same question governs the rhetoric of social documentary photography from the work of Riis to the Dust Bowl photographs of the 1930s. It is the "heart" of the middle-class viewer or reader that is at stake in the socially-conscious realistic or naturalistic fiction. Once that reader's feelings have been touched, he or she is meant to be moved to action, that is, to support reform, improvement, political change. The appeal by means of alternate doses of shock and sentiment works on the reader's sympathies and sense of outrage or guilt in a way that is little changed from the time of the novels of Charles Dickens in the 1840s, 1850s, and 1860s. The films of Charlie Chaplin between 1915 and 1935 took over directly the tone and humor of Dickens to represent poverty, immigration, and the world of modern labor and urban life.

One strange fact about the mechanisms of naturalism was that they worked almost as effectively at every level of social life. In Edith Wharton's greatest novel, and the single best New York novel of the first decade of the twentieth century, *The House of Mirth* of 1905, we watch an outsider lose her footing and accelerate her social descent until the novel ends with her solitude, drug use, and suicide. Although Wharton's is a novel of upper-class New York society, the mechanism of the plot is the story of an inexorable fall much like that of Dreiser's middle-class businessman George Hurstwood in *Sister Carrie* (1900), who flees to New York, where he remains a nameless outsider in steady decline. Finally, in a Bowery hotel he kills himself in an ending with much the same tone as the suicide that ends *The House of Mirth*. At the other extreme of the social scale from Wharton's novel, Stephen Crane's *Maggie* traces the grinding down, the "fall," and finally the death of its central figure. The report of Maggie's death that ends Crane's novella works out the same rhetorical formula as the death of Wharton's heroine and Dreiser's hero.

Wharton, Dreiser, and Crane are writing about three absolutely different social levels that range from the heights of New York society in Wharton's case, to the declining middle-class businessman in Dreiser's, to the squalid tenement-dwelling, working-class, hard-drinking family of Crane's novella. Yet in each case the novel's plot traces the snuffing out of a life. Each author poses the Darwinian question of survival or extinction. The answer is always given in the final scene of extinction.

The pattern for this type of urban novel was invented by Emile Zola in *L'assommoir* (1876), in which the history of Gervaise is the history of her decline, her brave moments of illusion, her dreams, and the underlying process of wearing out, like that of a shirt that in its lifetime of washings becomes ever thinner each time it is, for a time, made to look like new. The wearing out of vitality, the decline into lethargy and indifference, was one of the great subjects of the novel of naturalism. It made the novel into a study of energy rather than moral life with its choices, consequences, and responsibilities. With naturalism the topic of energy replaced the topic of good and evil. "Giving up" or "giving in," surrender; agreeing to fall into bed or into a world of drinking; a lethargy that no longer resists what is inevitable: these are what remain as a kind of sensuality of defeat within naturalism.

Within the naturalist novel we find ourselves again and again with characters who can be said never to have had a chance or, most important of all, never to have really lived. By contrast, the city novel after 1920 places at the center figures determined to live, hungry for experience, amoral in their individualism and in their egotistic relation to the possibilities around them. Dos Passos's *Manhattan Transfer*, Dreiser's *Gallery of Women*, and Miller's *Tropic of Capricorn*, along with the novels of F. Scott Fitzgerald, define a center for this representation of New York as a chaos of values and possibilities, a chaos of perception and sexual atmosphere in which, as in Joyce's *Ulysses*, the central consciousness within experience tolerates and lives off the very urban disorder that within naturalism, with its assumed background of middle-class normality (steady work, family life, home and children, economic improvement), had been lethal.

By 1925 the city novel had freed itself from loyalty or pretended loyalty to a norm of stable family life—marriage, children, home, and work. That family norm had haunted the urban novel from the time of Dickens and had permitted the realistic or naturalistic novel to display moral outrage at the many details of urban life that made that family norm more and more difficult to realize or preserve. The realistic and naturalistic novel in America was distorted in its account of urban life because it charged the city with a hostility to the norms of small-town or rural life. By 1925 this family norm had vanished and a new norm of the temporary, of free-wheeling individualism, of the search for experience and excitement, of the dreamer and the artist, had taken over. By 1925 New York City was, if anything, even more hostile to the possibility of a small-town norm of family life, but it was no longer being viewed by novelists through this single-minded frame of reference.

Models for the Social Novel: Conversation, Newspapers, Unseen Voices, Film

In the remainder of this chapter I will offer a series of models for social and, primarily, urban fiction. First, the domestic model of Howells's *Hazard of New Fortunes*. This might be called the model of the dinner table, since Howells in essence tries to extend the novel of manners so as to take in the variety of classes, social groups, ways of life, and manners that make up the complexity of city life. The round dinner table where all are equal is something of a central symbol for the novel of manners, and that is why I would like to think of this first model as an ever larger table where the varieties of culture can somehow find a common language in which to communicate and act together. This model of the novel of manners, but without its snobbery, social exclusion, and feminine emphasis, is nonetheless a hopelessly middle-class form of fiction, one based on the utopian project of imagining the entire urban world as eventually subject to middle-class norms and interests. Ultimately, the long discussion-like scenes of the novel of manners refer back to the drama. In the theater the fixed settings require long scenes of conversation, interrupted by entrances and exits. This in the novel of manners became the full-scale, real-time scenes of Austen, James, and Howells.

The second model that I will consider will be the modernist form of the social novel as we see it in Dos Passos's *Manhattan Transfer* and

U.S.A. The breakthrough of *Manhattan Transfer* involves the creation of a fragmented novel made up of nearly 150 short scenes, most of them two or three pages long. For Dos Passos the central model of experience is the newspaper rather than the dinner table. In the newspaper daily samples from every corner of the social world of the city are brought together side by side. The aesthetics of juxtaposition, rather than that of communication, could be called Dos Passos's goal. The novel presents itself as a chaos of "stories," glimpses, and conversations taking place over many years and involving more than a dozen equally important characters. The novel is a crowd of side-by-side, value-free, equal facts like the front page of a newspaper, where we glance in ten seconds at the football scores, the death of an actress, a new discovery in physics, an earthquake killing thousands in China, a three-alarm fire with no casualties, an investigation into government corruption, a story about a snowstorm that stalled traffic for three hours, the birth of quadruplets in Australia, and the launching of the first rocket to Mars. The newspaper reporter who, along with the detective, becomes the classic stand-in for the artist in the urban novel, and the format of the newspaper itself as a form of moral and intellectual disorder are important as a background image for the novel precisely because it is taken to mirror, in a deep way, the excitement and variety of urban life, a world of catastrophe and magic.

The third model that I will discuss is the new form of biography and story-telling that we can hear in Henry Miller, or earlier in the narrated lives that make up Dreiser's *Gallery of Women*, or in the Jason section of Faulkner's *Sound and the Fury*. This new talking life history, close in many ways to the endless egotistic self-description of psychoanalysis, places us so that we seem to hear, out of the silence and darkness, a single life history told by a speaking voice with a unique temperament and language.

This form of narration becomes popular within the novel at the moment when the technology of the radio is being introduced. The radio accustomed people to the intimacy of distant voices, whether that of the President of the United States talking from his office in Washington directly into every living room, or the voices heard late at night from cities far away, the jazz singer Billie Holiday singing in Chicago or a baseball announcer from Pittsburgh. Both psychoanalysis, which took hold in New York in the 1920s, and the new technology of the radio were forms of narrative dominated by the voice. The urban novel, in this same period, turned to the disembodied voice as a fundamental narrative tool.

In Dos Passos after 1925 this colloquial urban style often seems captured by a tape recorder or skilled stenographer since the voice or voices wander on without description or analysis in page after page of brief, spoken scenes. In later writers, the tirade, the rant, and the spiel produce an overall style of self-performance of the kind that Henry Miller, J. D. Salinger, and Saul Bellow made into a new style of urban intimacy not so different from hearing the life history of a stranger on a long Greyhound bus ride or a ranting voice at night over a radio. This feeling of an intimacy of strangers is one of the great achievements of the urban novel, since it accepts the urban solitude, the improvisational relations among people, the unexpected and often unwanted intimacy of urban life, and converts it into a narrative form.

In the American novel the urban wise-guy, the unstoppable Ancient Mariner of his own troubles and experiences, became the key permanent narrative form from the mid-1920s to the present. The masterpieces of this urban form of talk-narrative include Salinger's *Catcher in the Rye*, Bellow's *Herzog*, Philip Roth's many self-indulgent garrulous voices from *Portnoy's Complaint* to *My Life as a Man*, Ralph Ellison's *Invisible Man*, and Joseph Heller's *Something Happened*.

A final model within this period reflects the complex response of the novel to the Hollywood film, both the creation of novels as filmlike scripts and the creation of what I call "dark-screen" narratives, in which the visual exists only by implication and therefore carves out a unique territory for the novel that the film can never duplicate. For examples of these alternative relations to the film I will look at F. Scott Fitzgerald's *Tender Is the Night* as an example of the novel subservient to the new Hollywood techniques and then to Hemingway's use of dialogue as an example of "dark-screen" narration that clears away a space alongside film for the novel. I could also have used the opening section (the Benjy) section of Faulkner's *Sound and the Fury* as my example of "dark-screen" narration.

The Boardinghouse Dining Room Table of Realism: Howells's *Hazard of New Fortunes*

Although I will discuss mainly Howells's *Hazard of New Fortunes*, the form of the social novel that Howells uses is continuous from at least the time of Jane Austen through George Eliot and Henry James and was adapted by Howells and others to a complex urban experience that is intrinsically hostile to it. After Howells the great novels of Edith Wharton, from *The House of Mirth* (1905) to *The Age of Innocence* (1920), take up the novel of manners form for New York society. In 1925, with his novel *The Great Gatsby*, Fitzgerald not only wrote the last major work in this form, but also wrote the first novel that reflected the new relation of suburb to city, the first Long Island–Manhattan novel, where the urban world of bootleggers, love-nest apartments, downtown jobs, and drinks in the city is seen from the perspective of a carefully manicured private world of wealth and privileged isolation, a world that is nonetheless invaded by a distraught husband who leaves behind the glamorous body of Gatsby floating in the swimming pool.

The novel of manners has traditionally been a literary form in which conversation, and a social life defined by exchanges of visits and dining, the world of talk, dancing, courtship, and, ultimately, proposals of marriage make up the central business of the scenes. The novel of manners was traditionally a comic form based on stage drama with its conventions of entrances and exits, curtain lines and climaxes, all achieved within long unfolding scenes of conversation. The novel of manners served to police a uniform code of behavior and public life. At heart, the novel of manners is anthropological; its subject is the entrance into or expulsion from society. Marriage is, of course, the ultimate act of social inclusion. Banishing is, at the other extreme, the ultimate form of social death.

The conversation of the novel of manners has traditionally aimed at social judgments and evaluation that lead ultimately to inclusion or exclusion from the social group—the social set or circle—for those who are perceived as outsiders or strangers. The novel of manners has been about membership, the convergence of judgments, the preservation of society from dangerous outsiders, and the enlarging of a frozen, unanimous world by the inclusion of new members.

The attempt in American Literature to represent the more diverse, unmanageable differences of the city within the novel of manners can be seen in *Hazard of New Fortunes*. The central married couple of Howells's novel, the Marches, "migrate" to New York from Boston, but in this act they point to the wider urban fact of New York, a city of immigrants, a collection point for a variety of people born elsewhere, shaped under a variety of systems of manners, and brought together here to work out their lives in common. The novel of manners collapses in the face of this social mobility that brings together German immigrants, midwestern money, refugees from an impoverished post–Civil War American South, and New Englanders like the Marches.

The cliché of the city as a melting pot runs up against the city as a fixed society of manners and types. The novel of manners depends in its theory of society and in its functioning as a literary form on small-scale voluntary associations of four to eight people, like the magazine staff that Howells describes, or the people at a dinner table, or those who live together at a boardinghouse, or visit together for an evening. These small groups are based on the family as a model. The novel of manners failed in the face of urban experience, where this small-family style group was no longer central. In the city novel we find the solitary individual, the sexual couple, the crowd—seldom the middle-sized four-to-eight person group.

Howells's is an intangible, intimate world based on esteem and affection. Its center is the parlor or the dining room. Men and women are known first of all as hosts and guests, friends and suitors, potential husbands and wives, patrons and associates. Their business arrangements and their financial arrangements are added onto this world. People seem to be hired for March's new journal because, like Colonel Woodburn, they are found at the table of the boardinghouse where the promoter happens to eat, and where he will also find his fiancée. Relations are general, stable, and socially coded; they draw little from momentary events. They are also concentrated and overlapping to an artificial degree. Lindau,

March's old friend, is the artists' model for various characters. He becomes the translator for the journal, and he eats at the boarding-house that brings together all the other characters so conveniently. In other words, the same few threads are woven and rewoven into a number of small-scale patterns. The most unnatural and contrived of these is the moment in the street near the end of the novel that brings Conrad, Lindau, and March together during the streetcar strike. This moment leads to the death of Conrad and the conclusion of the novel. Such a closed world is the mark of the novel of manners, where a handful of characters from the "respectable classes" criss-cross their way through a set of visits, dinners, dances, and outings toward a set of marriages.

Howells's world, like the world of the novel of manners in general, is free of objects and things, free of detailed settings (or as the naturalist novel would call them: "environments"), and the novel looks closely at the outer world only in occasional, set-piece insertions like the house-hunting episode or a walk that is irrelevant to the pattern of events. The novel is free as well of decisive, large-scale matters like war, economic crisis, or other public events, and it works out the fates of its characters by means of quarrels, proposals of marriage, renewed friendships, and partings. It does so, until the strike at the end of the novel shatters this world rather than making up one more causal element within it. A type of narrative discretion or politeness sets up the model of communication, understanding, tolerance of differences, common effort, and human conscience that Howells imagines might make a tolerable, but diverse urban world. The outer world enters as a series of carefully prepared pictures, as it does in this brief scene on the elevated train in Chapter 10:

> At Third Avenue they took the elevated, for which she confessed an infatuation. She declared it the most ideal way of getting about in the world, and was not ashamed when he reminded her of how she used to say that nothing under the sun could induce her to travel on it. She now said that the night transit was even more interesting than the day, and that the fleeting intimacy you formed with people in second- and third-floor interiors, while all the usual street life went on underneath, had a domestic intensity mixed with a perfect repose

that was the last effect of good society with all its security and exclusiveness. He said it was better than the theater, of which it reminded him, to see those people through their windows: a family party of workfolk at a late tea, some of the men in their shirt sleeves; a woman sewing by a lamp; a mother laying her child in its cradle; a man with his head fallen on his hands upon a table; a girl and her lover leaning over the window-sill together. What suggestion! what drama! what infinite interest![1]

The outer world is seen as a set of inner worlds viewed through the window as the elevated train passes. What the passengers see is a set of photographs, a gallery of the picturesque, Dutch genre scenes, domestic Victorian family wall pictures. What Howells supplies is a quick formula, a sketch, a distant twilight of images and indirect narration. Even the conversation between the Marches is only reported and not literally represented. Those strangers seen at a distance for a few seconds are comforting in that their lives represent the same family values as the Marches' own genteel world: work, relaxation, young love, a child in its cradle, the laborer taking his well-earned rest. A pious and smug world, safely framed, and quickly passed, a glimpse into the "real" city without even a single disturbing detail. Certainly one of the houses that the Marches passed was not the drunken brawling home of Stephen Crane's *Maggie.* Crane's shocking novel was published in the same year as Howells's.

Novel and Newspaper: Juxtaposition, Scanning, and Following

The starkest contrast to the careful picturesque style and full-spoken scenes of the city novel, like Howells's that arose from the novel of manners can be found in the rich relation between narration and the phenomenological experience of reading a newspaper. Crudely put, for the novel the newspaper replaced the dining table with its conversation and careful manners as the model for the inclusiveness and the relations of society itself.

Perception in the city, especially in the street, has its basis in interruption, the breaking of the flow of attention from many sides, an interruption that does not close off attention or redirect it, but rather segments it into a finer and finer grain, reducing it, finally, to a set of glances. Our best training for this experience is the daily reading of a newspaper. In its history the newspaper between the mid-nineteenth and the mid-twentieth centuries was profoundly linked to the rise of the city and to the transformation of the experience of reading novels that we find in Hemingway, Dos Passos, Joyce, and Faulkner.

Column by column, weighted without regard to importance, the trivial and the heroic rest side by side on the front page of a newspaper. A fire in a vacant warehouse, the scores of last night's baseball games, a bomb killing forty people on a street thousands of miles away, a movie star's death, a traffic jam caused by an unexpected snowstorm: these are a typical set of front-page stories that we might find one day facing us in our morning paper. The front page of a newspaper is itself a crowd, a mass of individuals who remain strangers to one another. The front page trains the reader for the rapid alternations of experience, the panoramic mentality that permits an article on starvation in Africa to run down one column next to a large advertisement for the grand opening of a new restaurant. Neither space contaminates the other, neither suggests nor should suggest irony, outrage, or moral indignation. The newspaper is a training ground for the crowd and the city, a place where habits of perception are formed.

Explicitly, the newspaper is an image of the total structure of the city, which is in its turn a concrete image of the human psyche. Each newspaper is named for a city and had as its readers the citizens of that city. *The New York Times*, *The Philadelphia Inquirer*, *The Pittsburgh Press*. The newspaper is a discardable daily sampling of the world. It is one day's worth of life. The paper is an installment, a miniature, a total image of our psychic lives, as a day is, and given in direct proportion to our diverse appetites and interests. What is it that explains the scale—the "coverage," as it is called—and the shape of content in a newspaper? Why is there just this much space devoted to food, to death, to sports, to money, to stories of disaster or stories of luck and reunion? Why in some cultures and times would the newspaper report in detail on the sermons preached in church, while in others baseball games would be represented in great detail? Why would stories of danger in the streets or trials of murderers be prominent in the newspapers of one culture while stories of remorse or of religious miracles would be featured in another? The answer is that a newspaper, in its proportions and omissions, its attention and its blank spots, is an accurate reflection of the psychic economy of a culture, with money and love playing the parts that they play in life, sports and humor, crime and wisdom playing the exact parts that they also do.

The newspaper is dietary in that it replenishes daily the existing system of needs. In its use of sections—a financial section, a sports section, a section of death notices and obituaries, a food section, a movies and television section, a section on the weather—the newspaper orders experience by accepting the concrete social form in which events and information occur. In this way it acts as a handheld miniature of the city itself.

We read the newspaper, particularly its front page, by a set of glances and distractions from story to story. We read headline by headline, then dip a little into this story until we are interrupted by the picture next to the story. We glance away, return, read further, begin another story, maintaining all the while a divided attention that is alert to the swarm of disparate events on the total page, much as we act on a busy city street. The newspaper encourages the act of scanning that levels and braids together distinct events and sectors of reality.

Over time, day after day, we read the newspaper by means of two acts. The first is *scanning*. The second is the act of *following* a series of ongoing stories as they unfold over weeks or months or even years. The unfolding story of South Africa, the baseball season, the marriage of Prince Charles and Princess Diana, the Rodney King trials in Los Angeles, the ups and downs of the stock market, American-Japanese economic relations are stories that one might follow over days, months, or years. Every active reader of a newspaper has his or her set of quite diverse ongoing stories that he or she is "catching up" on each day. Sometimes a story moves into dormancy for a period; nothing new is happening. Then it flares up again in a new turn. This is the essence of the melodrama of narrative as we follow it in newspapers.

Scanning and *following* are the two kinds of reading that emerge in a society for which the newspaper is the fundamental map of social reality. Stories crowd together. *Juxtaposition* is the fundamental law of order. The novel and the short story in America came powerfully under the spell of the norms and habits of reading and organization created by newspapers in their great years from 1880 to 1950. We might say that the newspaper replaced the novel of manners as a model for social life.

One essential feature of the newspaper is the short, high-impact event. Typically the scenes of the novel of manners are full, unfolded social encounters lasting many pages. These full scenes we find in James, Howells, or Wharton. With the newspaper we more typically find experimentation with the shortest possible story or episode. In Hemingway's *In Our Time*, the most important collection of short stories published in the 1920s, we find the careful juxtaposition of dispatches ("stories" in the newspaper sense of the word) and extended, relatively eventless short stories. Hemingway alternated short stories with one-page narratives from the public wartime events of the period of World War I. A typical example is Chapter 5:

> *They shot the six cabinet ministers at half-past six in the morning against the wall of a hospital. There were pools of water in the courtyard. There were wet dead leaves on the paving of the courtyard. It rained hard. All the shutters of the hospital were nailed shut. One of the ministers was sick with typhoid. Two soldiers carried him downstairs and out into the rain. They tried to hold him up against the wall but he sat down in a puddle of water. The other five stood very quietly against the wall. Finally the officer told the soldiers it was no good trying to make him stand up. When they fired the first volley he was sitting down in the water with his head on his knees.*[2]

This complete story obviously draws on and plays off against a newspaper report of a public event. It is factual, and narrates the time, the place, and the event. It is of course more detailed than a story would be. It adds the detail of the pools of water and the dead leaves. The shutters of the hospital are nailed shut. We see the one minister sitting on the ground, and we do not have the final reporter's sentence telling us the ministers all died at once and their bodies were buried in an unmarked grave.

The brevity, tone, and subject of the paragraph—a political event involving six cabinet ministers—are clearly newspaper-like, as is the interest in violence and death. Hemingway is demonstrating how little change he has to do to make such an event brooding, symbolic, impressionistic. Emotion is hidden within factual details. No political side is taken. Were these evil and widely hated men or beloved leaders executed by the enemy? Were they French or Greek or Syrian or Turkish? The story is deliberately silent about anything that would orient ethical or political outrage or joy. We are not told the ministers' names. The story has been abstracted of these key facts. It is a meta-story in which the humanity of these six men, the bleak setting, the irony of being executed next to a hospital wall where one should be saved, the individualizing of illness (the typhoid of the one sitting minister), and the finality of the volley of shots are quietly brought to the surface.

The story is a newspaper story in its form, but a short story in what is told and what is withheld. Exactly those details most crucial in a newspaper story—the politics of the situation, whether these men in wartime were "ours" or "theirs"—have been removed. Nonetheless, the impact or the "punch" is that of a well-written, powerful piece about an event involving life and death. But the key fact about this story is that in Hemingway's *In Our Time* we encounter it between two completely unrelated stories about Nick Adams's youth: "The Three-Day Blow" and "The Battler." We are, in newspaper vocabulary, "following" the Nick Adams story episode by episode, but to do so we are forced to accept the interruption that this brief paragraph imposes on us. In the end we are "scanning" across unrelated materials, jumping from place to place, from time to time, from mood to mood in order to read the book. Hemingway has created here the juxtapositions, the glances of attention, the scanning and following, the reduction of stories to episodes that newspaper training—for the reader as well as for the writer—has made normative as the style of reading and attention within our culture.

The notion of "following" stories within a novel can be traced back to Dickens and his use of the braided plot, or multiplot narrative. In Dreiser's *Sister Carrie* the final third of the novel alternates chapters and attention between Carrie and Hurstwood. We "follow" her rise and career, a typical success story of a Broadway star, one of the very favorite topics of newspapers. Alternately, we follow the episodes of Hurstwood's decline to the Bowery and his final suicide. Each story is made up of episodes; each is unfolding before our eyes chapter by chapter like the day after day "coverage" of a financial crisis on Wall Street or baseball's World Series. Yet the two stories are juxtaposed, braided over each other. Carrie and Hurstwood are now strangers in the city, passing near each other but in different trajectories that the novel follows. This is the essence of the neutral narration of newspapers: fame and despair, triumph and collapse, sports and weather, war and a fire downtown. The genre is melodramatic in each strand. The fates are black and white—triumphant success, blackest failure. Boom and bust, glamour and poverty. Each is a matter of life and death.

If we glance back to Howells's *A Hazard of New Fortunes* we can see that his novel implies that a realm of liberal, middle-class values can be enlarged to take in more and more of the urban world. It can do so because that world is fundamentally the same in values and moral life. Already in 1900, in Dreiser's *Sister Carrie*, entirely different assumptions of representation had taken over. The second half of Dreiser's novel is set in a New York of polar extremes, a dynamic world of rising and falling lives. The middle has fallen out, as has the model of family life, conversation, marriage, and stable enterprise. Dreiser's is a world of Broadway and Bowery, of stars and has-beens. He created the fundamental narrative for American representation of the city: a narrative in which the two extremes of glamour and despair, dreamlike wealth and homeless, drifting self-destruction, replace the middle range. A narrative of juxtaposed extremes replaced a narrative of a hopeful and expanding middle class. It is for this dynamic of juxtaposed extremes that the newspaper model became crucial. Precisely because the middle had dropped out—both the middle-class family norm and the middle level of experience—that the extremes of newspaper narrative prevailed within the novel.

In keeping with the location of his material at the two extremes of the social scale, Dreiser made a key narrative invention. In the second half of *Sister Carrie* he learned to tell the simultaneous stories of two people in different worlds. He did this by alternating chapters that carried each life forward as an individual narrative, the one rising to stardom, the other falling to the Bowery and suicide. By juxtaposing each stage of Carrie's life to the corresponding stage of Hurstwood's, Dreiser created a narrative form for the tunnel existence of separate city lives. Symbolically linked at every level, parallel in surprising and subtle ways, the two life histories are free from any cheap ironic or moral relation.

It is this style of juxtaposition, of mere side-by-sideness, that Dos Passos would expand in *Manhattan Transfer* into an all-embracing way of writing. In the 1920s James Joyce in the "Wandering Rocks" episode of *Ulysses* had represented the city at one hour of the day by means of twenty brief scenes, each character caught up in the local drama of the moment. This is Dos Passos's style for his novel. In the opening of *Manhattan Transfer* we can see that this alogical style operates at every level.

The opening page is made up of three separated and discontinuous paragraphs. The first is a poetic description of the arrival of a ferryboat with gulls circling above a world of debris and garbage. The second paragraph describes a nurse in a hospital carrying a newborn child in a basket. The final line of the hospital paragraph reads, "The newborn baby squirmed in the cottonwool feebly like a knot of earthworms." The third paragraph, which is set now on the ferry itself, begins with the sentences, "On the ferry there was an old man playing the violin. He had a monkey's face puckered up in one corner and kept time with the toe of a cracked patent-leather shoe." Not only are the scenes harshly juxtaposed without logical connection or continuity, but within each scene we are forced into juxtapositions that are willful acts of the author. The baby is juxtaposed (by means of simile) to earthworms. The old musician is (by metaphor) a monkey and (by metonymy) juxtaposed to the close-up detail of the "toe of a cracked patent-leather shoe." The narration works by shock and by the arbitrary acts of the writer. In one page he brings together gulls, garbage, a baby, worms, an old man playing a violin, and a cracked patent-leather shoe.

Dos Passos collects a dozen characters to follow through 140 brief scenes. We come to know his people newspaper style, by means of tiny articles at widely separated, unexpected moments of time. Each new section of the novel is like opening a daily newspaper and seeing that a certain rock star or well-known criminal or nearly forgotten politician has, as we say, "turned up again." He is once again "back in the news."

What is an act of genius on Dos Passos's part is to have combined the conditions of remote knowledge with the technique of intimate close-up scenes. There is a flattening of intimacy and remoteness to his technique that has much in common with a police report. An urban toughness and cynicism marks our blunt intrusive intimacy with these people who always remain strangers. The newspaper, which is the classic form of this narrative style of short, juxtaposed stories, always works through summary, description, analysis, and response. What never occurs in a newspaper is dialogue or what is called in narrative theory an extended "scene." Dos Passos uses these close-up, intimate scenes within a newspaper's structure of side-by-side matter-of-factness. He implies that in the Manhattan world of 1900 to 1925 intimacy has taken on the brevity, the juxtapositions, the bluntness, and the rapid changes of the public world of baseball scores, fires, heat waves, political scandals, and juicy murder trials.

Like Dreiser, Dos Passos is still committed to telling us the life histories over time of a set of characters who rise and fall, commit suicide or become influential. He strings out for each person a set of two-page glimpses at widely separated periods of time. He operates, just as a newspaper does, with a set of types: the rising actress, the lawyer on the make, the criminal on the run, the politician, the once rich but now heavy-drinking drifter, the gilded youth, the newspaper reporter, the cunning immigrant, the speakeasy bartender.

The urban aesthetic that Dos Passos invented for the novel was that of the anatomy, the exposé. He takes us "behind the scenes" for a set of glimpses into the lives of the glamorous, the amoral, the powerful, the criminal. There is an element of *National Enquirer* tabloid voyeurism to this method. It depends on that modern hunger to know "the inside story," "the real dirt." When we trace Dos Passos's individual characters back from their endpoint we can see that they often end up as "stories" in the newspaper meaning of the word. Bud Korpenning jumps off the Brooklyn Bridge; an event that would appear as a tiny front-page story in the daily paper. Gus McNeil becomes a powerful political figure. Ellen Thatcher passes from lover to lover in her career as an actress; Stan Emery kills himself spectacularly; Anna Cohen dies in a fire in a dress factory. Each at the endpoint becomes newsworthy. George Baldwin runs for mayor as a reform candidate; the ruined Wall Street financier Joe Harland drinks his way around the city, begging quarters from strangers. What Dos Passos does is to satisfy that newspaper curiosity expressed in the sentence: "I would love to know the real story behind that!"

The novel then exposes the "real story" behind Bud Korpenning's jump from the Brooklyn Bridge, behind George Baldwin's rise as a lawyer, behind Ellen Thatcher's glamour as a star, behind Anna Cohen's death in a dress factory. The lurid and the glamorous, the corrupt and the "tragic" are the aesthetic categories of a newspaper age. Dos Passos, and those like Nathanael West who followed him in the thirties, took over literally the newspaper "layout" of juxtaposition; the newspaper narrative style of "following" a story; the newspaper melodrama of glamorous rise and violent fall; the newspaper equation of criminal, actress, politician, and financial wizard as all equally "famous."

When West in his novel about a newspaper, *Miss Lonelyhearts* (1933), tries to deepen the meaning of this urban form with symbolism, intellectual reflection, grandiose myth-making, and irony, he only manages to make it pretentious and mannered. His one great invention is to make use of a part of the newspaper that Dos Passos had never considered, the advice column that prints readers' letters in which ordinary people have a once in a lifetime opportunity to have their own misery, suffering, problems, and hard times appear as a "story" in the day's newspaper in their own words, to be read and talked about by millions of people. Ostensibly, the reason for these letters is that the writers are seeking advice. But as West's novel shows, these stories involve horrible lives that are beyond any intervention or small-scale first aid. Each letter permits one sufferer to be "famous for a day" even while remaining anonymous under the pen name "Broad Shoulders," or "Sick-of it all," or "Desperate."

The advice column was a mechanism for democratizing the short burst of fame that the newspaper had at its command. Dos Passos's characters, like Dreiser's before him, are typical of the classic "interests" of the newspaper reader: the businessman who robs his own safe to run away with his mistress and is found dead in a Bowery hotel; the small-town girl who becomes a Broadway star; the milkman who becomes a political power in New York; the country boy who kills his father, wanders around Manhattan, and then jumps to his death from the Brooklyn Bridge. What West did was to see that once the aesthetic of the newspaper had saturated the urban mind, every life could be conceived in terms of a two-page story, crude, melodramatic, "heart-wrenching."

Dos Passos also perfected the braided narrative style that I have been describing, and in so doing he wrote the great newspaper novels of the decades between 1920 and 1940. *Manhattan Transfer* and *U.S.A.* bring to perfection the use of brief, close-up episodes, separated mechanically by what the newspapers call "layout." His novels take life stories that could quite easily have been narrated as distinct short stories and break them up into episodes that we have to wait for the next installment of. We jump from person to person among the principal characters, then forty pages later get the next phase of each person's life, as in a story we see back in the papers after a week's absence. We "follow" the central characters and we scan from one type of narrative to another as Dos Passos juxtaposes them.

Dos Passos added the regularly appearing "columns" such as the Camera Eye that regularly recurs as a "voice" in the mix of narrative styles. A newspaper too has these anchoring, regular voices that personalize by means of "columnists," such as Walter Winchell in Dos Passos's day, the style and events of one small box within the paper to contrast with the latest news about this or that, the updating that is the real essence of story-telling in Dos Passos or in the newspaper.

Earlier and more explicitly, Sherwood Anderson in *Winesburg, Ohio* (1919) had invented the small town counter-newspaper, centered on the reporter George Willard. In this set of stories all the leading figures, achievements, events, and boosterism of the town that any ordinary small-town paper would reflect have been replaced by all the failures: the actress who never went on the stage, the schoolteacher thrown out for touching his students, the doctors who no longer practice medicine but sit in decaying offices, the store owner who always fails in business. What Willard gets is each person's story, in the newspaper sense. Each person is a ruined or crippled figure, and the narrative tells us "the story behind" the ruined individuality of the person. Just so might we look at a wrecked train or a burnt-out store and ask, "what happened here? What is the story behind this?" Here the writer has narrowed the overall meaning of the word "story" to limit it to the exposé, to curiosity, to whispered gossip, or once-in-a-lifetime confession. "What's his story?" a stranger in town might ask, pointing to one of Anderson's queer figures. The real newspaper would never print the "real story" behind ordinary stale or crippled lives. But Anderson has democratized failure; every story of defeat and failure can appear once, side by side in his negative newspaper. The successes and triumphs will have to wait for the other reporters to pay their usual attention and homage.

The democracy of suffering and the right of each victim to once and once only tell his tale of misery was perfected, in newspaper style, by Nathanael West in *Miss Lonelyhearts*, where the extraordinary letters telling in their own words of miserable and hopeless lives are printed in the novel as they would be printed even today in the advice columns of American newspapers. The letters in *Miss Lonelyhearts* show the exceptional force of each detail of the newspaper to ignite novelists and story writers to tap into the social fund of interest that the social form of the newspaper created. These ultimate and naked human stories, told in their own words, but strewn across the page of the daily paper next to advertisements for perfume, stock market tips, weather maps, and political gossip, are more extraordinary as part of the unmoralized structure of a daily paper than they are within the pretentious structure and religious symbolism of West's novel. West's letter writers speak in colloquial voices that remind us today of the callers on American talk radio, where the combination of the telephone and radio and real-time broadcasting has provided the explosive mixture that keeps radio alive in the 1990s, just as the mixture of newspaper and letters did in the later days of newspapers that West's novel records.

City Voices: The Radio and the Novel of Voices

T. S. Eliot's great poem of 1923, *The Waste Land,* was at first called "He Do the Police in Different Voices." The urban world appears by means of brief scenes, many of them scenes of free-floating voices.

> "My feet are at Moorgate, and my heart
> Under my feet. After the event
> He wept. He promised 'a new start.'
> I made no comment. What should I resent?"[3]

The disembodied voice became a means to assert a radical, free-standing experience. The voice decontextualized experience, freeing it from causality—that is, from antecedents and consequences. The free voice preserved individuality while sampling experience in a sharply truncated manner.

It was Dreiser who produced the first free-standing collection of what we today think of as urban oral histories. In his last great book, *A Gallery of Women,* Dreiser converted this project of the self into a series of bohemian life histories. New York became Greenwich Village rather than Broadway and Bowery. As a book of the twenties these fifteen stories tell of a different and more gritty Jazz Age. On one side they approach the razzle-dazzle take rich of F. Scott Fitzgerald's Gatsby and Daisy, but on the other they touch ground in the Greenwich Village of rope-sandaled poets, painters off to Paris, and young revolutionaries drawn to an American colony in the Siberia that the Russian Revolution would surely turn into yet another side of Paradise. That future was at first a promise, as Paris was for the young who wanted to paint in the new style of Picasso and Matisse, or as New York City was for every high-energy dreamer too big for small-town life, and on the run from the tedium of life once one "settled down." But the promise of all other promises was the erotic itself, for which the sex appeal of money, or politics, or fame, of Greenwich Village or Paris or Hollywood, was just an atmospheric setting. In this collection Dreiser wrote a dozen of the greatest stories of lives under the spell of love, sexual passion, and the variability of desire ever written in America. Like his contemporary, D. H. Lawrence, Dreiser designed a new, vitalist narrative in the aftermath of the first Freudian wave. These narratives are timed by the history of the energy of passion that glows incandescent, connects or fails to connect, but inevitably fades. Like the best of Lawrence's stories, these are accounts of lives in which the reality of passion and the reality of the aftermath of passion are the very texture of life history.

The stories of *Gallery of Women* are stories for a promiscuous world. Each story has the structure of a meeting with a new and, in the story's perception, intriguing woman. The reader who "meets" or is "introduced to" Albertine, Lucia, Ellen, or Esther by the story itself has an experience that Dreiser has designed as a parallel to the stage of getting to know someone through the fascinated gaze of a new affair. In the style of spoken history, Dreiser, along with Dos Passos, prepared the way for what we might call the city of talk, tirade, and self-performance that would follow in the work of Henry Miller, Philip Roth, Saul Bellow, J. D. Salinger, and Joseph Heller. Outside the urban novel, Faulkner used the same technique within *The Sound and the Fury* to create the voiced narrative of Jason Compson, the third section of the novel, and in the play of voices within the rest of the novel.

Film Treatment: *Tender Is the Night*

Alongside newspaper and radio, the Hollywood film, by the late 1920s, had already begun its rise to narrative domination of American culture. Where the novel might borrow from the newspaper, it found itself overwhelmed and ultimately displaced by the visual power of film narration and the rapid pace of story-telling possible in the movies.

Radio and newspaper were also verbal media, as was story-telling itself. With the film, novels and short stories faced a rival from which little could be borrowed other than the techniques of pacing, cutting, and scenic structure. As I look at this final medium briefly, I will be setting out two alternatives for the novel and story. The first is to adopt, as F. Scott Fitzgerald did, the ethos and practices of the film script. The second alternative is to devise an "unfilmable" or "blind" narrative style that no longer describes—as realism had done so exhaustively—the visual world, but rather insists on implying that visible world by means of what I call "dark-screen" narrative. If Flaubert was the ultimate visual and descriptive realist, then Hemingway and Faulkner began the new model of devisualized writing that might give an extended life to the word in what rapidly became an age of film and television.

It is a trivial fact about Fitzgerald's *Tender Is the Night* (1933) that one of its two heroines is a rising Hollywood starlet named Rosemary and that she had recently starred in a film called *Daddy's Girl*. Only one scene takes place in a French Riviera studio, but the novel is the first important American novel saturated by the influence of film and saturated, in particular, by how a narrative can be made up of dozens of tiny scenes, each following a certain film logic for its quick and glamorous effects. In *Tender Is the Night* Fitzgerald wrote the first movie novel, a book almost designed as what Hollywood calls "a treatment," the pre-script, or even the script itself, for a film. The novel is made up of fifty-one short scenes, on average less than five pages per scene. Most scenes take us to a fresh setting, a glamorous and famous setting, like the beach near Cannes on the French Riviera where the novel begins. As in all films, the places themselves are the first "star" that we see in each scene—glamorous, perfect, as much above the ordinary places of the earth as movie stars are above ordinary faces and bodies. From Cannes for a summer day on the beach, to Paris, to Zurich, to Gstaad in the Alps, Innsbruck, Munich, Rome, the beautiful places of the continent, alpine skiing, Parisian dining, swimming on the Riviera—these fifty-one brief scenes allow the narrative to cut back and forth among the photogenic sights and star locations of continental Europe.

Each scene has, in film vocabulary, its location. Each has its glamorous central actor—the leading man or leading lady—Dick

Diver, Nicole, or Rosemary, whose beauty, wealth, or fame in one of the glamorous professions—psychoanalyst or heiress or movie star—will dominate the scene and allow the other persons to arrange themselves as supporting actors and actresses around the glamorous central person.

The actual details of film reality are far more pervasive than these large matters. In each opening of a scene we get a classic set of movie tricks. In Scene XX of Book II, set in Rome, we begin:

> When Dick got out of the elevator he followed a tortuous corridor and turned at length toward a distant voice outside a lighted door. Rosemary was in black pajamas; a luncheon table was still in the room; she was having coffee.
> "You're still beautiful," he said. "A little more beautiful than ever."[4]

The setting of the elevator and corridor are precisely described as an approach shot. We take the point of view of the hero moving toward the beautiful "star." She is given a single physical detail, "black pajamas," her costume for the scene. She is sketched in against the dining table, the lighted door, and given a bit of stage business—having coffee. Dick then speaks, and the scene begins.

Location, costume, single detail, the stage business and prop, when taken together prepare the lines of dialogue that follow. This structure is fundamental to most of the scenes. The black pajamas that we see here are the telling detail, the striking costume. When Dick is skiing in the Alps at Gstaad the chapter begins:

> With his cap, Dick slapped the snow from his dark blue ski-suit before going inside. The great hall, its floor pockmarked by two decades of hobnails, was cleared for the tea dance, and four-score young Americans, domiciled in schools near Gstaad, bounced about to the frolic of "Don't Bring Lulu," or exploded violently with the first percussions of the Charleston.[5]

Against this setting, with this ambiance in place and Dick's costume and opening gesture indicating snow by slapping the snow from his dark blue ski-suit, the episode is ready to begin.

On the beach at Cannes we first see Dick through Rosemary's eyes as "a fine man in a jockey cap and red-striped tights." When

Nicole Warren first sees him in 1917 the location is an expensive psychiatric clinic near Zurich, where she sees him wearing the first American military uniform that she has ever seen. Diver is a hero, in an expensive setting, with his striking costume and World War I somewhere in the background of neutral Switzerland. After the war and outside the clinic, their first meeting is in a funicular cable-car near Montreux, where Diver watches "the little bug crawl down the eighty-degree slope of the hill." He is dressed in his bicycling costume—"leather shorts, an army shirt, mountain shoes"—and carrying a knapsack. Dick finds himself crowded into the cable car with Nicole Diver and their romance begins.

Montreux, Gstaad, Zurich, Paris, Cannes, Rome, or rather a beach near Cannes, a cable car in the Alps, the Gare St. Lazare in Paris, "a houseboat café just opened on the Seine" in Paris, the Ritz Bar, a sidewalk café in Munich, Innsbruck, and the battlefield outside Paris where trench warfare had recently ceased: Fitzgerald sets up a very expensive grand tour, a shopping trip of locations where his glamorous and rich figures can be placed in their wonderful costumes—black pajamas, a military uniform, leather cycling shorts and knapsack, a dark-blue ski-suit, a jockey cap with red-striped tights. These are the spurious and unnecessary exact details that create "the effect of the real," as Roland Barthes called it. They are precisely how every film scene operates. A special costume, a gesture, a stunning location, all to prepare for the gesture, the word, the event that makes up the heart of the scene. Then a quick cut to the next location, new costumes, stage business, and gesture.

At the Gare St. Lazare, the scene leads up to an irrelevant pistol shot. At Gstaad, Fitzgerald paints the whole world for the central Hollywood big kiss, which takes place "on the horseshoe walk overlooking the lake" just as "the stars began to come through the white crests of the Alps." Nicole can see "two thousand feet below. . . the necklace and bracelet of lights that were Montreux and Lausanne. From down there somewhere ascended a faint sound of dance music." The action within each short scene is a highly prepared gesture like a kiss, a pistol shot, a statement. In the final scene at Cannes the now failing Dick Diver makes the sign of the cross over the beach.

When the novel opened 250 pages earlier and 51 scenes ago, we saw the action begin with a false-specific stranger. "Before eight a man came down to the beach in a blue bathrobe and with much preliminary application to his person of the chilly water, and much grunting and loud breathing, floundered a minute in the sea." This unnamed quite specific bather sets up the entrance of Rosemary and then Dick and Nicole Diver, but it is his exactly visualized ritual and above all his blue bathrobe that convince us that we really are on a beach at the French Riviera.

It is often an incidental character, unimportant to the plot, and certain never to appear again, who generates the vividness of the scene. In one of the most exploitive scenes, the Divers and their friends visit a battlefield outside Paris. It is essential to understand that Fitzgerald does not state the location of the scene. The characters have not in the preceding pages discussed a visit to this place. Every new place and time is unprepared.

We suddenly find ourselves in the scene—as always happens in a film. We "cut" to this new and unprepared location. The scene begins with these words. "Dick turned the corner of the traverse and continued along the trench walking on the duckboard. He came to a periscope, looked through it a moment; then he got up on the step and peered over the parapet."[6] It is by means of these word-clues (trench, duckboard, periscope, and parapet) that we begin to know where we are. By means of these details we realize that we are on a World War I battlefield outside Paris. We begin, as all film scenes do, in the middle of an action—Dick's walk along the trench to the periscope.

Dick's use of the prop—the periscope—establishes the feel that this really is a battlefield. This entire scene leads up to nothing more than Diver's big speech: "'All my beautiful lovely safe world blew itself up here with a great gust of high explosive love,' Dick mourned persistently. 'Isn't that true, Rosemary?'"

Here are the beautiful people, sad and profound, within the glamorous setting, followed by a bit of action. Then we "cut" and a new scene begins with a new location, "a houseboat café just opened on the Seine."

In Fitzgerald we see the updating of the European travelogue novel that Henry James had practiced, but now under the spell of the visual and quick world of Hollywood. The American novel from James to Hemingway had often prized the setting and atmosphere of the tourist's Europe. Fitzgerald adds the mechanics of film-writing: the brief jumpy scenes, the sputters of plot, including the need for exciting moments—gunshots and kisses, a dead Negro found in Rosemary's bed in Paris. Fitzgerald accomplished this by forcing himself as a novelist to think first of those film questions: What interesting costume? What location for this bit of action? What stage business to make time and place real? What opening line of dialogue to start the scene? What climactic word or gesture? What last move before the cut to the next scene? Fitzgerald in 1932 had already mastered the technicolor techniques of the James Bond movies decades before there were technicolor movies or James Bond–like handsome rogue heroes to move around in a world which had become one very expensive set after another.

Film and Dark-Screen Narration

The explicit film-novel that Fitzgerald wrote in *Tender Is the Night* was not the only direction for the novel's conversation with the film. Hemingway's work in the twenties experimented with what we might call, in a visual age, "blind narrative," story-telling by conversation in which the author refuses to state the physical or visual details of place and action. Hemingway's dark-screen narrative forces the reader to imagine the setting, the gestures, the realistic facts of the situation; and furthermore, he creates a unique importance for novels and stories in a visual age—a film age—by defining them as the one work of art in which the visual must be imagined and supplied by the reader as a tacit and unstated set of facts. If these stories were filmed or if a narrator were to fill in by description or a statement of the facts the real circumstances, setting, and issues of the story, the delicate blend of hearing, reading, and imagining—the discretion that does not speak about the visual or the gestural—would collapse.

This technique I refer to as dark-screen narration is the opposite of silent films, where we find ourselves in a visual world without sound. In Hemingway, an audience trained in a culture where the visual is primary is deprived of the visual. Thus the dark screen is entirely different from no screen at all. What we hear and learn forces us to privately visualize the world implied by the conversation, but not to speak of it or refer to it in any way. We could think of this as reticence or discretion aimed at the visual. In a film the visual world is necessarily just there as fact. But in short stories or novels the visual world of things, persons, actions, and expressions can be unstated but nonetheless the subject of the reader's interest, curiosity, and imagination.

The story "The Snows of Kilimanjaro" opens in a typical way without any clue to place, time, persons, or their relations. We could say the story refuses to introduce itself. Hemingway will not state the setting, the look and feel of the world, the characters of the persons, or their circumstances or relations:

> "The marvellous thing is that it's painless," he said. "That's how you know when it starts."
>
> "Is it really?"
>
> "Absolutely. I'm awfully sorry about the odor though. That must bother you."
>
> "Don't! Please don't."
>
> "Look at them," he said. "Now is it sight or is it scent that brings them like that?"
>
> The cot the man lay on was in the wide shade of a mimosa tree and as he looked out past the shade onto the glare of the plain there were three of the big birds squatted obscenely, while in the sky a dozen more sailed, making quick-moving shadows as they passed.[7]

In the novel *A Farewell To Arms* (1929) the experiment with devisualizing is far more extreme. Chapters are made up of long sequences of brief spoken exchanges. The reader feels located in real time, like an eavesdropper outside a room, hearing the words spoken intimately between the people inside the room—usually Catherine and Lieutenant Henry. The atmosphere of intimacy and eavesdropping is conveyed by the fact that the characters can see the scene, sometimes a scene of lovemaking, but we cannot. Our existence as readers is defined by our blindness in this world that we can only imagine. Important uses of dark-screen narrative in the 1920s and

1930s include the Benjy section of Faulkner's *Sound and the Fury*, the many Hemingway stories, such as "The Killers," that are dialogue driven, and the main effects of *A Farewell to Arms*.

Dark-screen narrative, back-and-forth spoken words, requires real-time narration. The scene covers a few seconds or minutes of consecutive time, fully recorded; then after a gap we move to another few seconds or minutes of real time. The pace is slow; conversations in time are completely and exactly reported. The page fills up with quotation marks. The world itself is being tape-recorded. The words are given importance by being exactly re-corded and completely recorded at the expense of everything else. The reader overhears this world.

The great invention of *A Farewell to Arms* is the refinement of a dark-screen narration of conversation from which the physical de-scriptions and psychological or visual frame have been blanked out. Page after page of dialogue—a play without a stage, visible actors, costumes, or gestures. Hemingway wrote a devisualized set of scenes between lovers and friends with only the voices remaining, but because it was an intimate world of hotel rooms and hospital beds that he opened up, we read the dark-screen narrative as though we were overhearing through the door from the hotel corridor, or just outside a window where we can see nothing but hear everything. The intrusion into intimacy is one unexpected effect of devisualizing. Hemingway makes us feel that we are pre-sent in some special way where all we can do is to hear—as though this were a wiretapped telephone call or a tape-recording played later in another time and place.

Hemingway's intention was not to remind us of eavesdropping or overhearing. He used an unpictured world to force us to imagine it, to see it by means of omitting to state it. This is a part of discretion, of a decorous respect for the bodies and expressions and thoughts that should not be intruded upon, and that we must think about without seeing or know about without hearing.

His goal was the opposite of Fitzgerald's in *Tender Is the Night*. Both writers were working in the first years of the film revolution that would displace the novel as the primary form of narrative entertain-ment. Both saw that the visual along with the brief, cut scene was the key to the pace and pleasure of the new medium. Fitzgerald imagined ways in which the novel might duplicate and compete with the effects of Hollywood. Hemingway and Faulkner began to open up the alternative of an unvisualized world, but one located now at the margins of narrative that would be, after the film, inescapably screened, whether with the screen bright or darkened.

Conclusion

The literature of an unfinished land, early in time and expecting a future only in part imaginable from the present, favors lightly sketched lines of personality and obligation. America a hundred and fifty years ago could be called unfinished because it was only partly settled and, from the perspective of farming, only partly cleared and fenced. Today we can call the same country unfinished and new in time for a very different reason. Innovation, rapidly changing kinds of work from generation to generation, and an ever new blend of population driven by expanding immigration from every continent of the world have created a permanent meaning to the idea of a never finished society.

If our national census were to list both persons and things, uses of land as well as occupants of the land, ghost towns and unused paths, rusted miles of track as well as new airports and interstate highways, radios gathering dust as well as cable television connections, instruments no longer played along with personal computers, clubs with declining membership alongside newly founded e-mail chat groups, language rusty with disuse next to numbers of new terms entering ordinary vocabulary within the ten years since the previous census, then the facts of mobility and a restless shifting of the machinery of life would strike us as even more turbulent than they do now. How many of the ten most important cities in the United States economy of 1800, 1850, 1900, or 1950 would remain on a similar list for the year 2000? What remains of the traditional ideal of culture once the act of handing on skills and knowledge to the next generation has become riddled with questions? From anthropology we have taken in an idea of culture that best describes small homogeneous, tradition-rich groups living in the same location whose work, crafts, beliefs, habits, and language remain stable over many generations. If these are the presumptions of culture, then can we even say that a modern, mobile society of innovation and immigration like the United States has a culture?

Immigration, renewed in later acts of what Mark Twain referred to as "removal," became in the United States a life form and not simply a onetime act. Removal is both a selective deletion of the past, as bankruptcy or going away to college at eighteen is, and a confident act whose preoccupying horizon is the future. Removal is a cultural or personal act of creative destruction.

In this book I have attempted to give a deliberately provocative, fresh account of American culture drawing on the idea of creative destruction—the favoring of the future over the past within economic and social life. My claim is that in America we should view generational life as a series of renewed acts of immigration into a new world. Along with the actual flood of immigrants from an ever-changing mix of cultures, technological change brings about what I refer to as an immigration of objects and systems, ways of life and techniques for the distribution of ideas and representations. Our national embrace of immigration and technology creates in the United States a new kind of cultural life in which the transmission of knowledge and ways of life from parents to children matters less and less. Transmission of an existing way of life came to be replaced by an ever new economic and cultural world into which the members of each generation—made up of the young and of the newly arrived—settled and defined themselves.

Most people now line up on opposing sides of a debate between multiculturalists and defenders of a traditional unified culture. They ask that we choose between two pictures drawn from anthropology: a unified central culture passed on from generation to generation or a set of side-by-side cultures each of which is also passed on successfully. I hope that in this book I have changed the terms of this debate by looking at the underlying core facts of American experience that make either of these alternatives of little value. I have set out to change the use of the word "assimilation" by arguing that the young of each successive generation, and newly arrived Americans create together a new world and that their own new world becomes the most strongly defined feature of culture in their lifetime. One important consequence is that a split between generations is one of the most intractable features of American life. In this feature, once again, it is the life experience of recent immigrants, where the generations often do not share even the same primary daily language, that gives the best pattern for the culture as a whole.

In the twentieth century, a strongly marked generational culture has often found entirely new channels for the cohesion of culture: the radio generation, the generation of silent films, the movie generation, the television generation, the computer generation, the generation in which telephone calls were easy and inexpensive so that even the lives of teenage friends could be knit together through hours of telephone talk or the generation that first learned to connect with e-mail.

Assimilation in the United States today does not mean the surrender by some of a culture that they feel to be their authentic culture so as to take on the stable culture of some other dominant group. It means instead the active discarding of large parts of the past in the name of a future that is equally new to everyone. Within phases of our lives the same moment of discarding a way of life happens with the same strong effect. Every retired person moving to Florida from New Jersey or Chicago or Pittsburgh has to be seen as an immigrant, leaving behind a neighborhood, friends, habits, and other family members. An eighteen-year-old going away to college does the same.

It was to describe in a convincing way the consequences of its being still the new world in America that I wrote this book. Literature and the entire landscape of representation change their purposes and tactics within a culture more committed to the future than to the past. I have used the project of Whitman's poetry throughout this book as a leading instance because I am certain that his was a profound invention within the history of poetry, one that was demanded by the novel society he set out to celebrate.

Abstraction, understood as the concentration on minimal, widely shared traits, on activity that is recognizable because common-place, on types and on what is everywhere thought or known, has been described in this book as one essential kind of representation or art in a culture of creative destruction. The philosophy of Emerson, the poetry of Whitman, Wallace Stevens, and T. S. Eliot or John Ashbery are important examples of abstraction, as are the styles of painting within, postwar American abstract art, associated with Jackson Pollock, Jasper Johns, and Frank Stella, and the New York paintings of Piet Mondrian. Abstraction designs the air-conditioned skyscraper suitable for any climate or terrain, the interstate highway system, and the identical airports on the outskirts of a hundred different cities. The personal computer is what we call a commodity because of the workings of abstraction, the similarity of traits, the indifference to differentiation. In design as well as in art and literature abstraction is the fundamental aesthetic category and the key alternative to modern varieties of realism.

I have attempted to spell out the resources in our culture for giving an account of what counts as real. Those resources I have called abstraction, regionalism, and three distinct models of realism—a realism that I termed pictorial, another that I described as based in states, and a final variety that drew evidence from the exact mimesis of the speaking voice. I have tried to show how abstraction and realism serve similar goals in a culture where what is to be represented is the individual person, not the community, the family, or the way of life of groups. Both abstraction and realism are in the end kinds of art for a culture of democratic individualism.

Realistic representation as we find it in novels or poems has existed for more than a hundred and fifty years in complex and evolving rivalry with the story-telling and the representation of individual personality found in newspapers, films, photographs, the voices heard over the airwaves and captured on radio, the images and stories on television or within recorded song. Ordinary representation finds itself, because of media culture, also set over against the magical, ultra-representation of persons, places, and things that we think of as stars, brand-name objects, larger-than-life places like Hollywood, Silicon Valley, Yellowstone National Park, Wall Street, or Harvard University.

How realism held its ground within this landscape of ever stronger rivals within other media of story-telling and representation has been the subject of the final third of this book. The key invention of a new intimacy and witness-like self-representation in what I have called voice-based realism allowed literature to claim a ground that film or other visual media could not invade. It is important to see that the experiments of Hemingway and Faulkner with what I have called dark-screen narration opened up a new territory that would never have to be contested with film or photography.

Abstraction and a realism grounded in the close replication of tone, accent, idiom, and personal style in the speaking voice are the two essential aesthetic discoveries of a culture in which creative destruction rules, in which the future, not the past, is the reference point for present thought and action, and, finally, in which the free individual, not the community or group, is the heart of the matter of representation.

This book was written to affirm my conviction that in America in the year 2000 it is still the new world.

Notes · Acknowledgments · Index

Notes

Introduction

1. Mark Twain, *The Adventures of Tom Sawyer,* in *Mississippi Writings,* ed. Guy Cardwell (New York: Library of America, 1982), chap. 2, p. 19.
2. Ibid., chap. 2, p. 20.
3. Arthur Rimbaud, letter to Paul Demeny of May 15, 1871, in *Collected Poems,* trans. Oliver Bernard (Baltimore: Penguin, 1962), p. 9.
4. Ibid., "Délires II," p. 329.
5. Robert William Fogel, *The Union Pacific Railroad: A Case in Premature Enterprise* (Baltimore: Johns Hopkins University Press, 1960).
6. Ralph Waldo Emerson, "Circles," in *Essays and Lectures,* ed. Joel Porte (New York: Library of America, 1983), pp. 410–411, 413
7. Ibid., pp. 407–408.
8. Ibid., pp. 403–404. Emphasis added.
9. Ralph Waldo Emerson, "The American Scholar," in *Essays and Lectures,* p. 65
10. Emerson, "Circles," pp. 410–411.
11. Stanley I. Kutler, *Privilege and Creative Destruction: The Charles River Bridge Case* (Baltimore: Johns Hopkins University Press, 1971).
12. Charles Neider, ed., *The Autobiography of Mark Twain* (New York: Harper Perennial, 1959), p. 1.
13. Ibid.
14. Alexis de Toqueville, *Democracy in America,* vol. I, trans. Henry Reeve, ed. Phillips Bradley (New York: Vintage Books, 1960), p. 328.

15. Alexis de Toqueville, *Journey to America*, trans. George Lawrence, ed. J. P. Mayer (London: Faber and Faber, 1959), p. 262.
16. Ibid.
17. Ibid. Emphasis added.
18. Philip Fisher, *Making and Effacing Art: Modern American Art in a Culture of Museums* (New York: Oxford University Press, 1991).

1. Democratic Social Space

1. Montesquieu's central discussion of climate occurs in Book XIV of *De l'esprit des lois*.
2. Walt Whitman, "Song of the Broad-Axe," in *Complete Poetry and Collected Prose*, ed. Justin Kaplan (New York: Library of America, 1982), sec. 3, p. 332. Subsequent references to Whitman's poetry will be given in the text by section number and title of poem, referring to the 1891–92 deathbed edition of *Leaves of Grass*.
3. For an important discussion of the consequences of this grid for American architecture and city planning see Leonardo Benevolo, *History of Modern Architecture*, 2 vols. (London: Routledge and Kegan Paul, 1971).
4. Daniel J. Boorstin, *The Americans: The Democratic Experience* (New York: Random House, 1973), p. 89. The whole of Boorstin's book is a chronicle of the place of objects in the formulation of American life. Parts Two, Five, Seven, and Nine contain the core of his evidence. See also Siegfried Giedion, *Mechanization Takes Command* (New York: Oxford University Press, 1948), and David A. Hounshell, *From the American System to Mass Production, 1800–1932* (Baltimore: Johns Hopkins University Press, 1984).
5. Karl Mannheim, *Ideology and Utopia* (New York: Harcourt, Brace & World, 1955).

2. Whitman and the Poetics of a Democratic Social Space

1. Allen Grossman, "The Poetics of Union in Whitman and Lincoln," in Walter Benn Michaels and Donald Pease, eds., *The American Renaissance Reconsidered: Selected Papers from the English Institute, 1982–83* (Baltimore: Johns Hopkins University Press, 1985).
2. Walt Whitman, "Song of Myself," in *Complete Poetry and Collected Prose*, ed. Justin Kaplan (New York: Library of America, 1982), sec. 1,

p. 188. Subsequent references to Whitman's poetry will be given in the text by section number and title of poem.

3. For a full analysis of Stowe's novel and the relation of sentimentality to slavery see Philip Fisher, *Hard Facts: Setting and Form in the American Novel* (New York: Oxford University Press, 1985).

3. Transparency and Obscurity

1. Jürgen Habermas, *Legitimation Crisis* (Boston: Beacon Press, 1975).
2. David Hounshell, *From the American System to Mass Production, 1800–1932* (Baltimore: Johns Hopkins University Press, 1984), pp. 189–216.
3. James MacGregor Burns, *The Workshop of Democracy* (New York: Alfred A. Knopf, 1985).
4. Herman Melville, *Great Short Works of Herman Melville*, ed. Warner Berthoff (New York: Harper & Row, 1969), p. 241. Subsequent references to *Benito Cereno* will be given in the text.
5. Walt Whitman, "As I Ebb'd with the Ocean of Life," in *Complete Poetry and Collected Prose*, ed. Justin Kaplan (New York: Library of America, 1982), sec. 1, p. 394. Subsequent references will be given in the text.

4. Hierarchical Social Space

1. Stuart P. Sherman, "Roosevelt and the National Psychology," reprinted in Morton Keller, ed., *Theodore Roosevelt: A Profile* (New York: Hill and Wang, 1967), p. 37.
2. Herbert Adams Gibbons, *John Wanamaker* (New York: Harper & Brothers, 1926), p. 133.
3. Fred W. Lorch, *The Trouble Begins at Eight: Mark Twain's Lecture Tours* (Ames: Iowa State University Press, 1968).
4. For an extraordinary analysis of the physical and structural reality of *The Gross Clinic*, see the essay by Michael Fried in *Representions*, 9 (Winter 1985), 33–104.
5. The physical presence of the painter within the scene of the painting and the interpretation of action given by the parallels between the physical acts of surgery and painting are major points made by Fried in *Representations*. For the use of the body to certify and make real political and other socially abstract facts, see the brilliant analysis of war and torture by Elaine Scarry in *The Body in Pain: The*

Making and Unmaking of the World (New York: Oxford University Press, 1985).

6. Keller, *Theidore Roosevelt*, pp. 67, 100.

7. John Milton Cooper, Jr., *The Warrior and the Priest: Woodrow Wilson and Theodore Roosevelt* (Cambridge, Mass.: Harvard University Press, 1983), pp. 28–29.

8. For an analysis of *Sister Carrie*, see the final chapter of Philip Fisher, *Hard Facts: Setting and Form in the American Novel* (New York: Oxford University Press, 1985). The concept of performance and its consequences for a social account of personality are given there in detail.

9. William Dean Howells, *My Mark Twain*, ed. Manlyn Austin Baldwin (Baton Rouge: Louisiana State University Press, 1967), p. 6.

10. David Nye, *Image Worlds: Photography at General Electric, 1890–1930* (Cambridge, Mass.: MIT Press, 1985).

11. Michael B. Miller, *The Bon Marché: Bourgeois Culture and the Department Store, 1869–1920* (Princeton: Princeton University Press, 1981), p. 167.

12. Daniel J. Boorstin, *The Americans: The Democratic Experience* (New York: Random House, 1973), p. 115.

13. Thorstein Veblen, *The Theory of the Leisure Class* (New York: Macmillan, 1899), p. 71, pp. 71–72.

14. William Allen White, "Theodore Roosevelt," in *Masks in a Pageant* (New York: Macmillan, 1928), p. 283.

15. Ibid., p. 284.

16. Howells, *My Mark Twain*, p. 80.

17. Mark Twain, *The Adventures of Huckleberry Finn*, edited and with an introduction by Lionel Trilling (New York: Rinehart and Co., 1948), p. 19. All further references to the novel will be given in the text.

18. Henry James, *The Bostonians* (New York: Random House, 1956), pp. 60–61. All further references to the novel will be given in the text.

19. For an account of the transfer of reality between the physical and the political realms, see Scarry, *The Body in Pain*.

20. Boorstin, *The Americans*, pp. 93–94.

5. Membership and Identity

1. Clifford Geertz, "'Ethnic Conflict': Three Alternative Terms," *Common Knowledge*, 2, no. 3 (Winter 1993), 54–65.

6. Episodes of Regionalism

1. Richard Brodhead, *Cultures of Letters: Scenes of Reading and Writing in Nineteenth-Century America* (Chicago: University of Chicago Press, 1993).

7. Realisms of Detail, State, and Voice

1. Anton Chekhov, "My Life," in *The Tales of Chekhov, Volume 8: The Chorus Girl and Other Stories*, trans. Constance Garnett (New York: Ecco, 1985), sec. 9, p. 110.

2. Georg Lukács, "Raconter ou décrire?" in Philippe Hamon, ed., *La description littéraire* (Paris: Macula, 1991), p. 226.

3. Gustave Flaubert, *Madame Bovary*, trans. Alan Russell (Baltimore: Penguin, 1950), p. 79.

4. Paul Valéry, *Degas, Manet, Morisot*, trans. David Paul (New York: Pantheon, 1960), p. 76.

5. Roland Barthes, "L'effet de réel," in Tzvetan Todorov, ed., *Littérature et réalité* (Paris: Editions du Seuil, 1982). Translated as "The Reality Effect," in Tzvetan Todorov, ed., *French Literary Theory Today*, trans. R. Carter (New York: Cambridge University Press, 1982).

6. Chekhov, "My Life," sec. 3, p. 66.

7. Flaubert, *Madame Bovay*, p. 30.

8. Oliver Wendell Holmes, "The Stereoscope and the Stereograph," *The Atlantic Monthly*, June 1859, p. 746.

9. Charles Baudelaire, "Une charongne," in *Oeuvres complètes*, ed. Claude Pichois (Paris: Gallimard, 1975), p. 31.

10. Jane Addams, *Twenty Years at Hull-House* (New York: New American Library, 1960), chap. 4, p. 69.

11. Walt Whitman, "Song of Myself," in *Complete Poetry and Collected Prose*, ed. Justin Kaplan (New York: Library of America, 1982), sec. 15, p. 200. Subsequent references to Whitman's poetry will be given in the text by section number and title of poem, referring to the 1891–92 deathbed edition of *Leaves of Grass*.

12. Stephen Crane, Maggie: *A Girl of the Streets*, in *Prose and Poetry* (New York: Library of America, 1984), chap. 13, p. 55.

13. Mark Twain, *The Adventures of Huckleberry Finn*, in *Mississippi Writings* (New York: Library of America, 1982), chap. 23, pp. 777–778.

14. Harriet Beecher Stowe, *Uncle Tom's Cabin*, in *Three Novels*, ed. Kathyrn Kish Sklar (New York: Library of America, 1982), chap. 18, pp. 255–256.

15. Nathanael West, *Miss Lonelyhearts and Day of the Locust* (New York: New Directions, 1962), pp. 41–42.

8. Inventing New Frames for Realism

1. William Dean Howells, *A Hazard of New Fortunes* (New York: Signet, 1965), p. 66.
2. Ernest Hemingway, *In Our Time* (New York: Collier, 1986), p. 51.
3. T. S. Eliot, *The Waste Land,* in *The Complete Poems and Plays, 1909–1950* (New York: Harcourt, Brace, 1959), lines 296–299, p. 46.
4. F. Scott Fitzgerald, *Tender Is the Night* (New York: Scribners, 1933), p. 209.
5. Ibid., Book II, Scene XIII, p. 171.
6. Ibid., book I, Scene XIII, p. 56.
7. Ernest Hemingway, "The Snows of Kilimanjaro," in *The Short Stories* (New York: Scribner's, 1995), p. 52.

Acknowledgments

I have been fortunate to have the support and generosity of many colleagues in American literature at a number of institutions where I have taught. At Brandeis I profited for many years from the ideas and conversation of my friends Michael Gilmore and Allen Grossman. Among my many debts to Harvard colleagues I especially want to acknowledge here the past ten years of rich exchange with Dan Aaron, Sacvan Bercovitch, Lawrence Buell, and Helen Vendler.

In 1981 I first went to the Kennedy Institute in Berlin to teach for a semester. Since then, for almost twenty years I have presented most of my new work to the research colloquiums and conferences of the Kennedy Institute. To Winfried Fluck, Ursula Brumm, and Heinz Ickstadt, I owe sharp engagement with my work and a context, created by them in Berlin, where the best possible European version of American Studies exists in ever more vital ways.

Earlier versions of some sections of Chapters 1–3 appeared in *Representations*, 24 (Fall 1988), 60–101, and in Philip Fisher, ed., *The New American Studies: Essays from "Representations"* (Berkeley: University of California Press, © 1991 the Regents of the University of California); and earlier versions of some parts of Chapter 4 appeared in *Reconstructing American Literary History*, ed. Sacvan Berkovitch, Harvard English Studies 13 (Cambridge, Mass.: Harvard University

Press, 1986), pp. 155–188. I am grateful for permission to use this material.

Final work on this manuscript profited from the care and close attention of several research assistants. My thanks to Mark Greif, Sara Yellen, and Lynn Lee. At Harvard University Press I was fortunate to find in Nancy Clemente an editor of patience and discernment. Her help with the nuances of the search for the best possible final book made infinitely easier the many hours of guiding two very different books through publication.

Index

Index

Index

Index